IMAGES
of America

CHESTER COUNTY

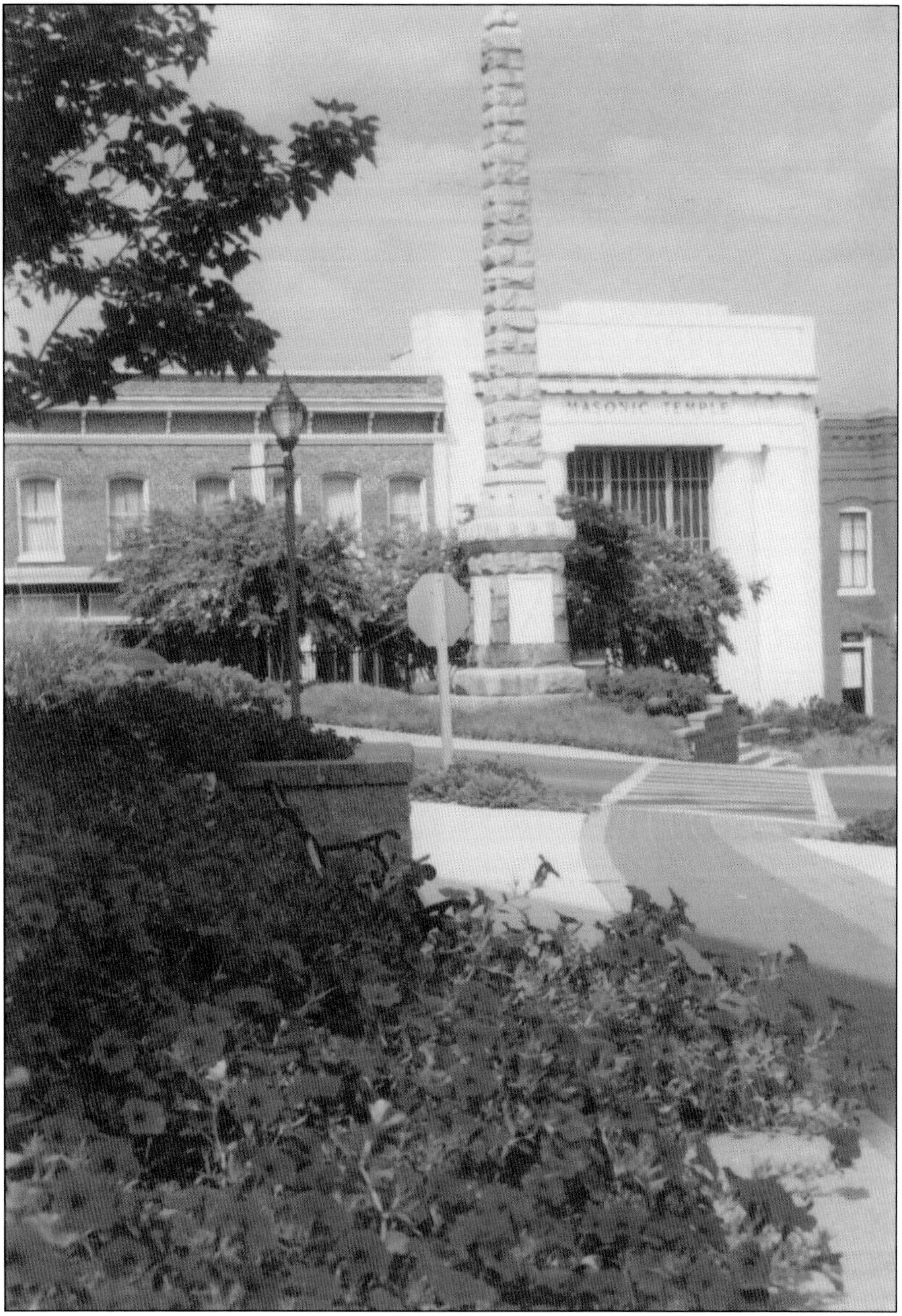

Downtown Chester, seen here on a beautifully sunny, summer day, is filled with history and heritage.

IMAGES
of America

CHESTER COUNTY

Glinda Price Coleman and Gina Price White

ARCADIA
PUBLISHING

ISBN 978-0-7385-0649-4

Published by Arcadia Publishing
Charleston, South Carolina

Printed in the United States of America

Library of Congress Catalog Card Number: 00-107120

For all general information contact Arcadia Publishing at:
Telephone 843-853-2070
Fax 843-853-0044
E-Mail sales@arcadiapublishing.com
For customer service and orders:
Toll-Free 1-888-313-2665

Visit us on the Internet at www.arcadiapublishing.com

To Anne and Laura Coleman,
who can now have Mama and Aunt Gina back.

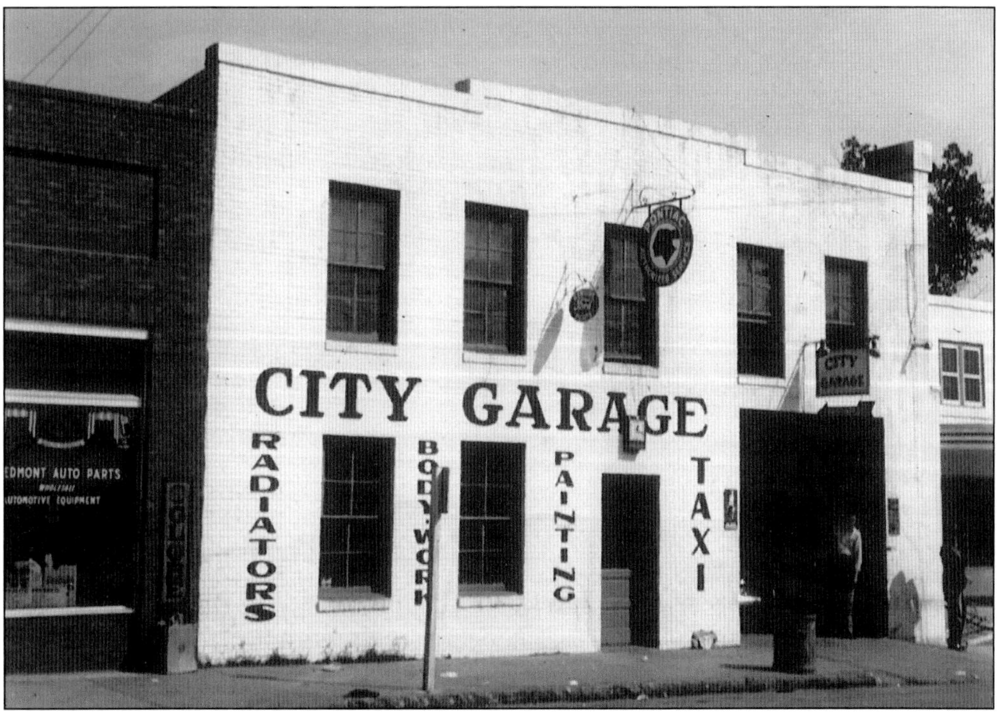

City Garage, next to Piedmont Auto Parts downtown, is shown here in the 1940s.

CONTENTS

ACKNOWLEDGMENTS

We wish to thank the following people for all their help and support:

Chester News & Reporter
the late Ward Pegram
Russell & Company, Inc.
Chester County Historical Society
Dot and Dock Price
Bob and Maurice Bennett
Bill and Ruth Bennett
Donna and Eddy Jordan
Blair and Jenell White
Heyward Gourley
Sam Grant
Mary Brown Powell

and especially our husbands and children, who have put up with a lot:

Russ White
Scott Coleman
Anne Coleman
Laura Coleman

INTRODUCTION

The area between the Broad and Catawba Rivers in upstate South Carolina was first widely settled by the white man in about 1750 when the Scotch-Irish from Pennsylvania and Virginia made their way into the area. The Native Americans, however, especially the Cherokee and the Catawba, had used the fertile lands between the rivers for centuries as a neutral hunting ground. The settlers first built their homes along the banks of Fishing and Rocky Creeks. Seeking religious freedom, these settlers established meeting houses, which later became churches, and the wilderness began to become more populated. Two of the county's oldest landmarks are Fishing Creek Presbyterian Church and Old Catholic Presbyterian Church.

Originally part of Craven County, a large region that encompassed much of Upstate South Carolina, Chester County came into its own in 1785. That was the year the state was divided into 37 minor judicial districts. The first courthouse was established in 1776 at Walkers, now known as Lewis Turnout, and was moved to the top of the hill in Chester shortly after 1785. The present courthouse, located in downtown Chester, was built in 1852.

During the Revolutionary War, British general Lord Cornwallis is said to have camped in many sections of the county. There were at least four battles in the county during the Revolution, all of which were forerunners of larger battles and turning points in the war, namely Kings Mountain and Cowpens in 1780.

Aaron Burr, passing through Chester en route to his trial for treason, made a speech from a rock at the top of the hill in town, appealing to the citizens of the area for his release. His appeal fell on deaf ears, and he was whisked away by soldiers to Lewis Turnout where he spent the night at the Lewis Inn, now a private residence. The Aaron Burr Rock stands today in Monument Square in downtown Chester.

In 1803, Henry Dearborn, secretary of war to President Thomas Jefferson, laid the cornerstone for an arsenal and magazine on the banks of the Catawba River near Great Falls. The arsenal existed only a short period of time and only the ruins of Mount Dearborn Military Establishment exist today.

The railroads came to Chester in 1852 and changed the sleepy little town almost overnight. During the War between the States, Chester served as a quartermaster depot for the Confederacy; many warehouses full of military supplies were in existence. Famous diarist Mary Boykin Chesnutt was a refugee here and entertained many well-known persons of the day, including Confederate First Lady Varina Davis and her children. Four Confederate cannon were unearthed in 1986 and have been restored, two of which are now on display downtown. One is part of a traveling exhibit and can actually be fired.

A school for freed slaves begun by the Presbyterian Church became an important part of Chester following the war. Brainerd Institute would become one of the most important schools for African Americans in the state and the region before closing as a junior college in 1939.

After Reconstruction, the railroads helped to rebuild Chester County, and the town became a railroad hub early in the 20th century. At one time Chester was included in the ten largest cities in South Carolina.

In the fall of 1941, the U.S. Army held maneuvers in Chester County and the soon-to-be-famous Gen. George Patton came through town and spoke here.

Once a primarily agricultural area, Chester County and its cotton production led to textiles being the reigning industry. Now, however, diversification has led to development, and the county is growing and prospering.

This is by no means an all-inclusive representation of the photographs of Chester County. It is, however, a collection drawn from local families and newspapers, with a few others picked up along the way. Our goal has been to bring to light photographs that few have seen for years and others that may have never had a public viewing. Chester County is rich in history, culture, and heritage. These photographs basically cover the past 130 years, since the development of photographic techniques. The many different aspects of the county is one of the things we tried to focus on as we chose what to go into this book. We had fun going through the old photographs. We hope you have as much fun viewing them as we did.

Glinda Price Coleman and Gina Price White

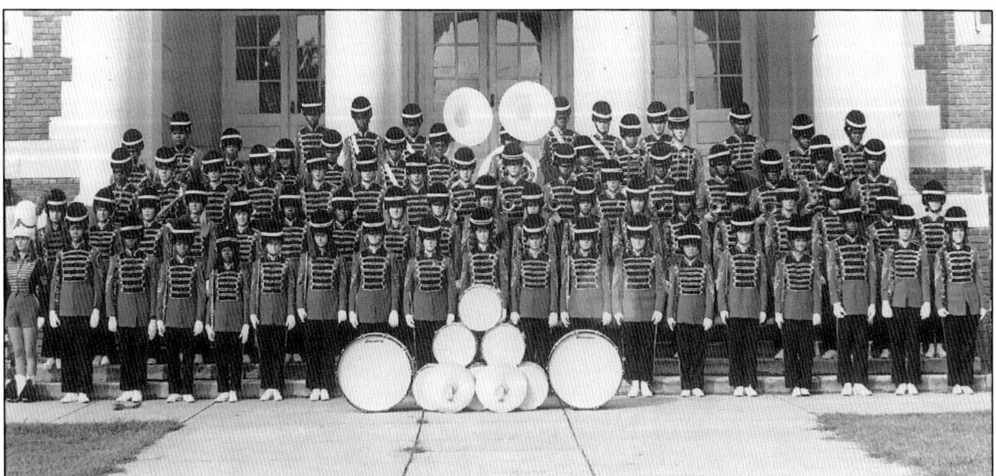

Pictured here is the Chester High School Marching Band in 1972.

One

HOMEFRONT

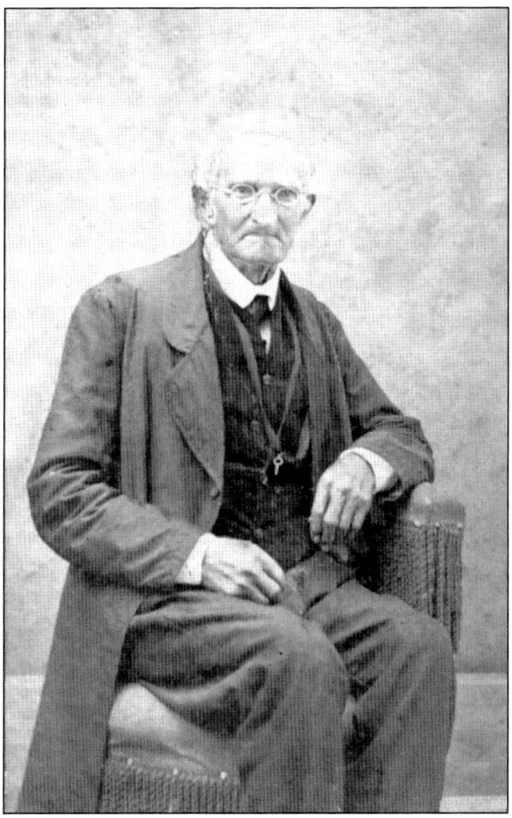

One of the innovations of the 1850s was photography. The average citizen could have a portrait of himself and his family members for a fraction of the cost of the traditional painted version. Photography studios cropped up in big cities and small towns alike. This gentleman is James Bailey Sr. in a portrait taken by Van Ness, a photographer in Chester, South Carolina, in the late 1860s to early 1870s.

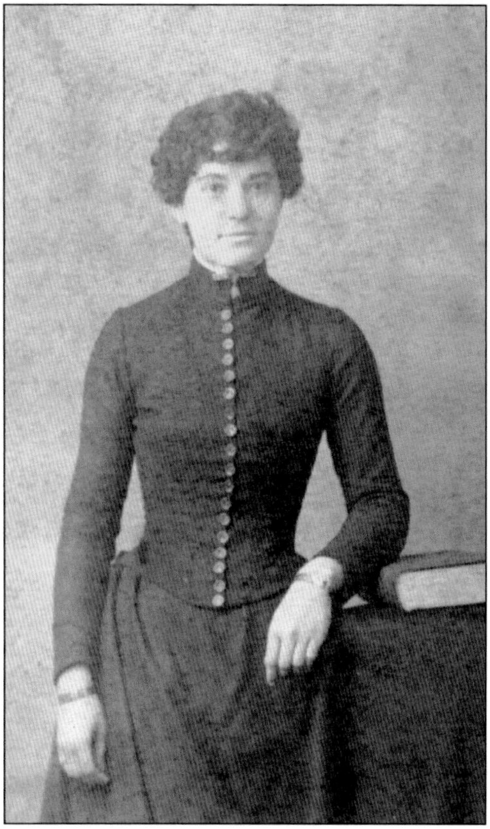

This unidentified young lady, standing in a classic pose, *c.* 1870s, had her likeness captured by Baker & Johnson, artist photographers, Chester, South Carolina.

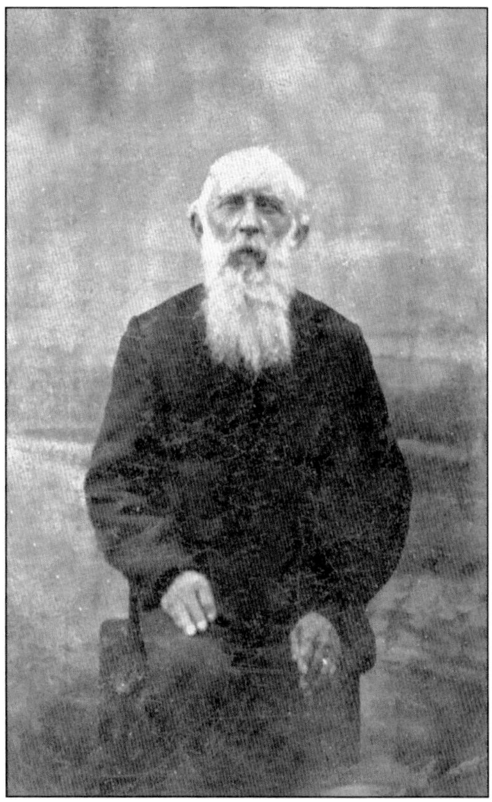

Tintypes were a durable, early medium of photography. They were particularly popular during the War between the States because soldiers could carry likenesses of their loved ones without fear of destroying them. This image, *c.* 1860, is of a Mr. Robinson, possibly John Harvey, the father of Chester County resident Eli Frank Robinson of the Baton Rouge community.

A tenant farmer stands in the doorway of his home on the Walker place near Walker's Branch in western Chester County. Sidney, one of the Walker sons, sits on a table by the stoop around the turn of the 20th century.

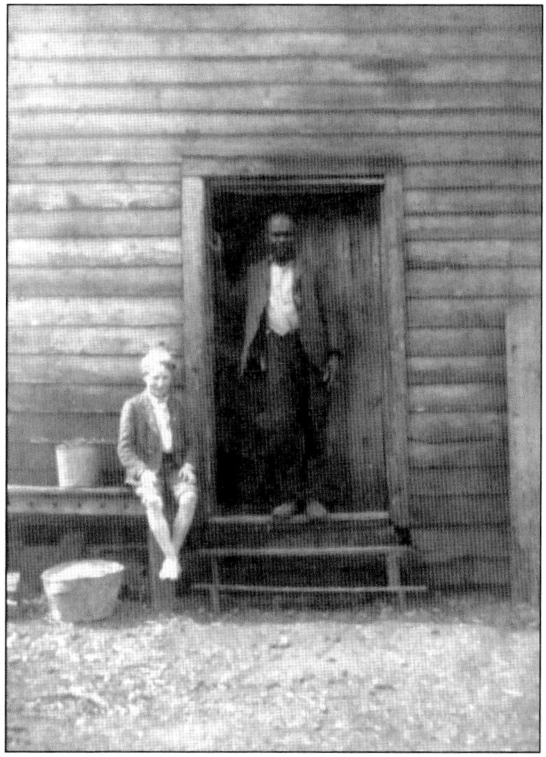

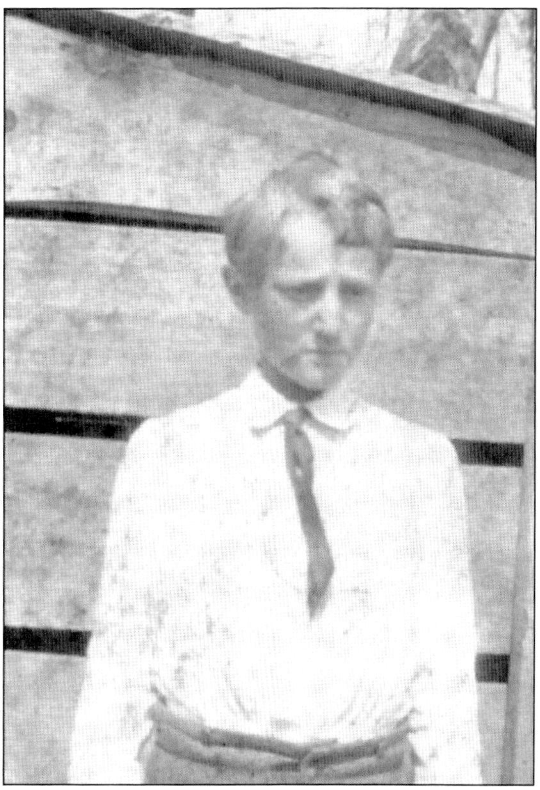

Shown here is a portrait of Sidney Walker in front of one of the outbuildings on the Walker place. This view was probably taken about the same time as the photograph above.

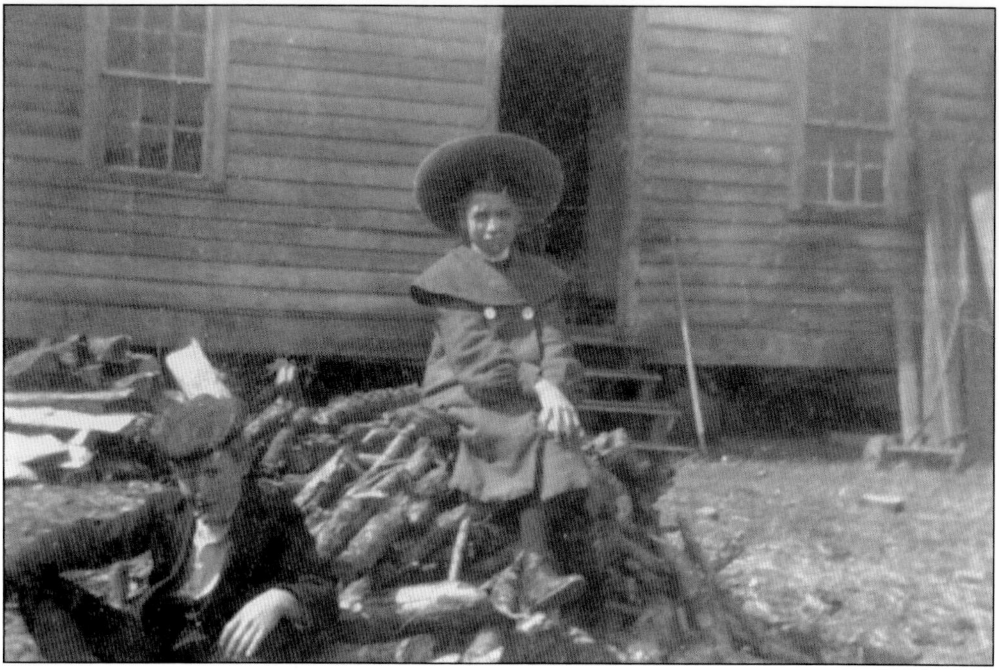

Woodcutting and gathering were typical chores for children around 1900. These two appear to be contemplating the work to be done after they have changed from their Sunday clothes.

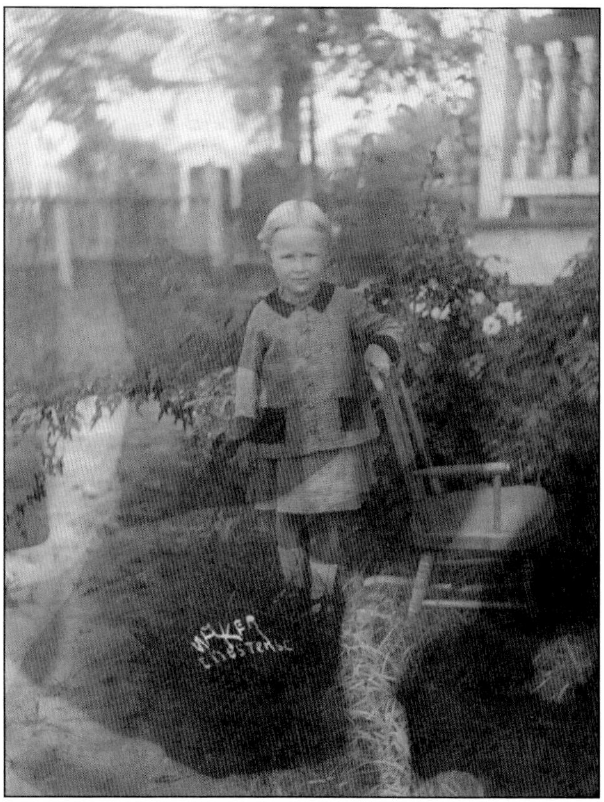

In the 19th century, parents parted little girls' hair in the middle and little boys hair on the side. This is a convenient way of discerning the gender of children in photographs because, very often, they wore similar clothing until the age of three or four. This little girl poses in a rose garden by the porch of her home, c. 1900. Note the signature of the photographer at the bottom.

Isabel Owens was about 20 years old in this photograph, which was taken in the 1870s. She was born in Chester County in October 1851. As was typical of the daughters in the farmer class in upcountry South Carolina, she married in her 20s (to John Bennett) and had six children.

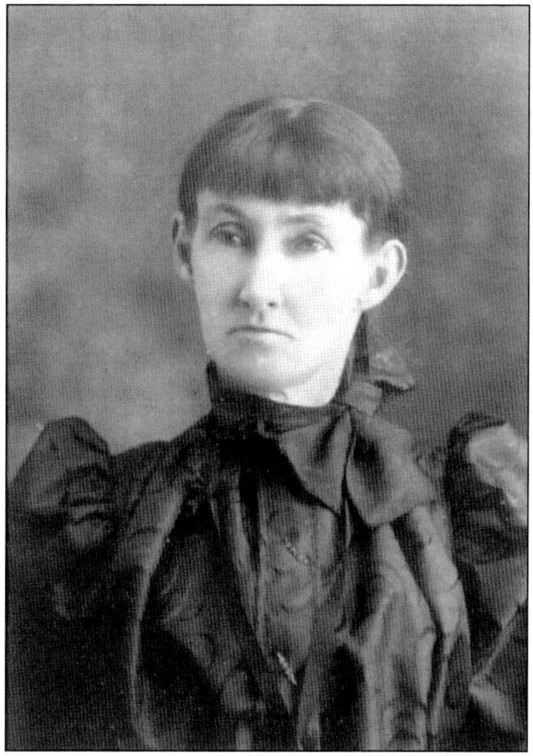

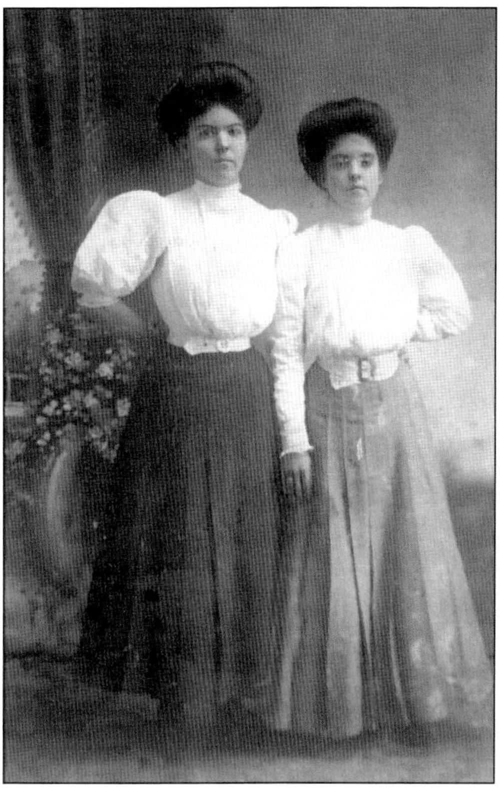

Annie Sidney Robinson and Daisy Viola Robinson pose for a portrait at a Chester studio, *c.* 1908. The only two girls in a family of ten, the sisters were very close. They were dressed in their Sunday best for this portrait, which was taken in front of a painted backdrop.

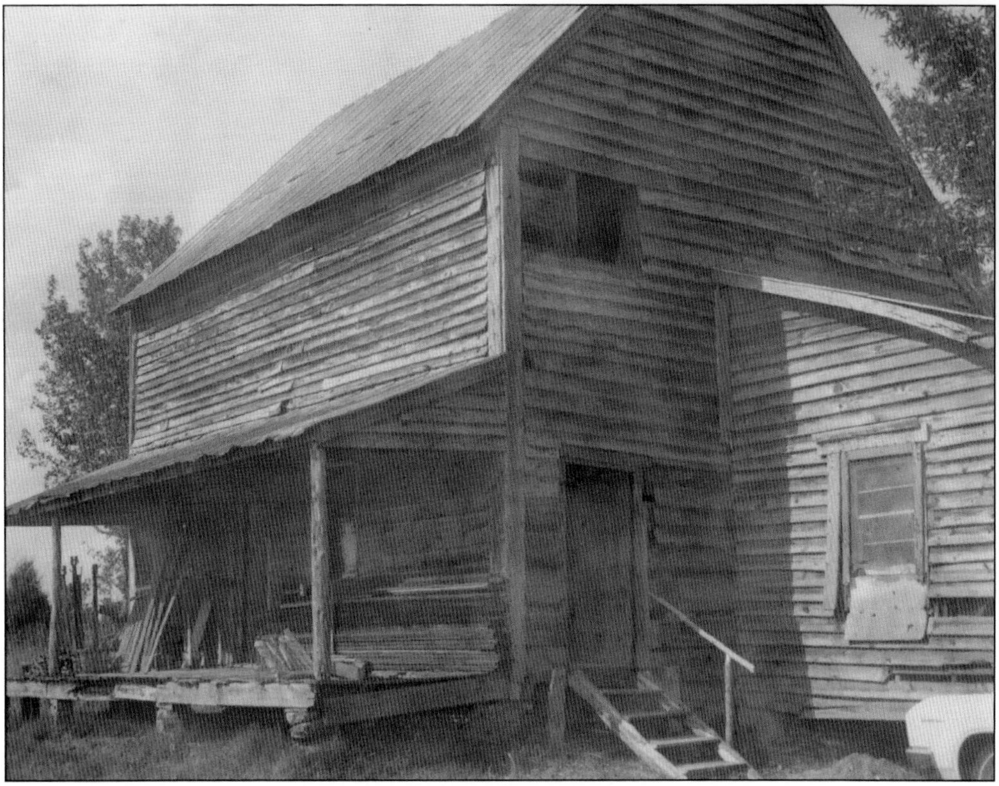

This cabin, formerly located 1 mile north of Richburg on SC 9, was built prior to the American Revolution. Once owned by the Chester County Historical Society, the cabin, which had a central chimney considered a rarity, was moved in 1998 to the Mendenhall property at Brattonsville, just across the Chester County line. The original part of the house, made of logs, is 20 feet wide by 28 feet long.

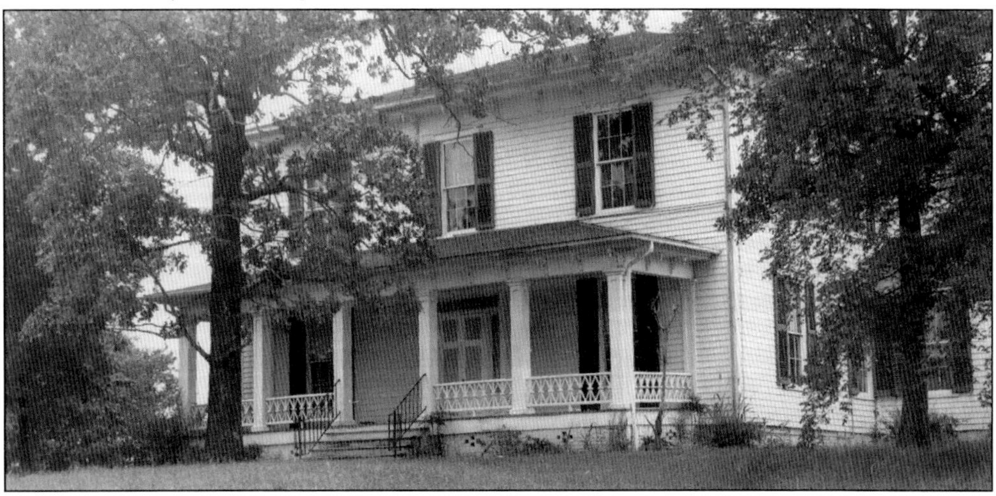

Gen. Alexander Walker built this house in 1859 featuring a one-story porch across the front with an unusual balustrade railing designed to resemble Mexican lace work. Walker, a Confederate lieutenant colonel, became a general in the state militia following the war. He served in the State House of Representatives and the Senate. The house was torn down in the mid-1970s.

Life in rural Chester County in the first couple of decades of the 20th century moved at a much slower pace than it does now. John Harvey Robinson and his wife, Dora Anne Allen Robinson, stand next to the Saye House, built c. 1825, in Rodman. Alongside the buggy in the yard is parked a touring car (with a license plate dated 1922)—a portent of change.

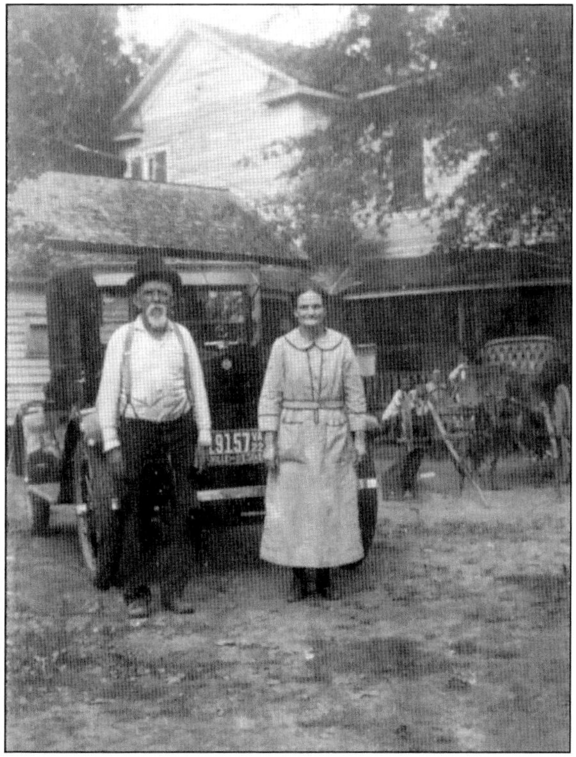

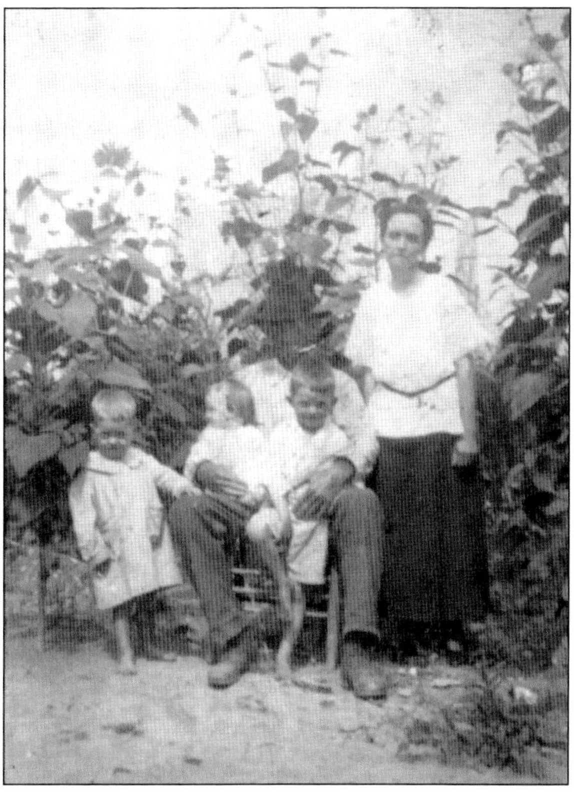

In this 1922 image, John and Daisy Bennett pose with their children, from left to right, Robert (Bob), Dorothy (Dot), and J.L. Jr., for a family portrait in front of some mid-summer flowers at the home of Daisy's parents in Rodman.

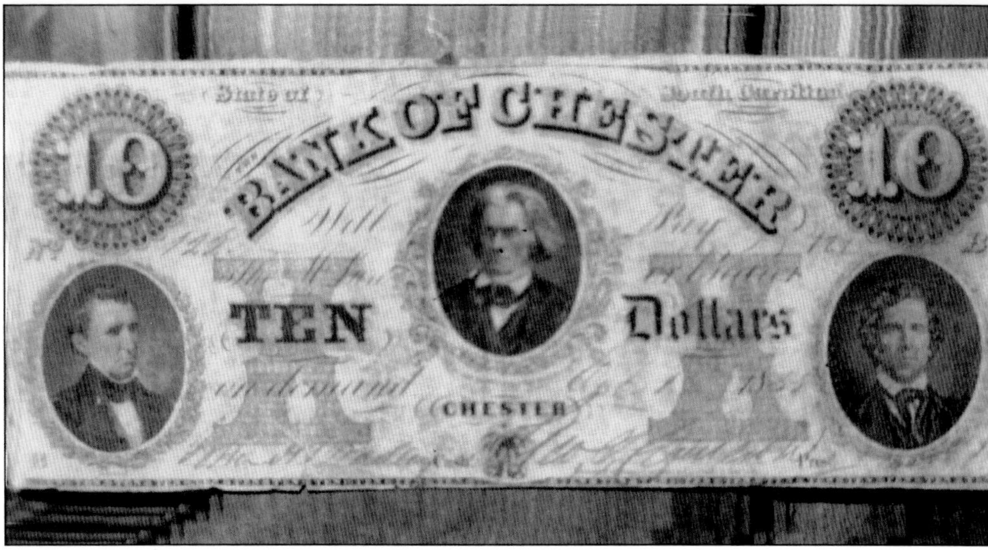

It was common in antebellum America for the local banks to print their own money. Here is an example of a note printed by the Bank of Chester in the 1850s.

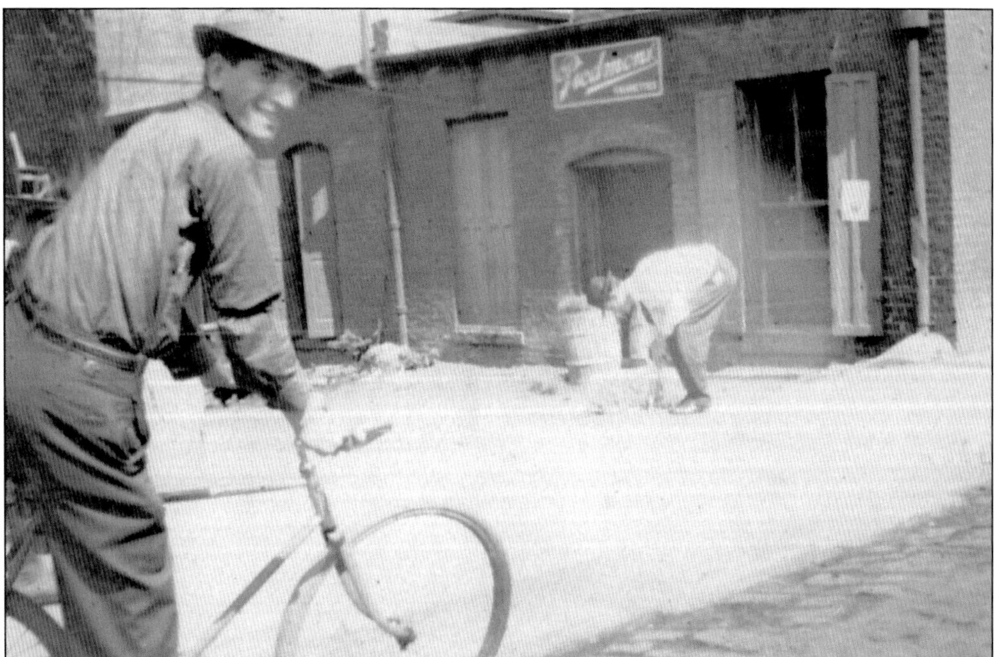

Bicycles were a favorite mode of transportation around Chester in the early half of the 20th century. Here, an unidentified young man bicycles past a warehouse on the outskirts of town in the 1920s.

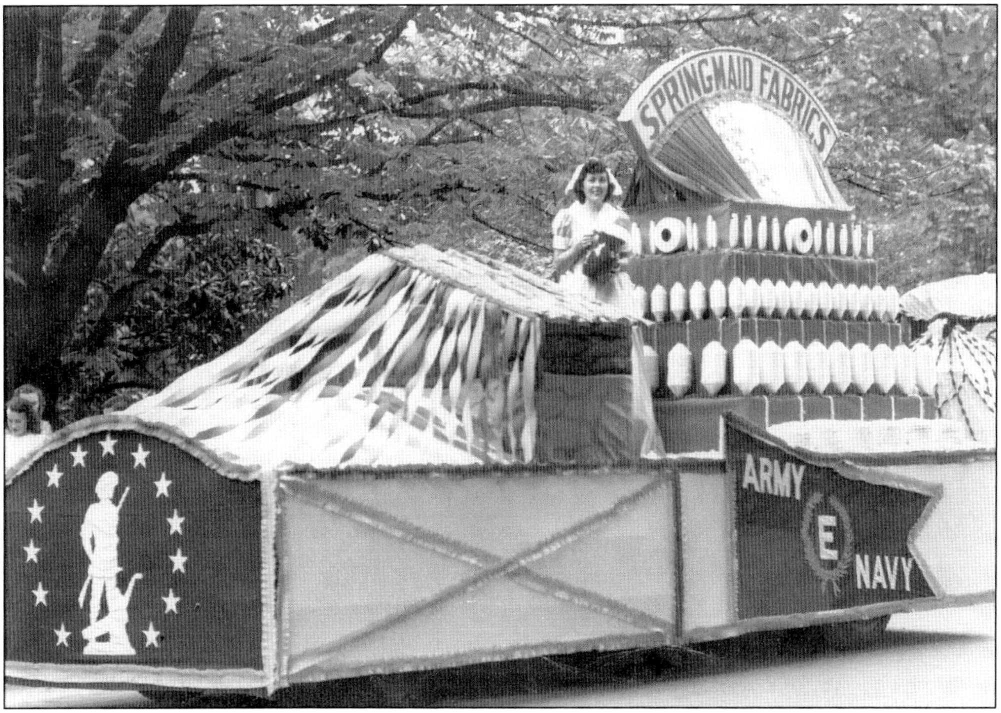

Parades have been and continue to be popular events in Chester County. This photograph is of Springs Mills float in the Guernsey Festival parade in Chester, and riding on the float is Billie Etters. Springs Cotton Mills was a heavy influence in the area. Because of the abundance of dairies in the county, the county established the Guernsey Festival in the 1940s.

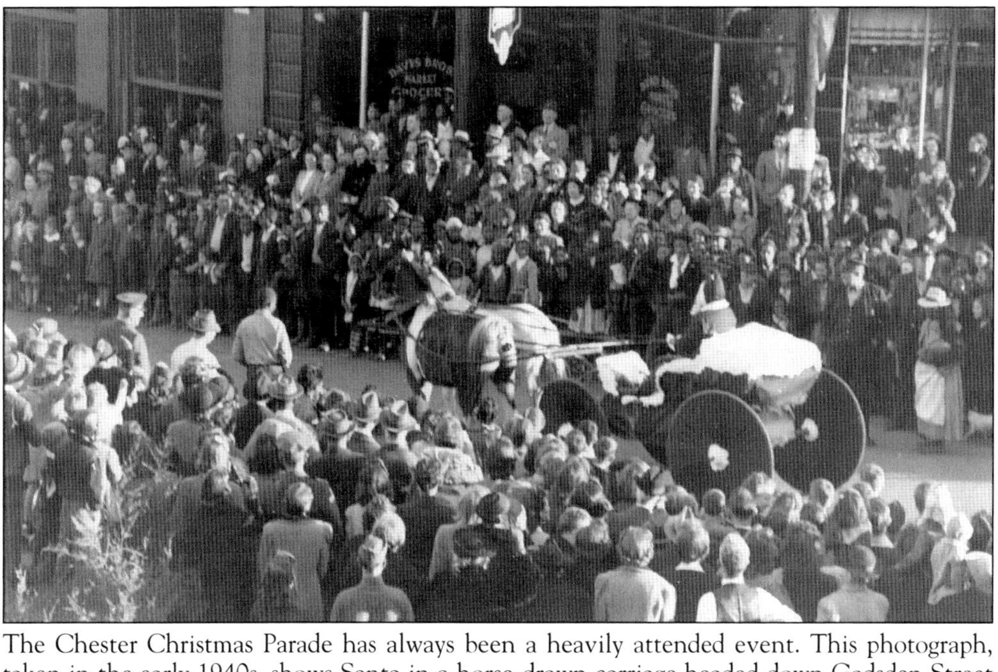

The Chester Christmas Parade has always been a heavily attended event. This photograph, taken in the early 1940s, shows Santa in a horse-drawn carriage headed down Gadsden Street toward the Valley.

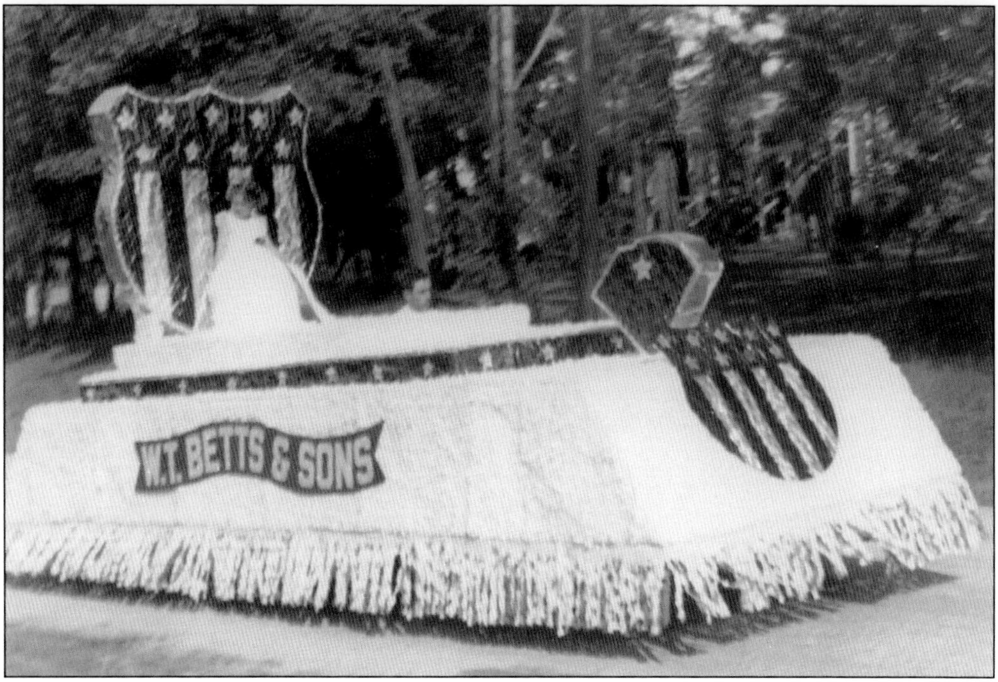

Little Betty Betts graces the float of her grandfather's company, W.T. Betts and Sons, at the Guernsey Festival.

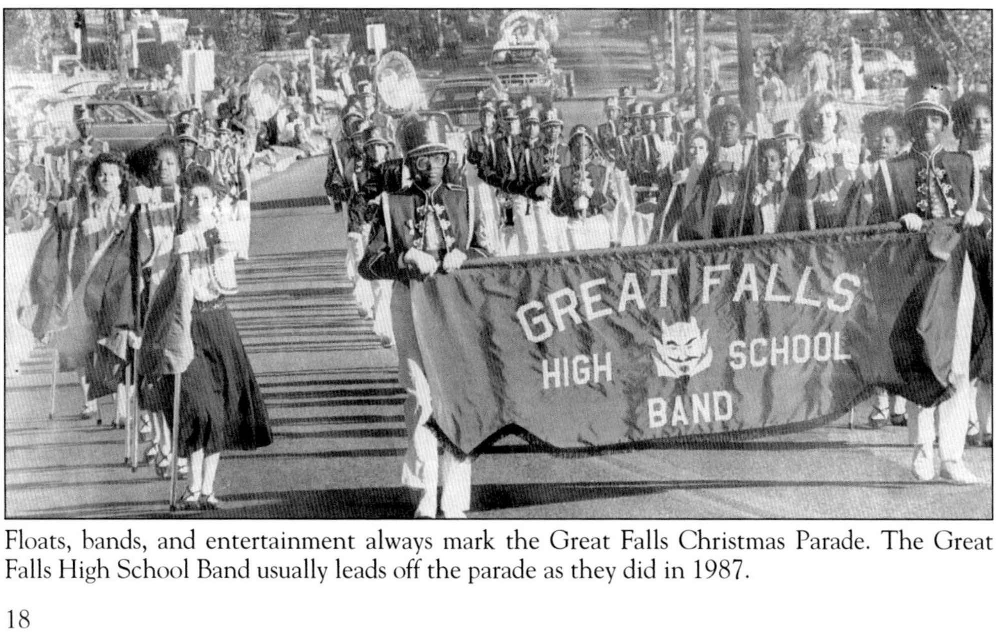

Floats, bands, and entertainment always mark the Great Falls Christmas Parade. The Great Falls High School Band usually leads off the parade as they did in 1987.

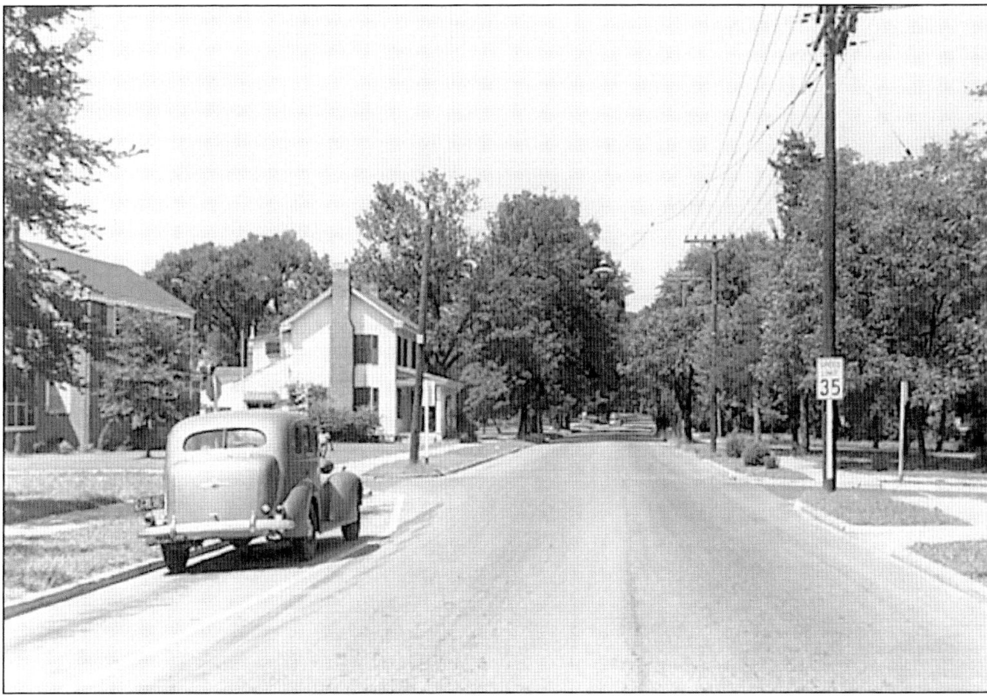

The tree-lined residential areas of Chester have always been much admired. This photograph, looking north on York Street, was taken in July 1952.

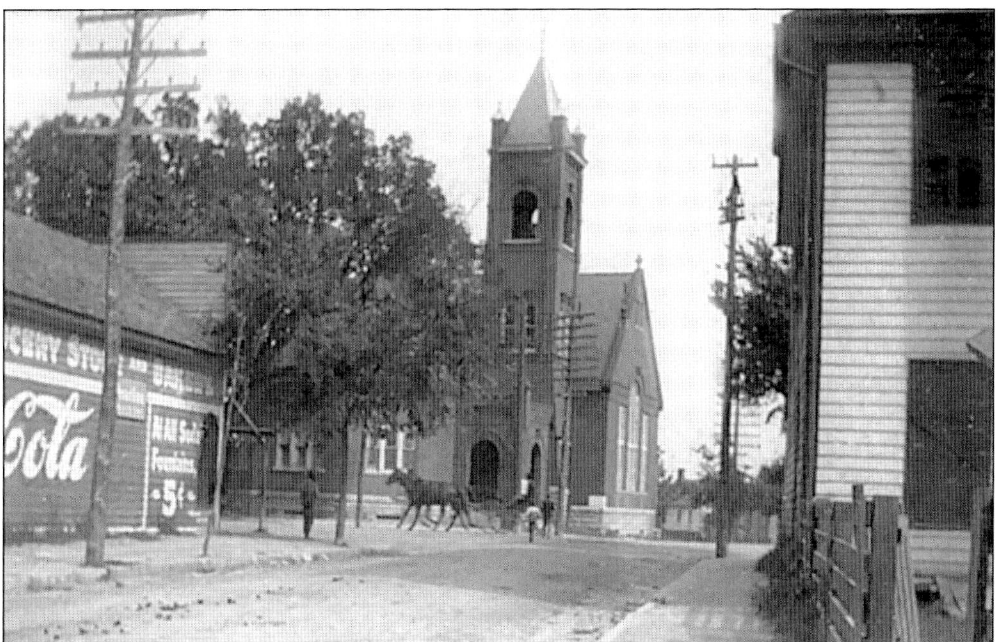

This photograph was taken, prior to 1907, from Wylie Street looking toward the Associate Reformed Presbyterian Church. Note the horse and buggy traveling along Main Street and the grocery store, at left, that occupied the corner before the post office was built in 1908.

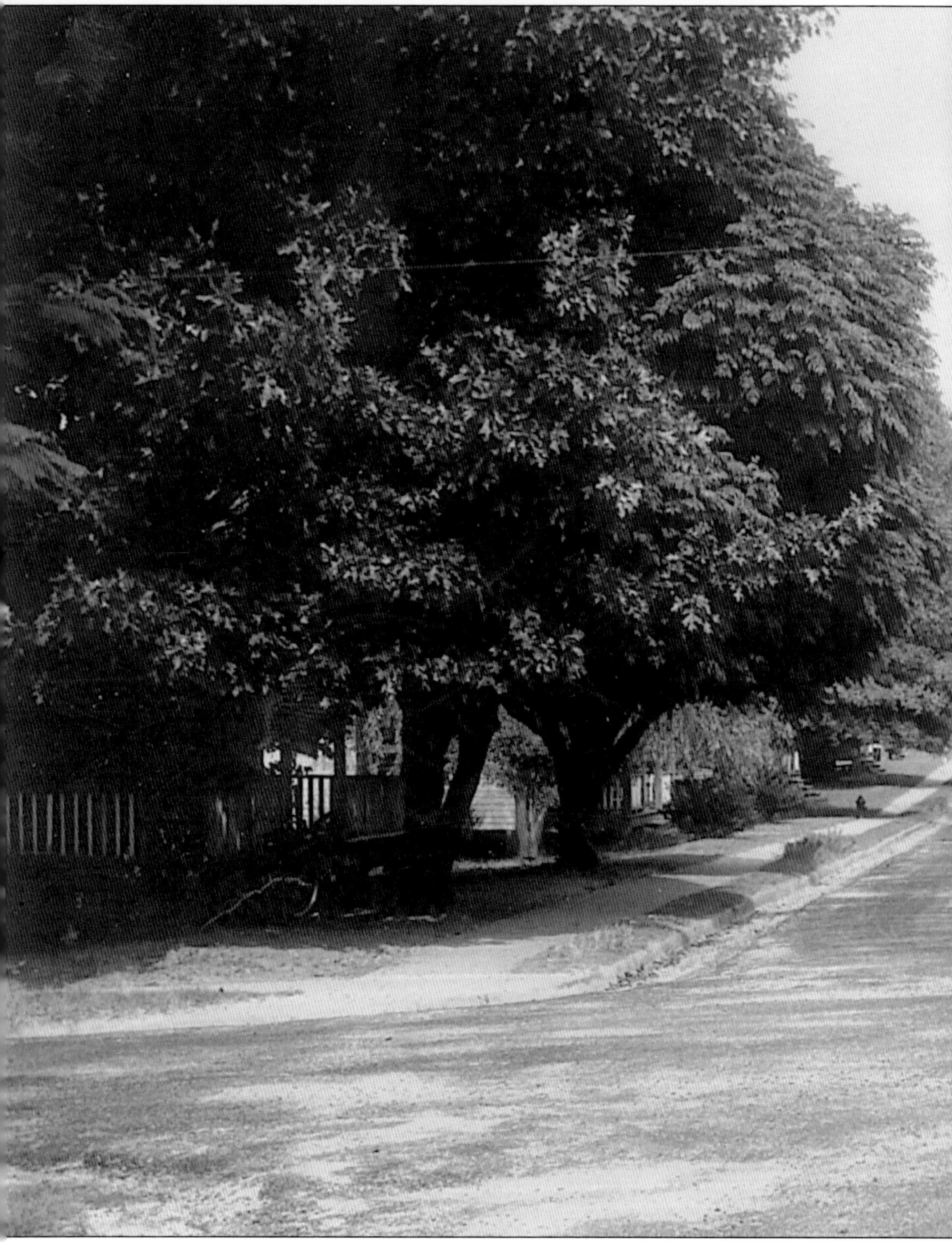

Textile mills were the main employers of people in Chester County through most of the 20th century. Springs Mills had a number of plants in the county, and the mill villages were a central

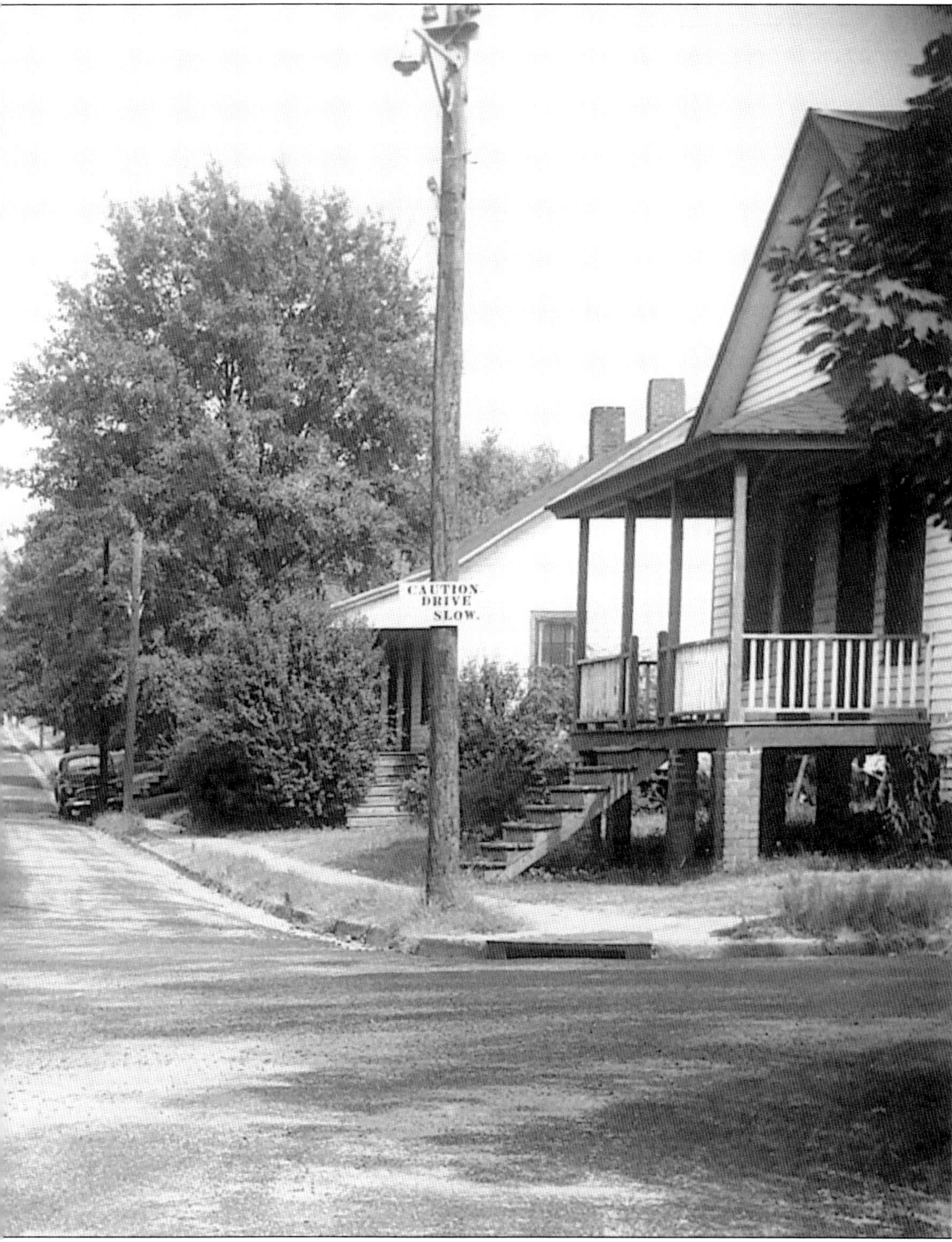

part of life for many residents. This is a scene of the newly paved street in the Gayle mill village on the northwestern side of town in August 1948.

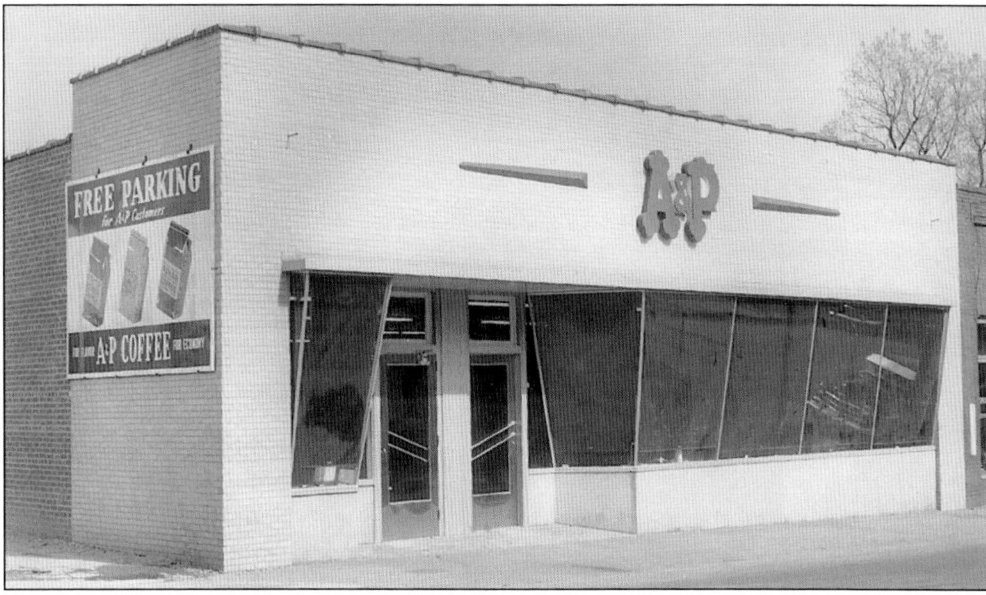

The A&P Store in Chester had several locations before it closed in 1986 at its last location on York Street. This photograph shows the store in the early 1950s when it was located at 130 Hudson Street, the present location of the Hazel Pittman Center. In the 1960s the building housed a Sears catalog store and, in the 1970s, a Western Auto.

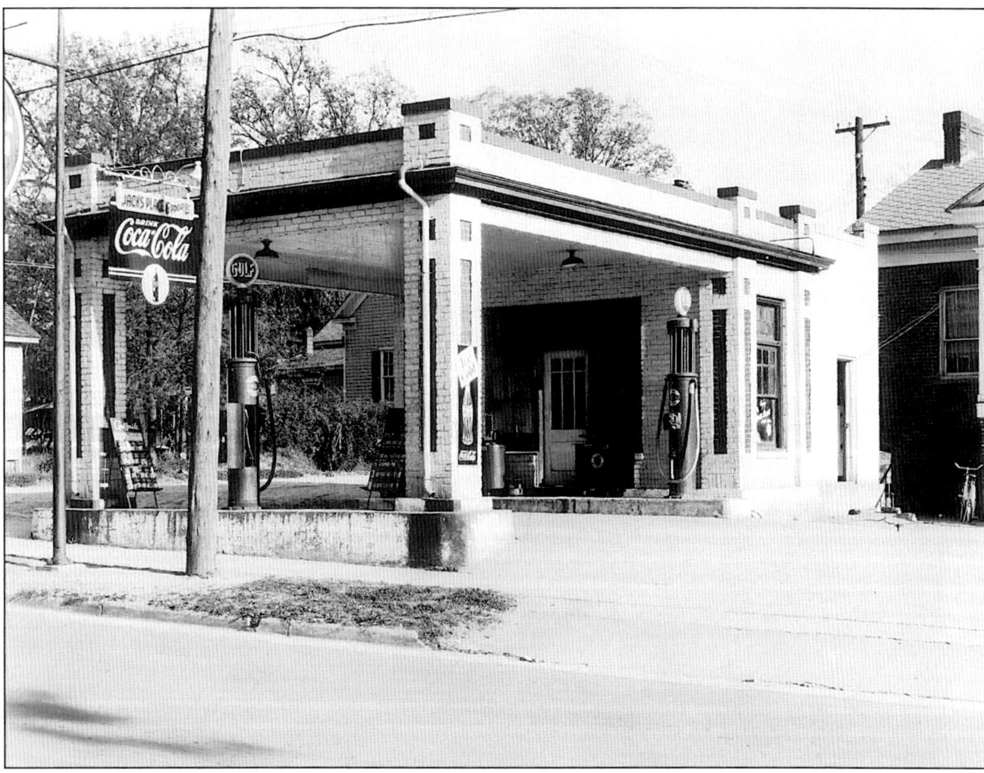

Many Chester County men got their first jobs in gas or "filling" stations in the area. This Gulf station, seen in the late 1930s, was located on Lancaster Street.

In 1942, the Belk Hudson building in downtown Chester burned. It could not be replaced until after World War II when rationing was suspended. The Belk building was demolished (seen at right) before being replaced with a more modern structure.

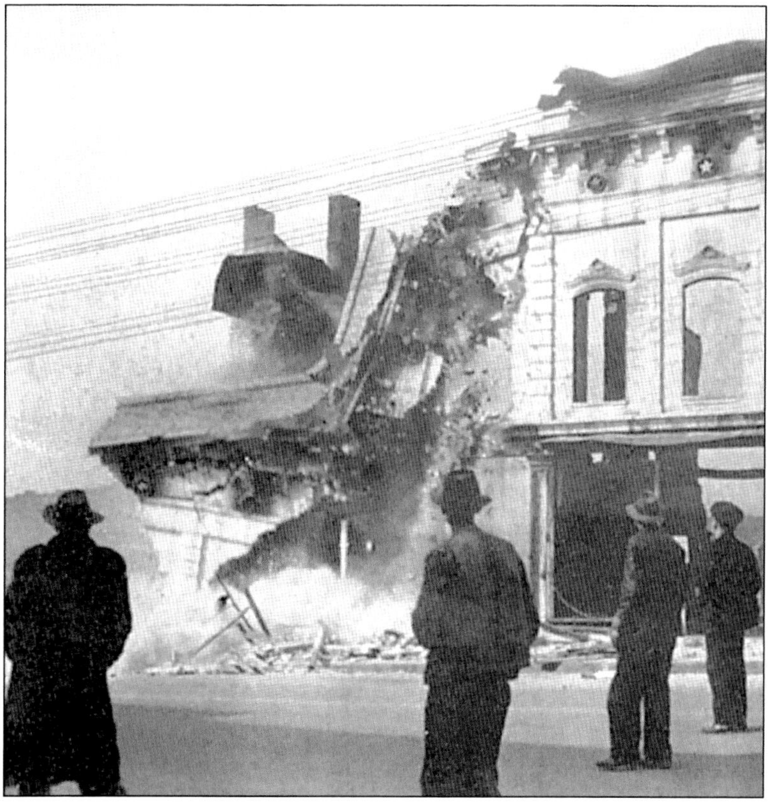

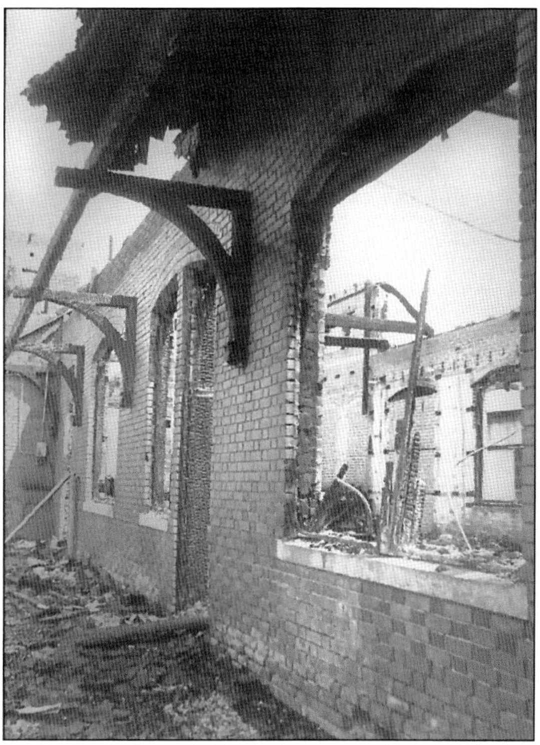

At left, another landmark was destroyed by fire in a later decade. The abandoned Norfolk Southern depot burned to the ground in August 1993.

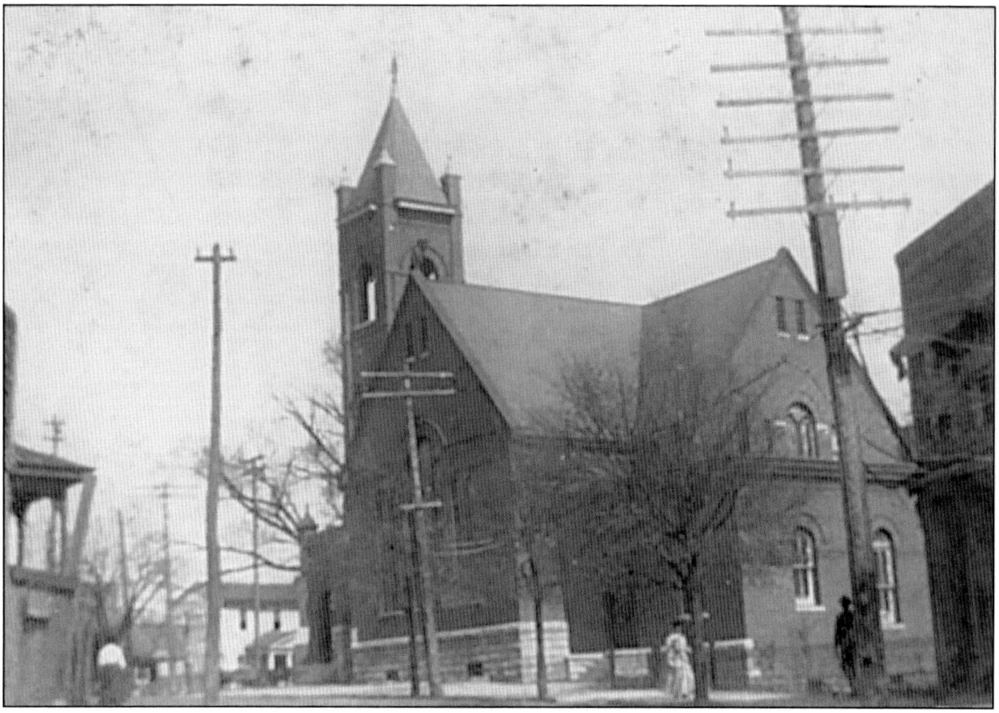

Organized in 1869, the Associate Reformed Presbyterian Church has stood on the corner of Main and Wylie Streets in Chester since 1898. This photograph was taken sometime around the turn of the 20th century. Note the white frame building across from the church.

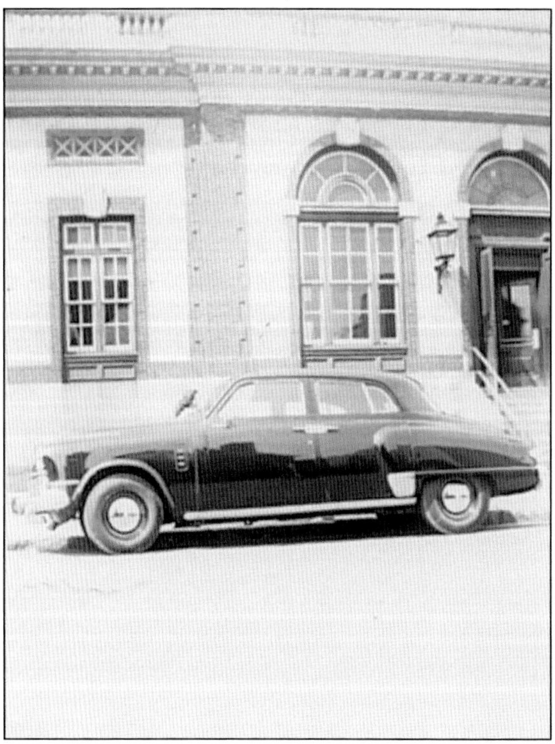

The Chester Post Office, seen here in the 1940s, was located in this building from 1908 until the mid-1960s.

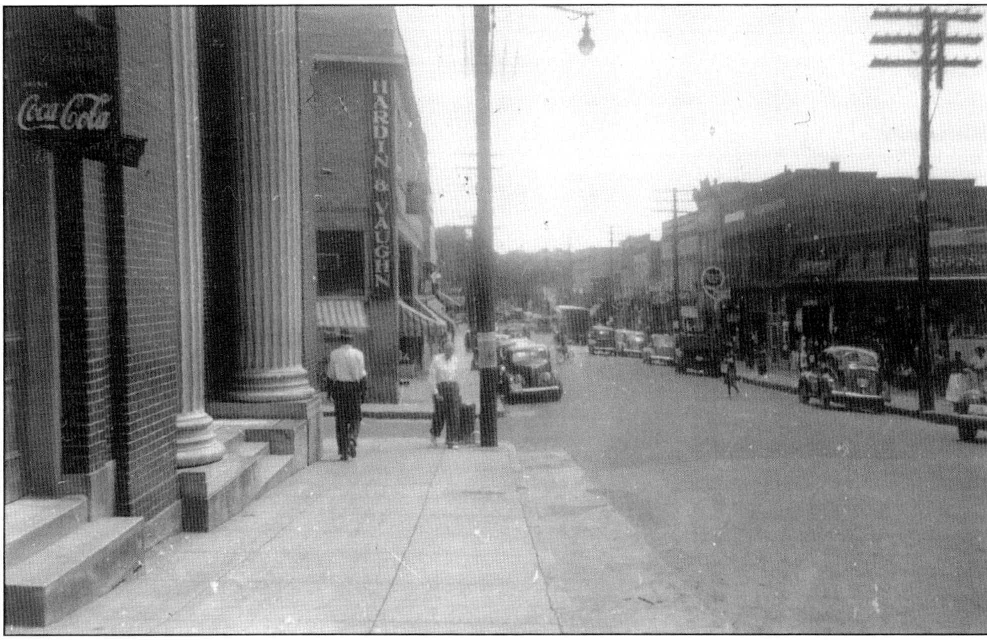

This is a picture of Gadsden Street, looking north, in 1938. Notice Hardin & Vaughn Department Store on the left and the early stages of construction on the new McCrorey's Dime Store on the right.

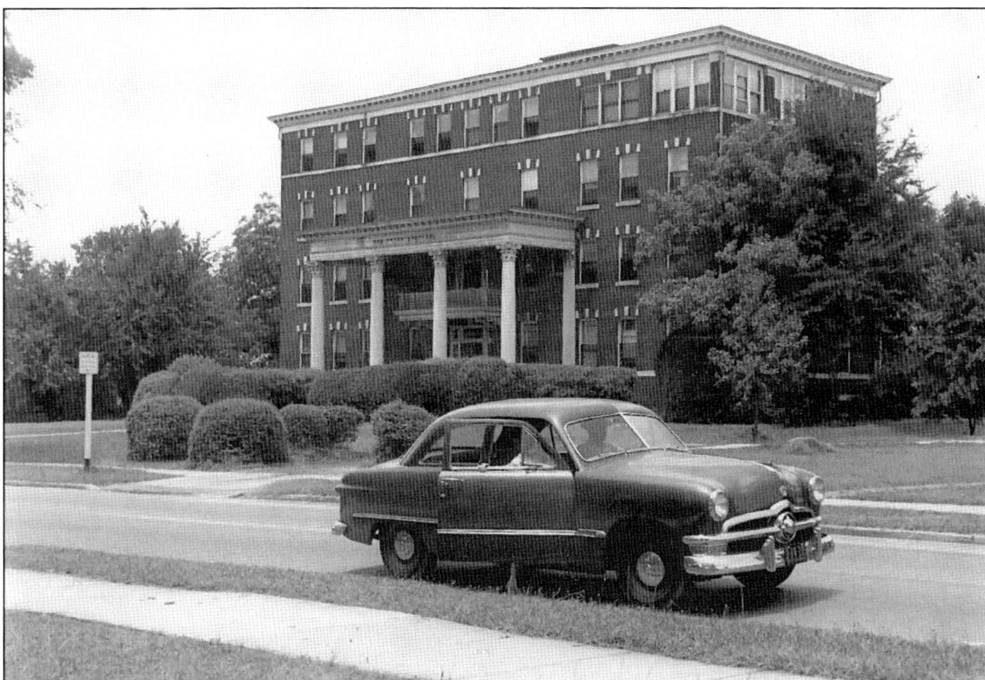

Pryor Hospital was located on York Street in Chester for 36 years, from 1916 to 1952. This photograph was taken just prior to its move to a location on Great Falls Road about 2 miles south of town.

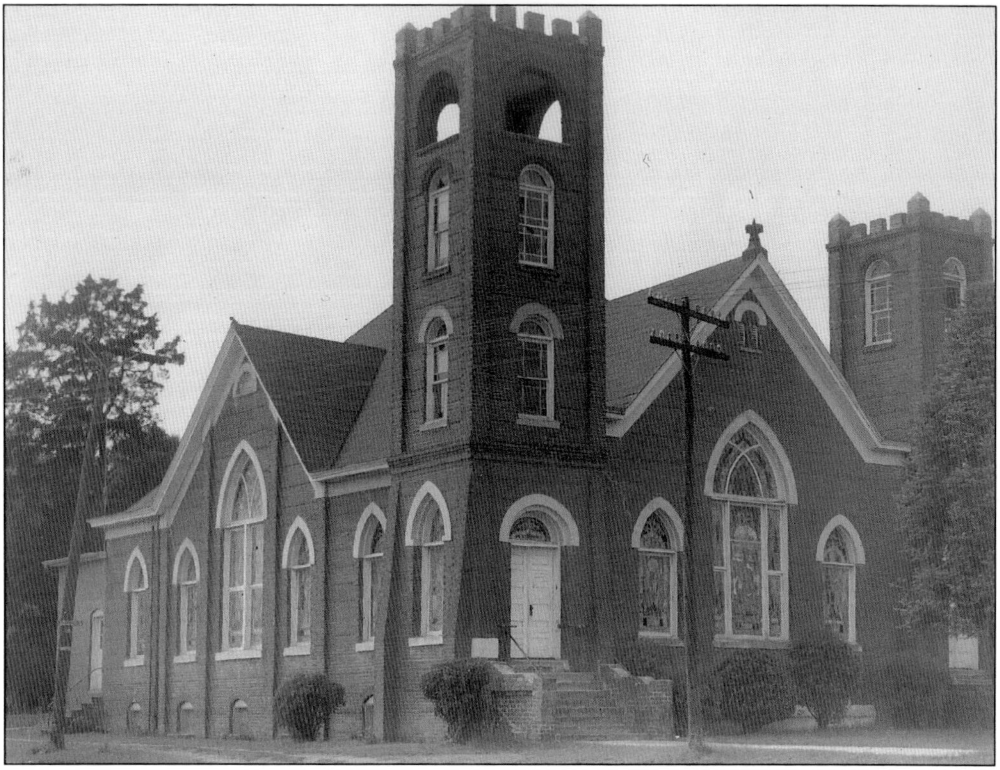

Metropolitan A.M.E. Zion Church on York Street was organized in 1866 and first met in a brush arbor. Eventually, the congregation built a wooden church on the same site as the current building, which was constructed in 1914. This photograph was taken in the 1960s.

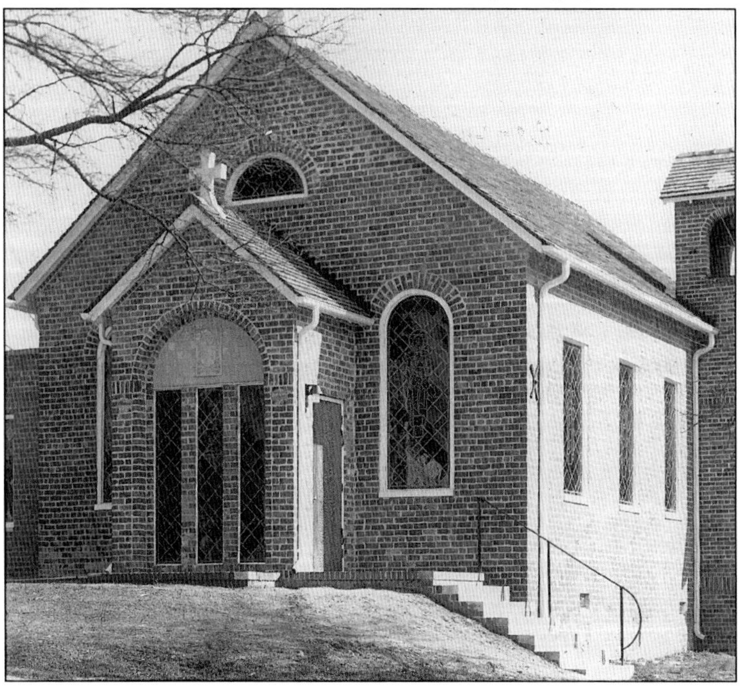

The St. Joseph Catholic Church building was built by the Purity Presbyterian Church congregation as a lecture room in 1839 because their main sanctuary was located 2.5 miles southeast of town. Purchased by the Catholic Diocese of Charleston in 1854, the building has undergone extensive renovations. It is the oldest church building in the town of Chester.

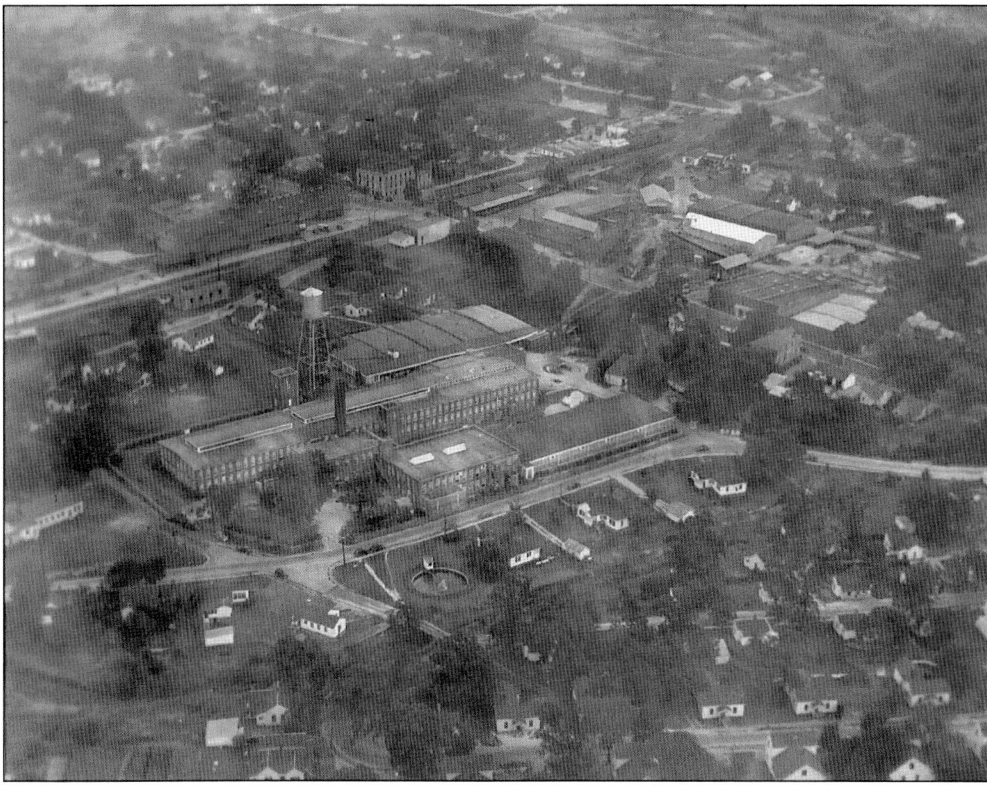

This is an aerial view of Springsteen Mill and the Lancaster Street area of Chester. Notice the Nicholson Hotel in the top center of the photograph just to the right of the Southern Depot.

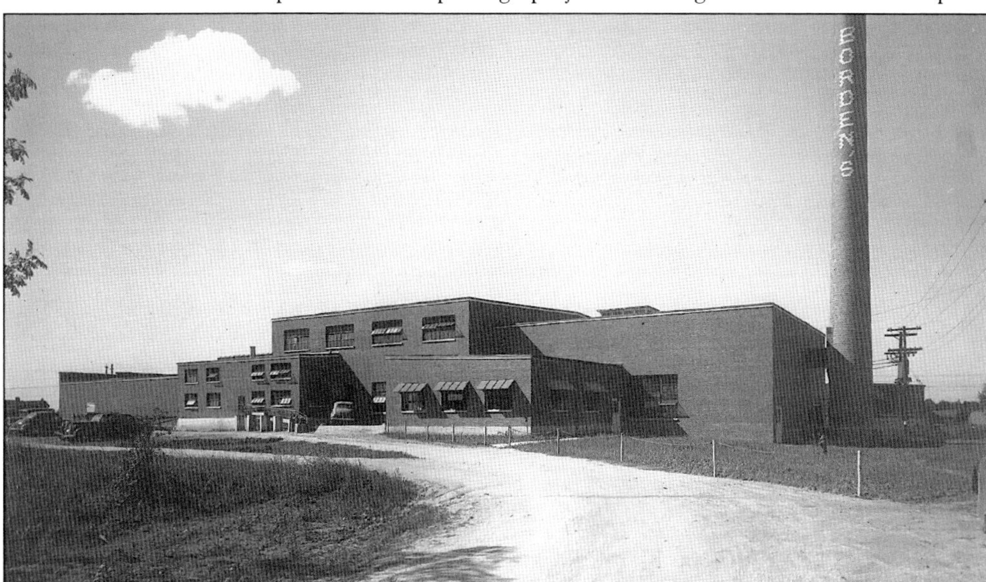

The Borden Evaporated Milk Plant located on Saluda Street opened in Chester in 1940. It operates today as Eagle Family Foods. The smokestack was torn down in 2000. This photograph was taken about the time the plant opened.

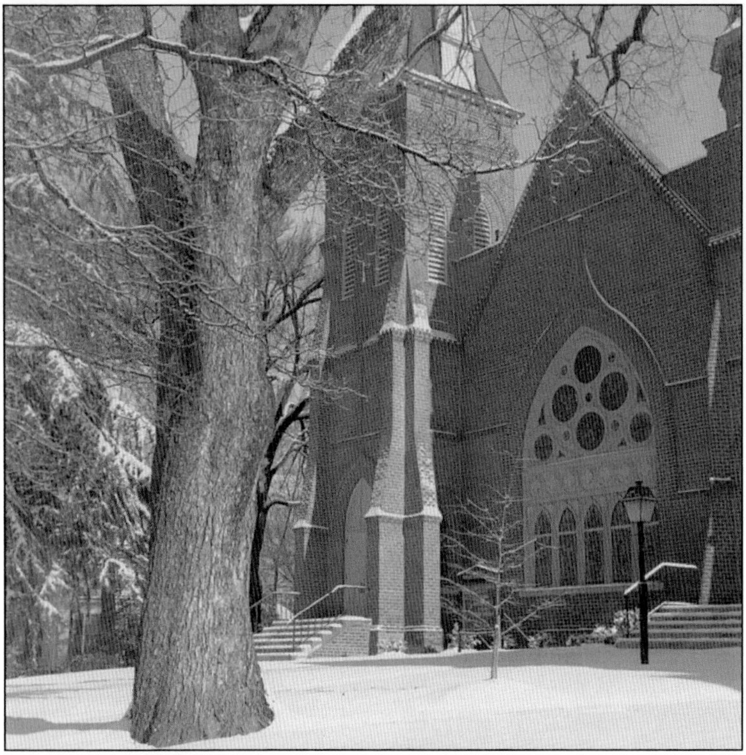

In 1787, Purity Presbyterian Church was established 2.5 miles southeast of the courthouse. The present building on Wylie Street was dedicated in 1855. A snowstorm in 1966 provides the lovely setting for this photograph.

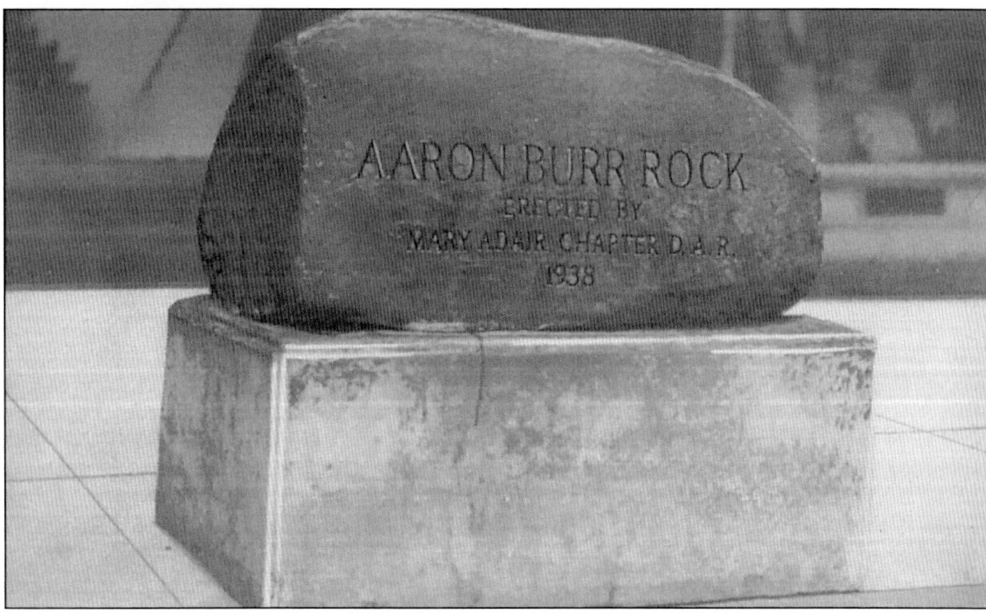

Aaron Burr, former Vice President of the United States, was captured in 1807 and charged with treason. He passed through Chester County under armed guard on his way to stand trial in Richmond. When he and his captors reached town, Burr jumped from his horse, leapt upon a rock near a tavern, and plead to the citizenry of Chester for asylum. No one heeded his appeal. The rock has been preserved and was erected as a monument by the Mary Adair Chapter of the Daughters of the American Revolution in 1938.

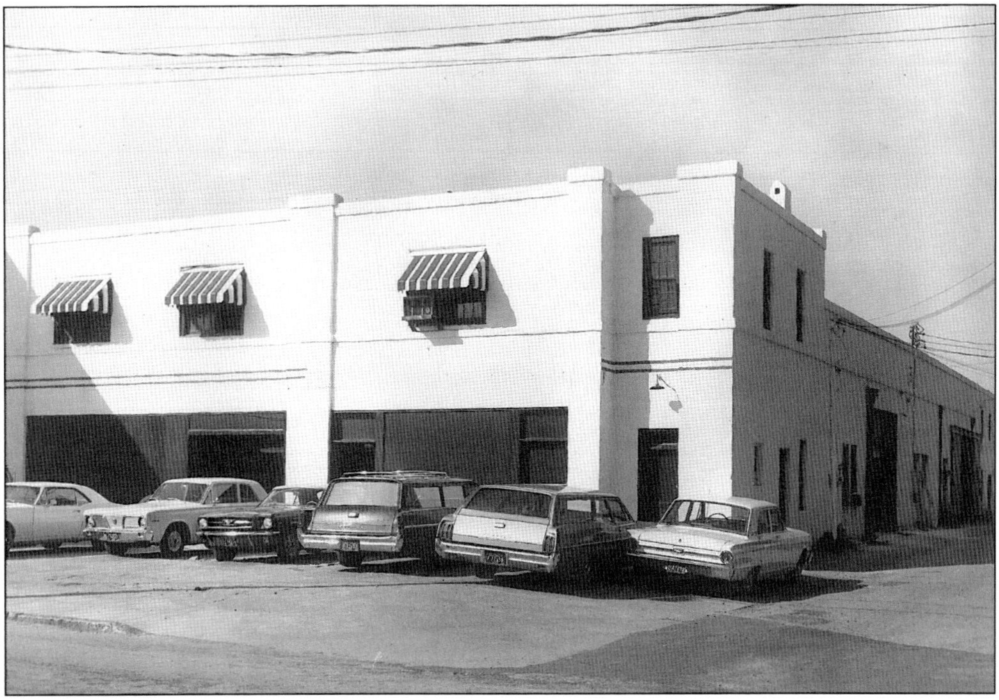

The Chester Foundry was located at the corner of Hudson and Irwin Streets. The building was torn down in the 1970s, not too many years after this 1968 photograph was taken.

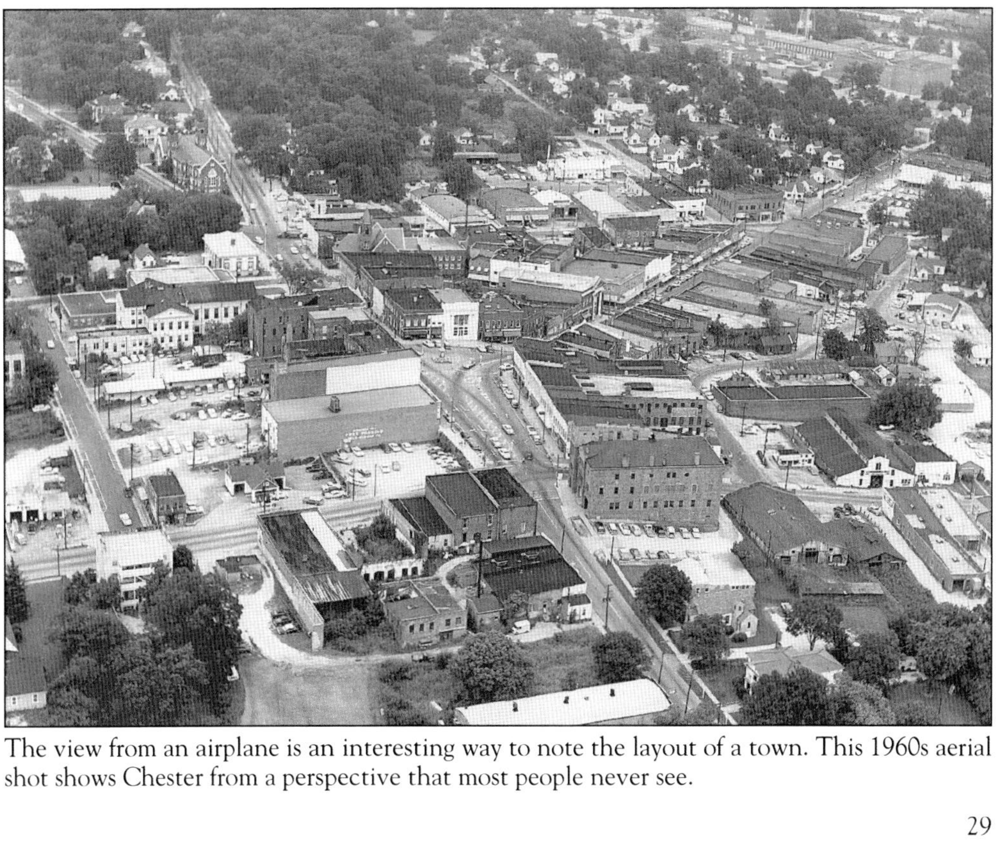

The view from an airplane is an interesting way to note the layout of a town. This 1960s aerial shot shows Chester from a perspective that most people never see.

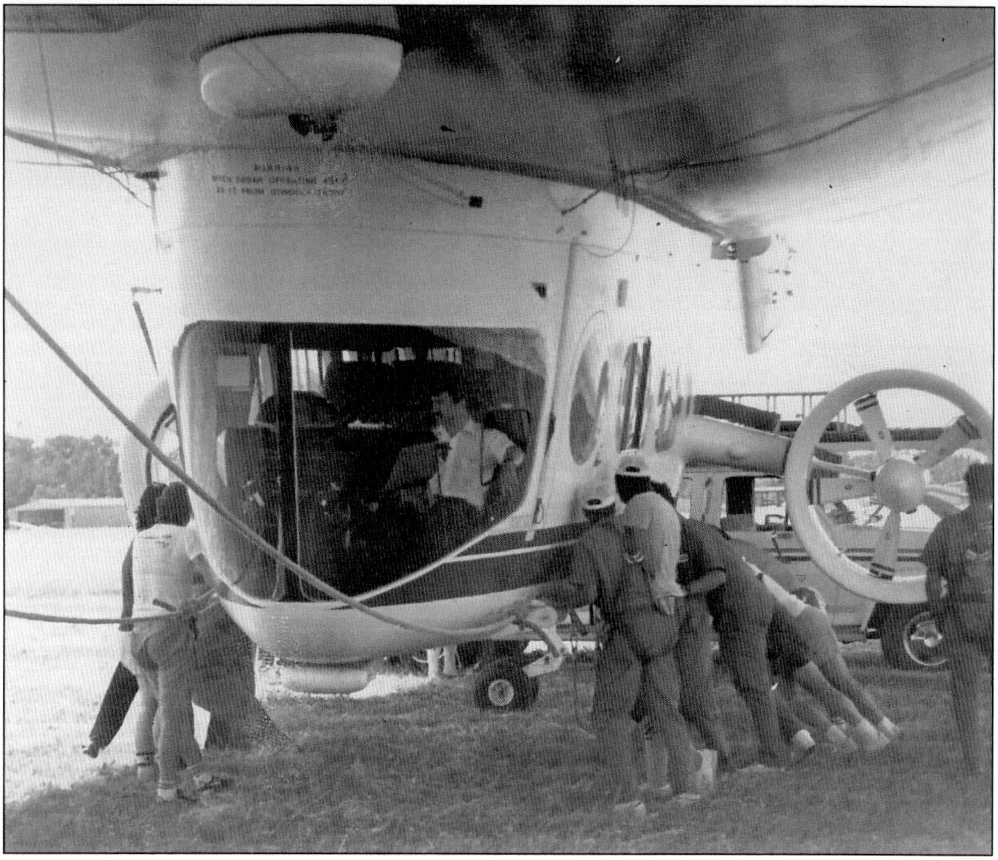

In the late 1980s, Chester Airport was used to house a blimp for a few days, and some newspaper photographers were asked to take a ride. Above are passengers piling into the gondola and, below, is a view of Chester while the blimp is airborne.

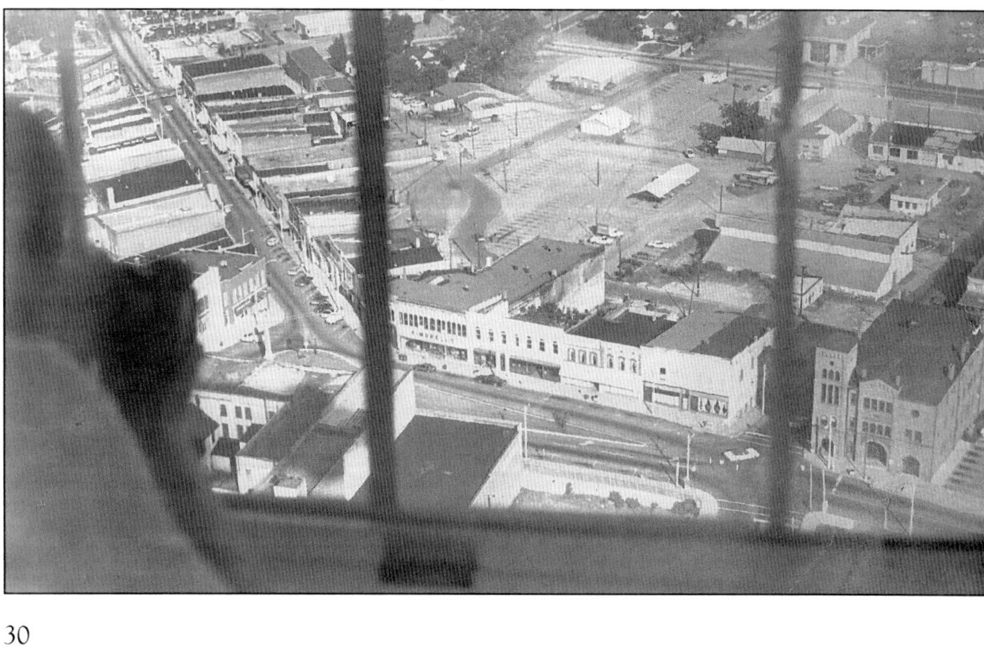

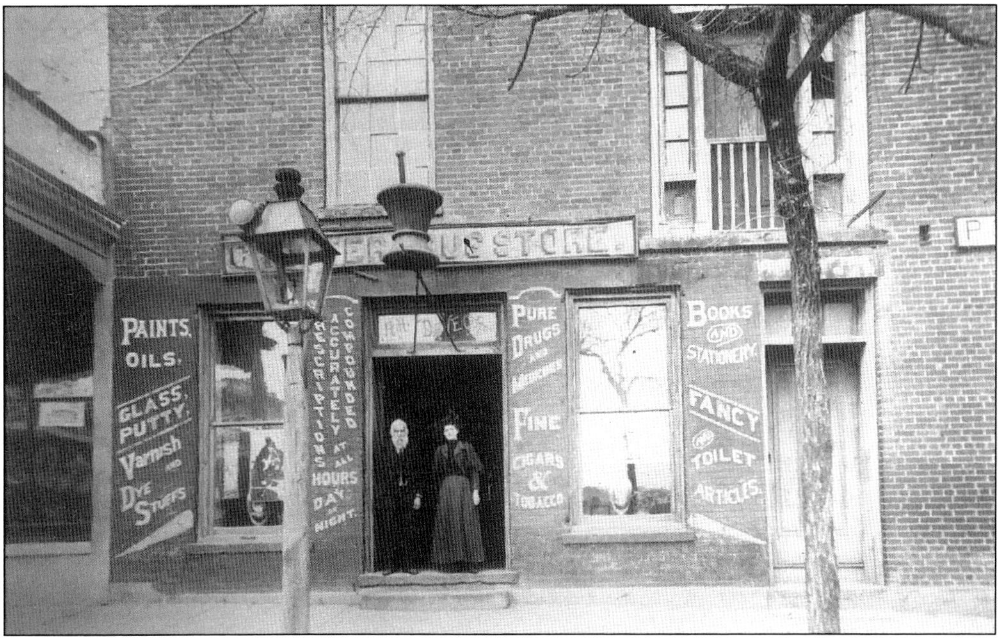

The Chester Drug Store was owned and operated by Dr. A.H. Davega, posing here with his wife in front of the establishment. Located on top of the hill, the store offered more than just medicine as can be seen by the signs around the door. The third floor of this building was the home of Civil War diarist Mary Boykin Chesnutt for several months in 1865.

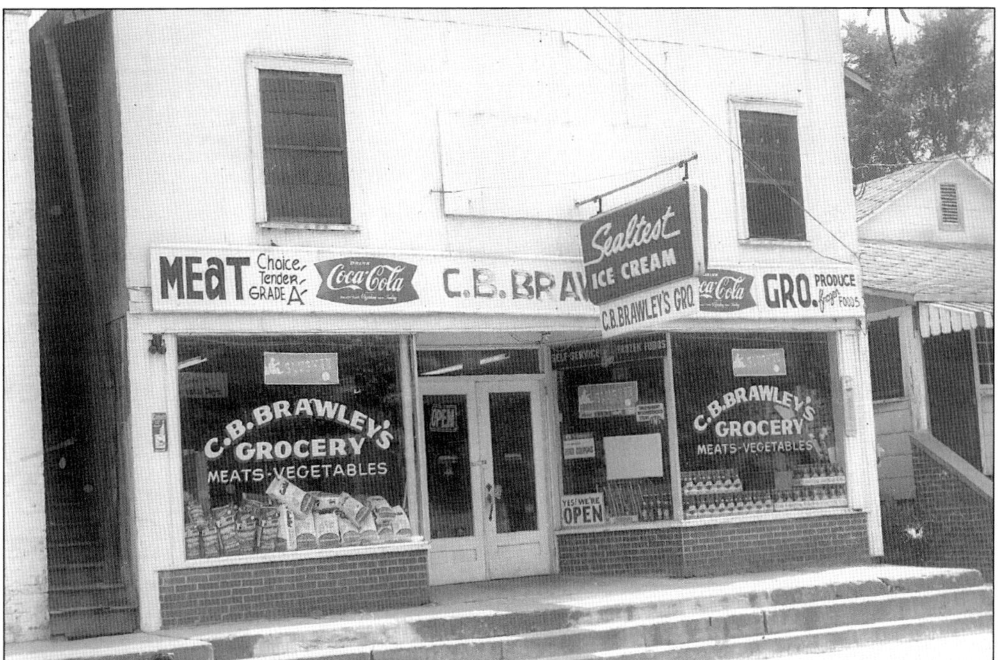

About 100 years later, this store on Pinckney Street shows how retailing had changed but also stayed the same over the years. C.B. Brawley's Grocery displayed some of their wares in the large windows across the front. Signs, however, still help advertise the merchandise within.

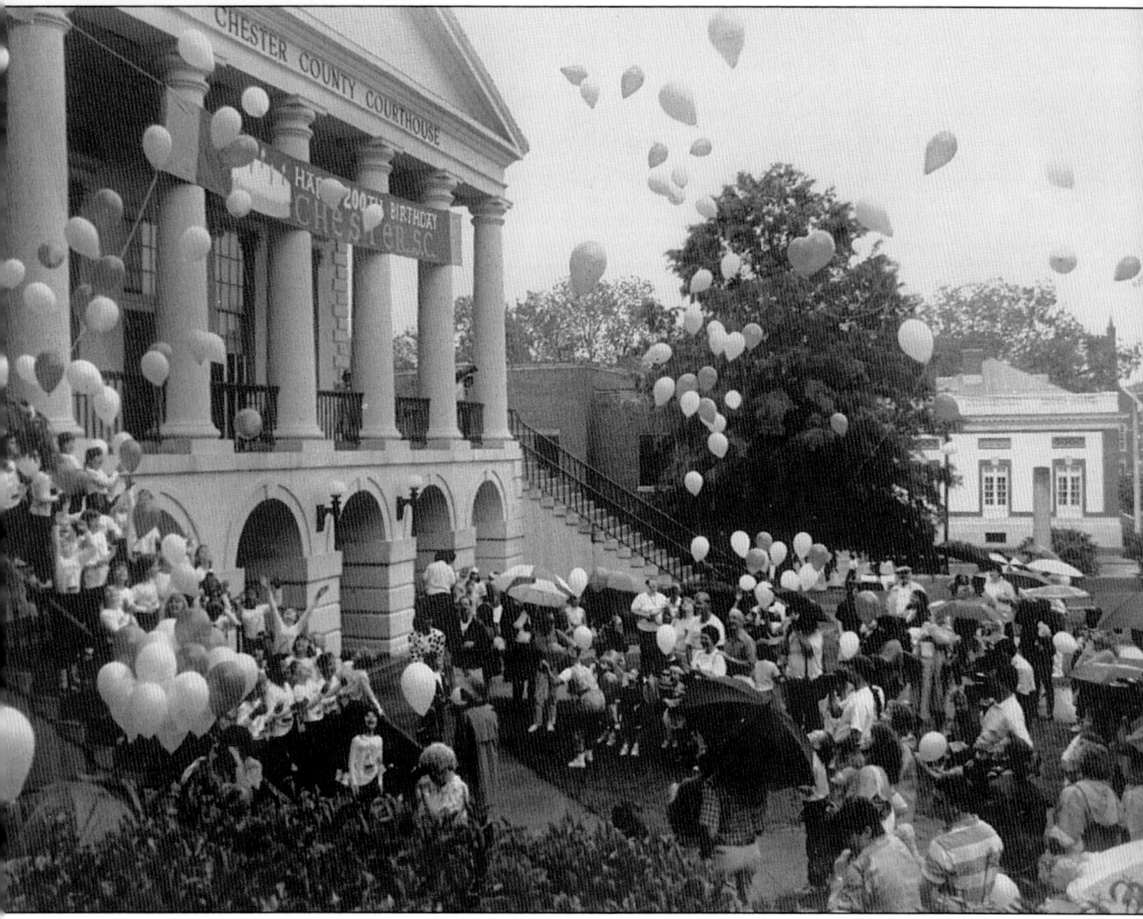

Chester County celebrated its bicentennial in 1985 and the City of Chester marked its 200th year in 1991. The balloon launch, seen here, was held on the courthouse lawn to commemorate one of these occasion.

Two

RURAL

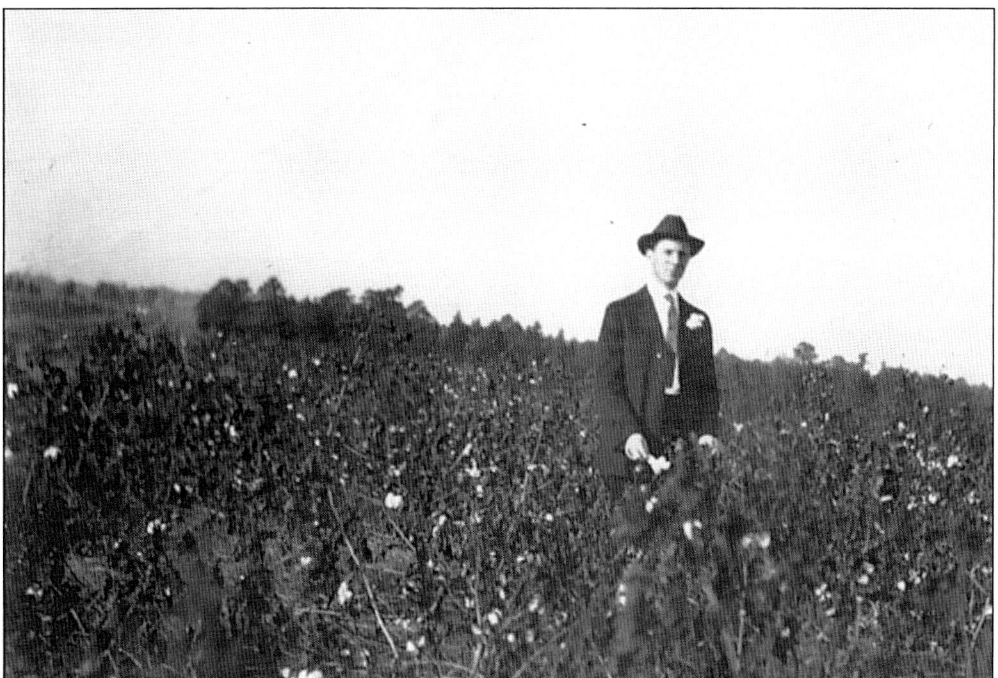

In days gone by, cotton was the main cash crop in Chester County. You couldn't drive more than a couple of miles without seeing a cotton field, and cotton warehouses were plentiful. Albert Walker stands in a cotton field, c. 1920.

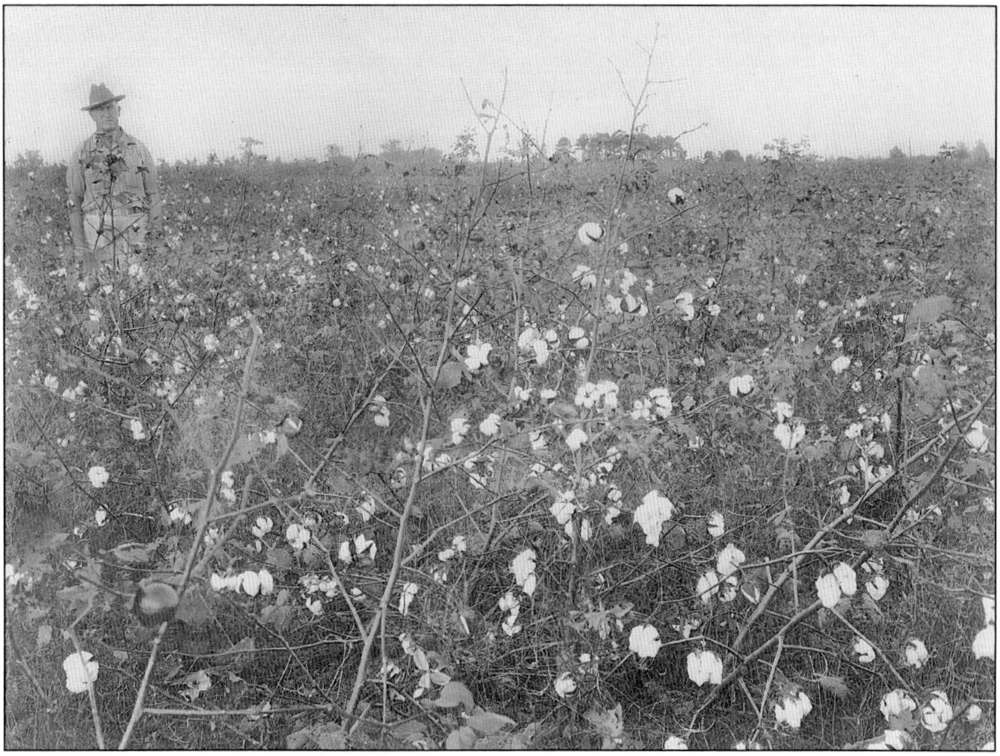

Buck White looks over his stand of cotton in the 1940s.

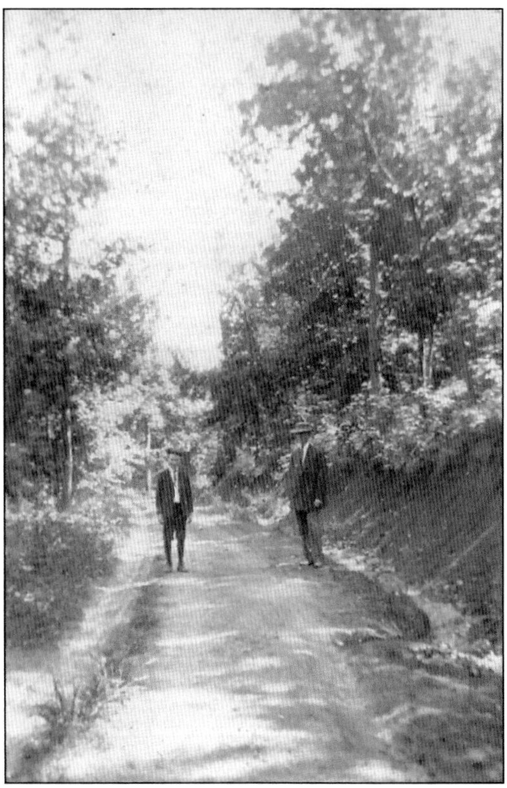

As we speed along on our interstate highways today, it is difficult to believe that less than 75 years ago most rural roads looked like this unpaved lane pictured c. 1920.

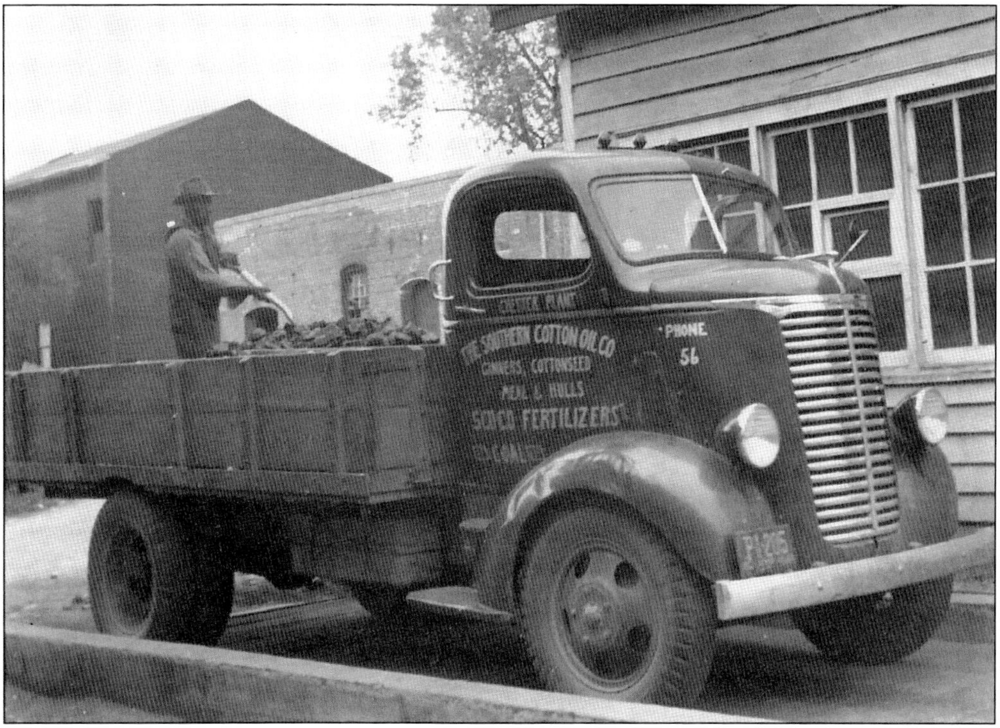

Fifty to sixty years ago, many folks across Chester County heated their homes and businesses with coal. Southern Cotton Oil Company was one of the distributors. Here, a worker shovels coal off of the back of a truck in the late 1930s or early 1940s.

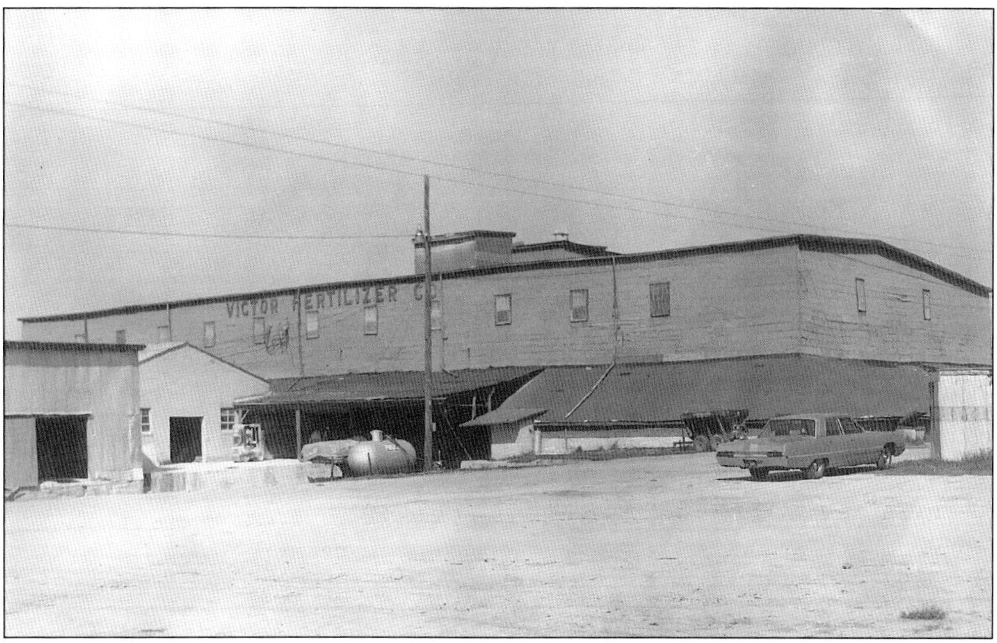

Victor Fertilizer Company was one of several plants in Chester County. Located on York Road, it used the C&NW (Carolina and Northwestern) rail line to transport its product. This photograph was taken in the early 1960s.

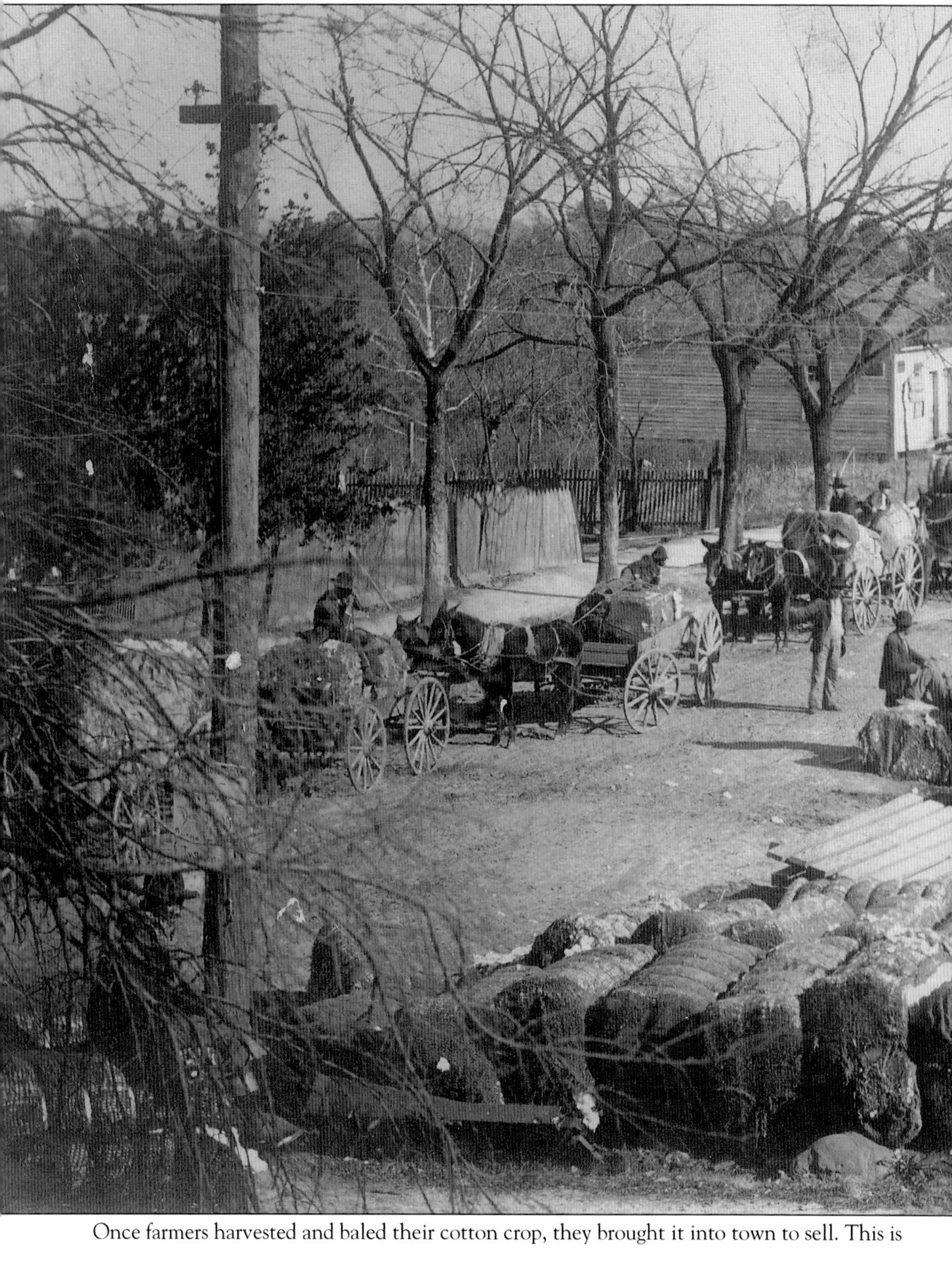

Once farmers harvested and baled their cotton crop, they brought it into town to sell. This is

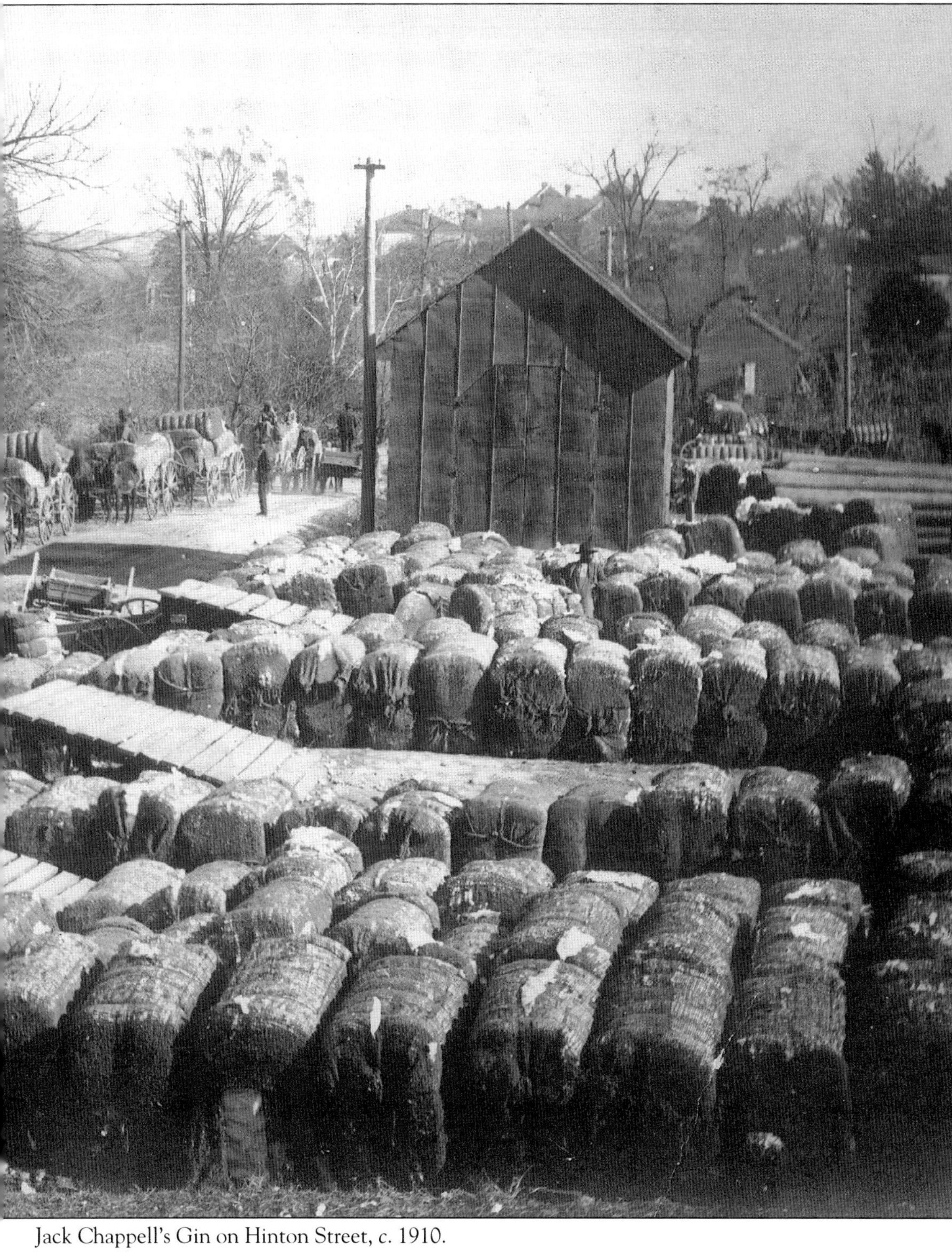

Jack Chappell's Gin on Hinton Street, c. 1910.

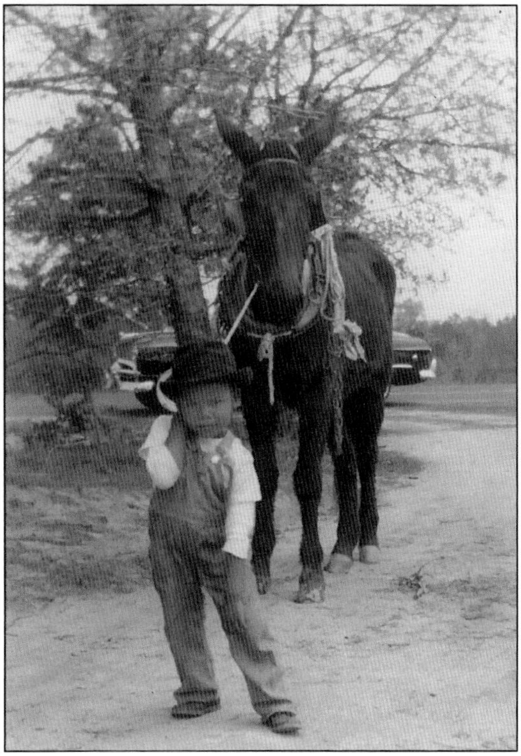

Throughout the better part of the 20th century, people used mules to plow their fields. This little boy hauls a stubborn mule home from the fields in the 1950s.

Agriculture became increasingly mechanized as the 20th century progressed. Chester High School agriculture teacher John Parris, right, looks over freshly plowed fields with farmer Adron Logan in north central Chester County in the early 1960s.

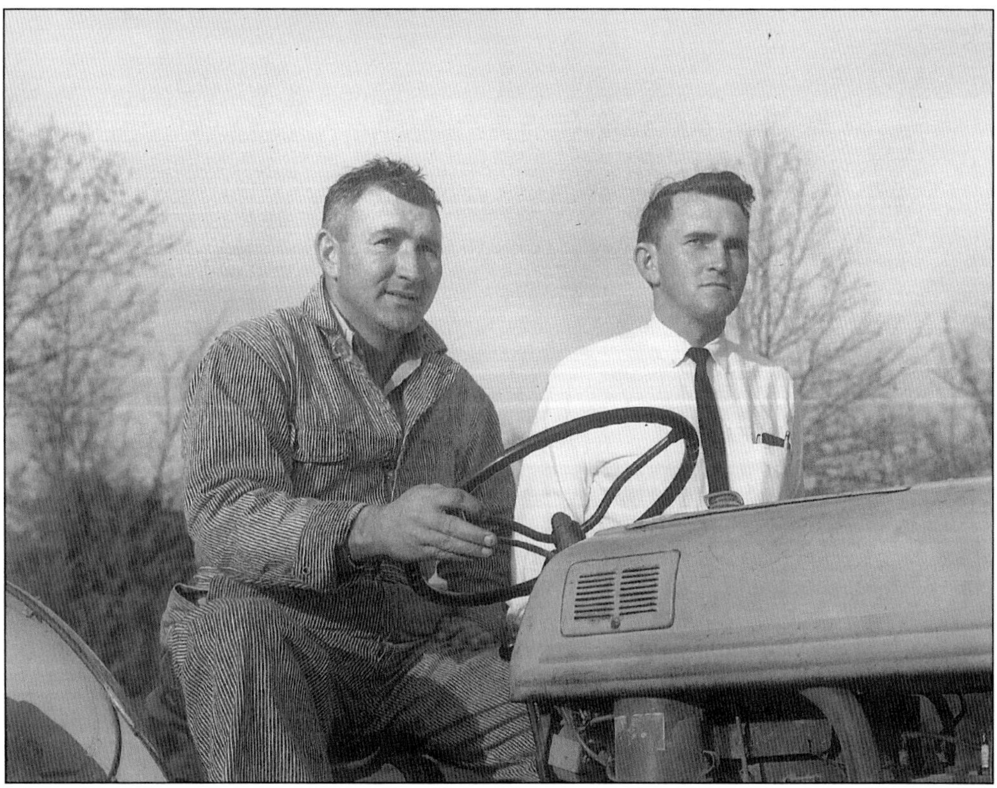

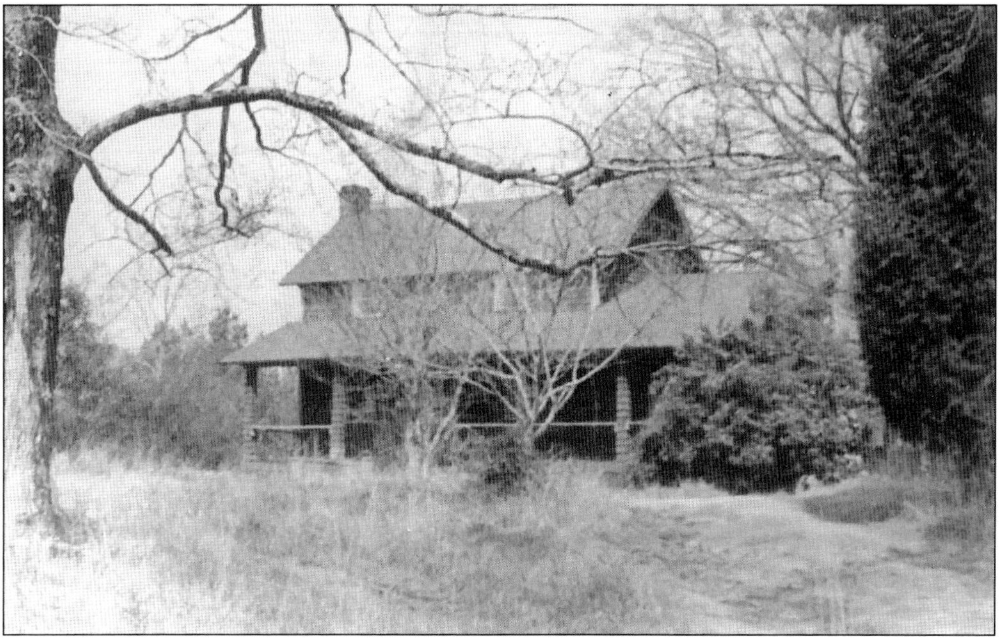

There were a number of colonial-era inns in Chester County and several still exist. The Lewis Inn, located near the Lewis Turnout community, is one of them. It gained fame when it housed former Vice President Aaron Burr as he was brought to trial in Richmond for high treason in 1807. Many of the original features of the pre-Revolutionary structure still exist.

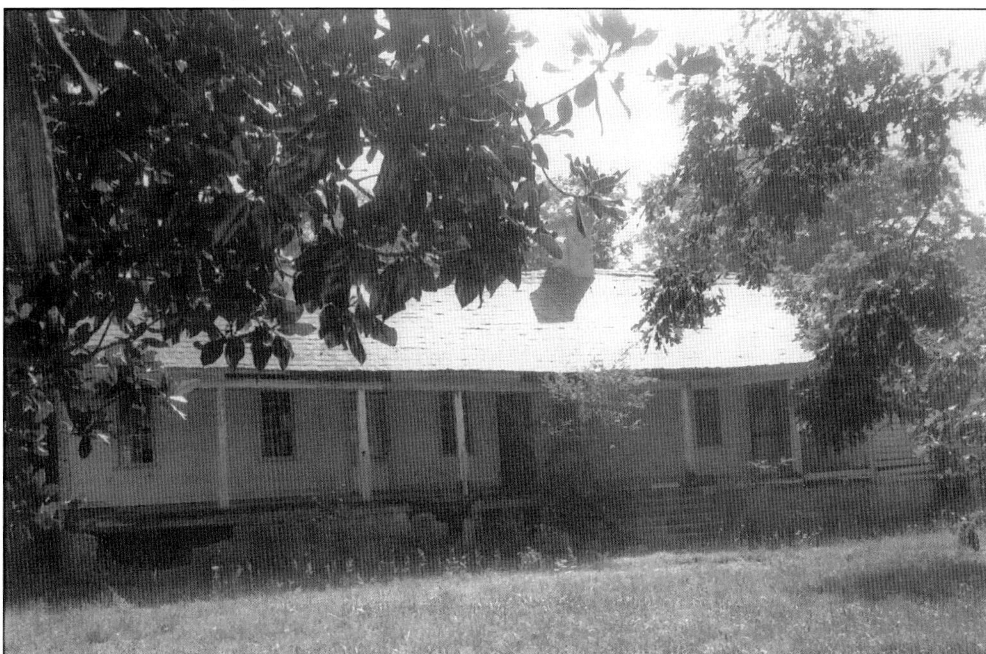

Elijah Cornwell built the 17-room Cornwell Inn in 1841. The stage coach was a common mode of long-distance transportation until the railroad came along in 1851, and when that happened the inn served rail travelers. Among its most famous visitors were South Carolina statesman John C. Calhoun and Gen. Wade Hampton.

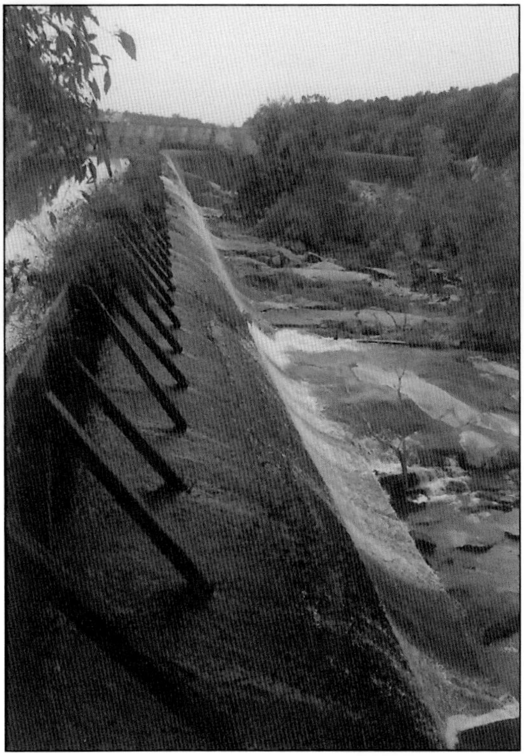

The spillway at Great Falls is just one of the places that the mighty Catawba River has been impeded to harness its power for electricity. James B. Duke had a great impact on the development of Great Falls and eventually created the Duke Energy empire.

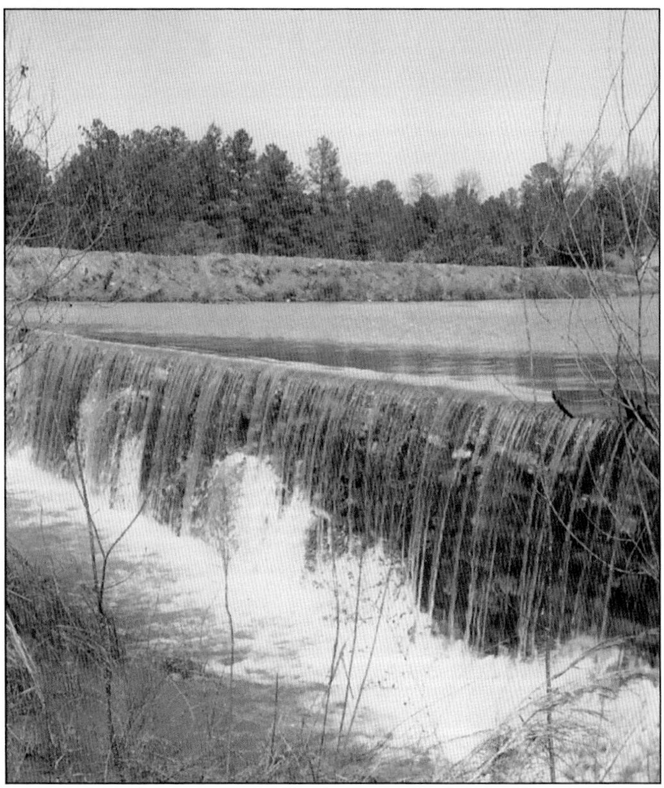

Pictured here is another of the Catawba River's spillways in Chester County.

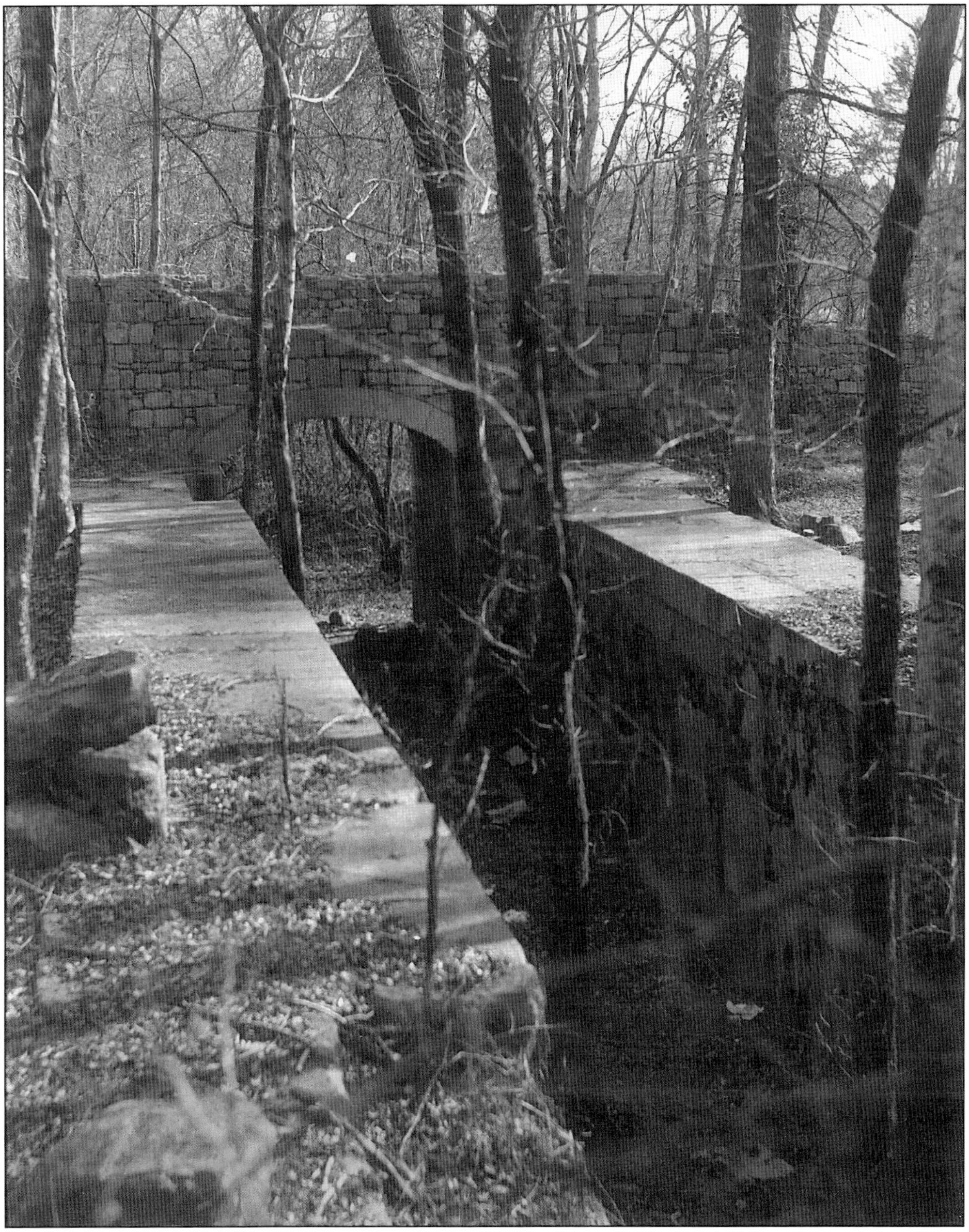

Famous architect and then South Carolina state engineer Robert Mills designed Landsford Canal along the Catawba River in Chester County in an effort to connect Charleston to the Mississippi with a series of waterways. Completed in 1832, the building of the canal was overseen by chairman of South Carolina Public Works Joel Poinsett and contractor Robert Leckie. Portions of the canal can still be seen, and the area was developed into a state park in 1975.

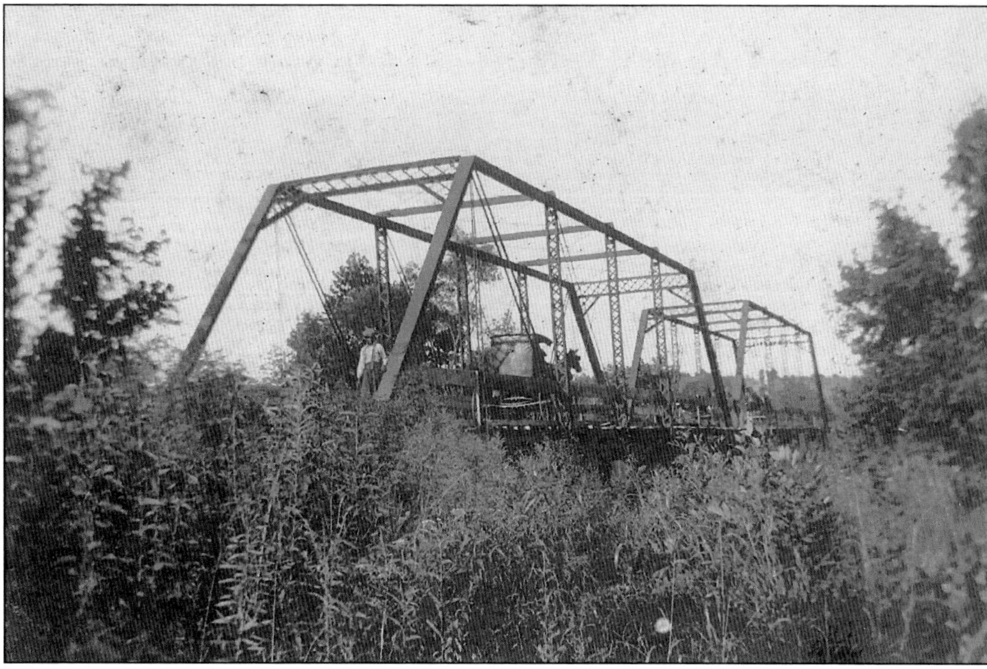

Bridges made traveling from place to place in rural Chester County much easier. This steel frame bridge, *c.* 1910 (above), is one of the examples of bridges in the county, but this wooden plank bridge (below) was much more common.

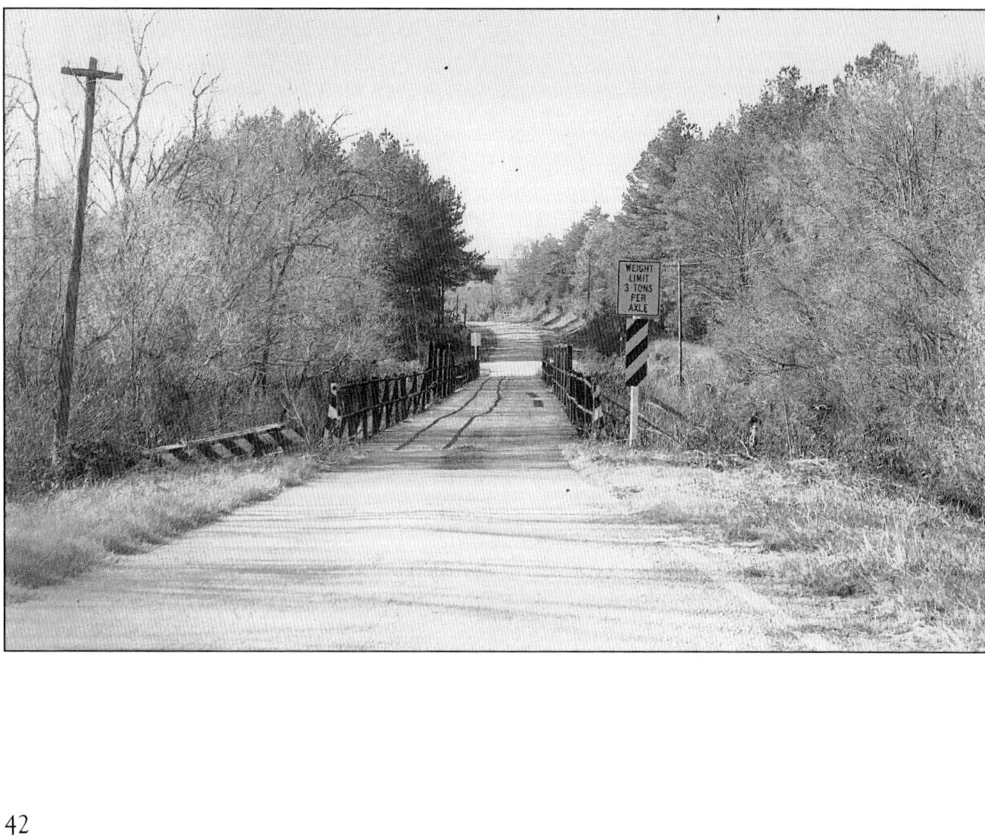

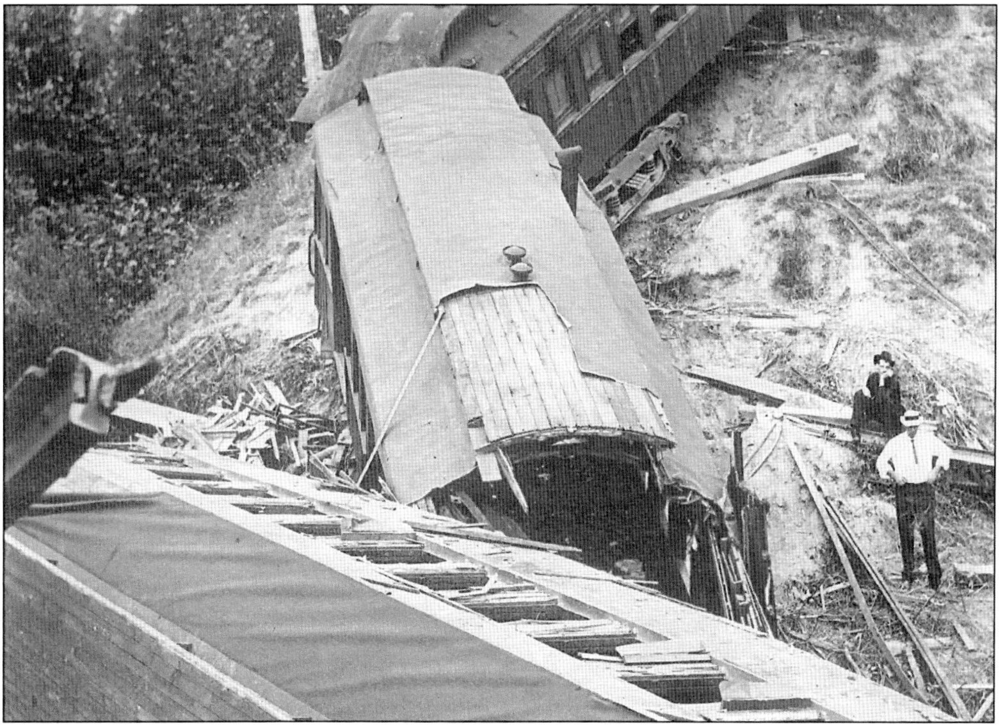

In the spring of 1913, the Lancaster & Chester Railway ran a special train to take baseball fans from Chester and Lancaster to Dillon for a special game. At the Hooper's Creek Trestle, a freight car jumped the track and the three passenger cars plunged down the embankment into the creek. Five people died. After that accident, the L&C carried very few passengers and eventually made the decision to be a freight line only.

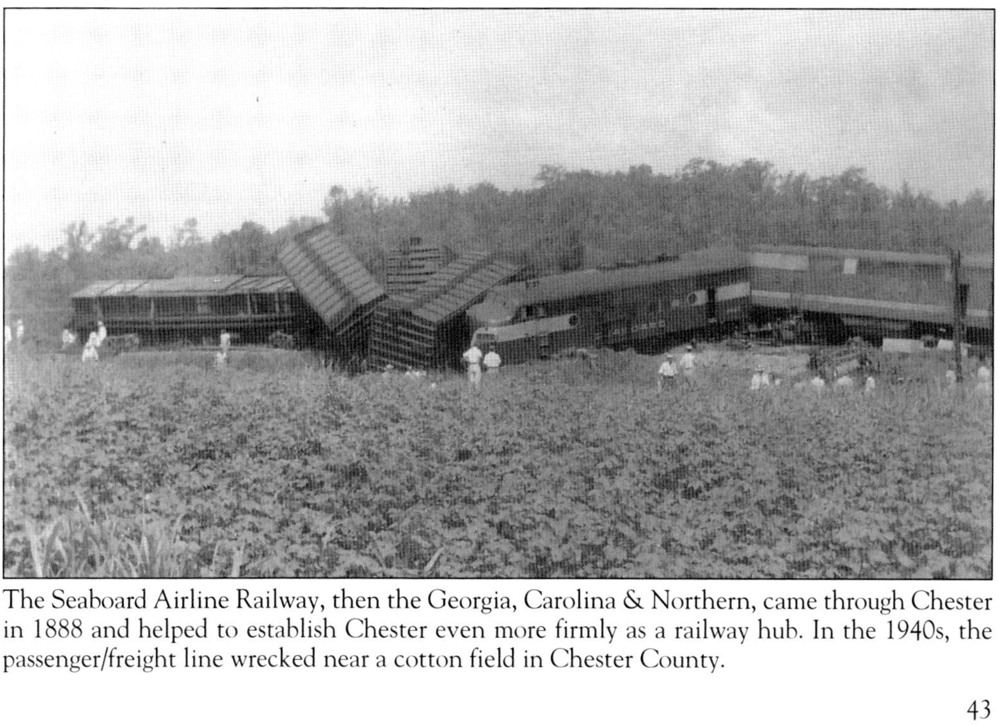

The Seaboard Airline Railway, then the Georgia, Carolina & Northern, came through Chester in 1888 and helped to establish Chester even more firmly as a railway hub. In the 1940s, the passenger/freight line wrecked near a cotton field in Chester County.

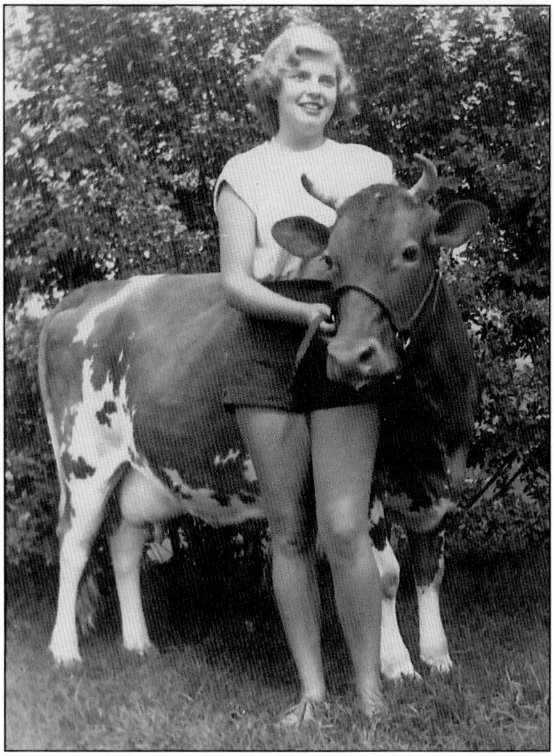

Guernsey cattle and dairies had a major impact in Chester County for decades. The Guernsey Festival and a large portion of the economy were all derived from the gentle-eyed milk cows. Here, Ginger Archer shows off one of the pride of the herd in August 1948.

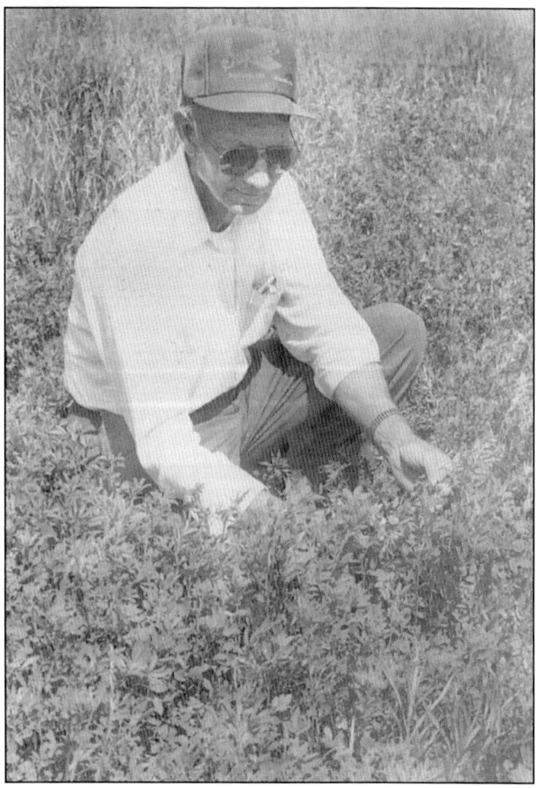

Farming was a major occupation in Chester County in previous years. Although agriculture is still practiced by a good portion of the population, few make their sole living at it. Here, Eugene Logan kneels beside a good crop of soybeans he planted at his farm off Peden Bridge Road in 1987.

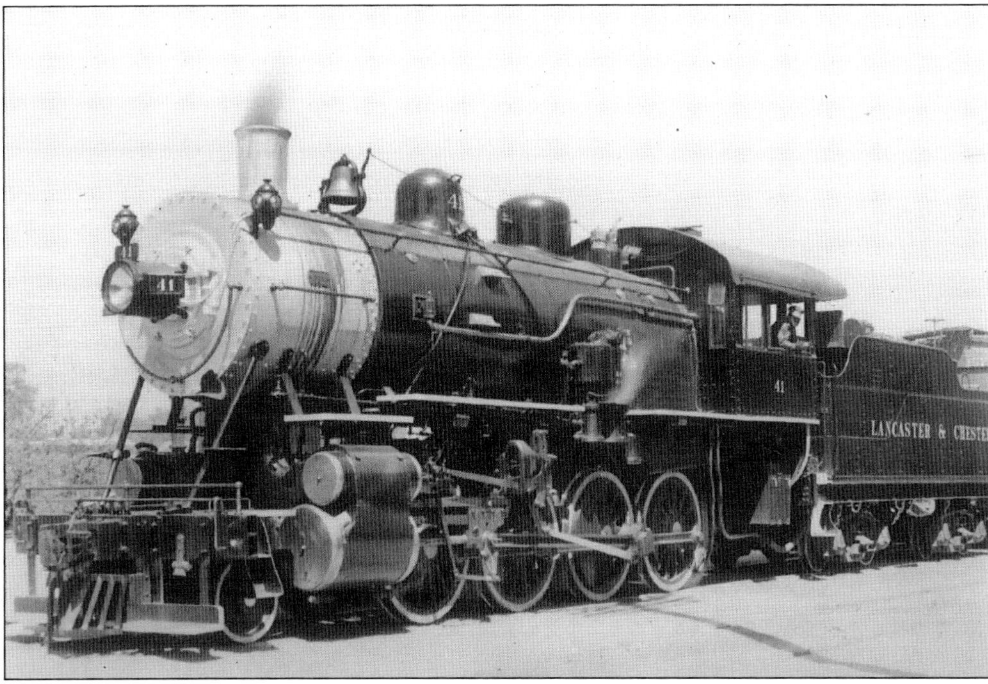

The Lancaster & Chester Railway was an integral part of transportation in the county. Although the company, owned by Springs Mills, mainly hauled freight over the years and still does, many rural families along the L&C line would catch a ride in the caboose to come to town.

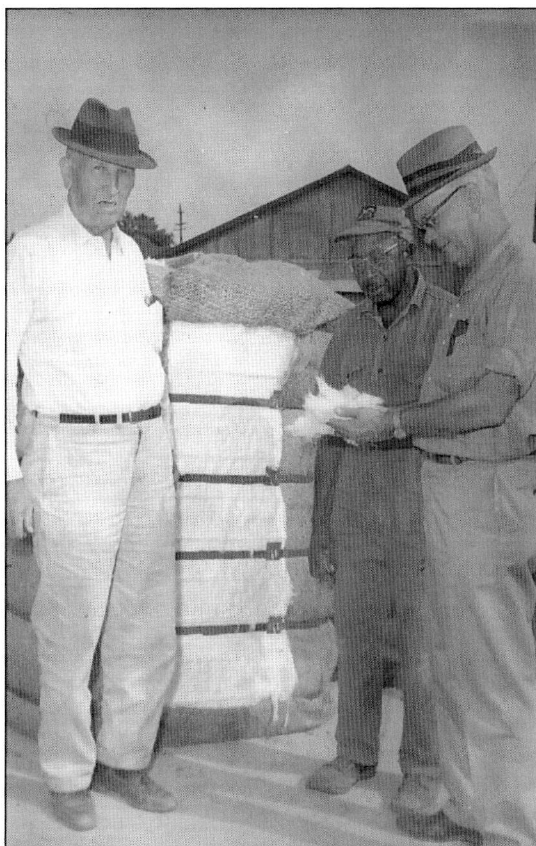

The bringing in of the first bale of cotton was a much anticipated occurrence in rural areas of the South, and Chester County was no exception. A cash prize usually accompanied the honor, and farmers took great pride in producing a quality product. These unidentified gentlemen display the first bale in the late 1950s.

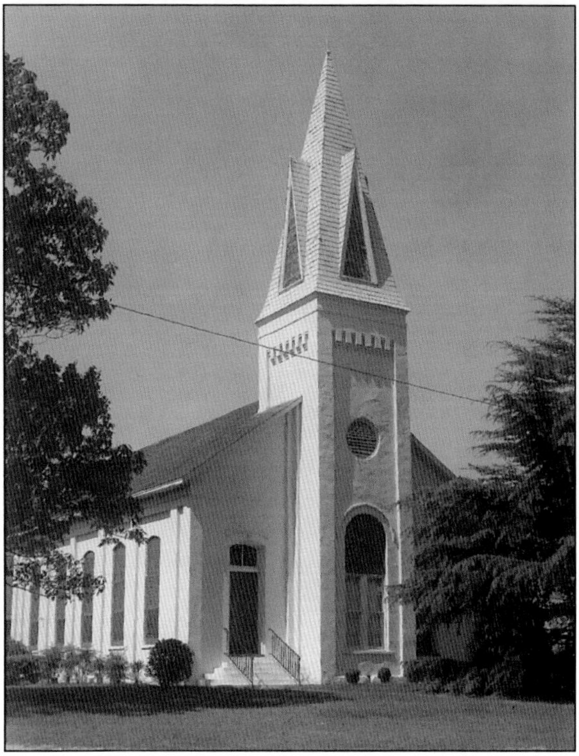

Zion Presbyterian Church is located in the center of Lowrys. The church had its beginnings in 1850 and was originally located approximately 1 mile northeast of its current site. The present sanctuary was dedicated in 1895, and this photograph was taken in the 1960s.

The earliest record of Methodism in the New Hope community in western Chester County occurred in 1794 when Bishop Francis Asbury preached there. For years there was no church building; the community was visited by circuit riders. This building was constructed in 1861 with changes made in 1884 so that the entrances would be on the side toward the roads. The building was brick veneered and an educational building was added between 1931 and 1940.

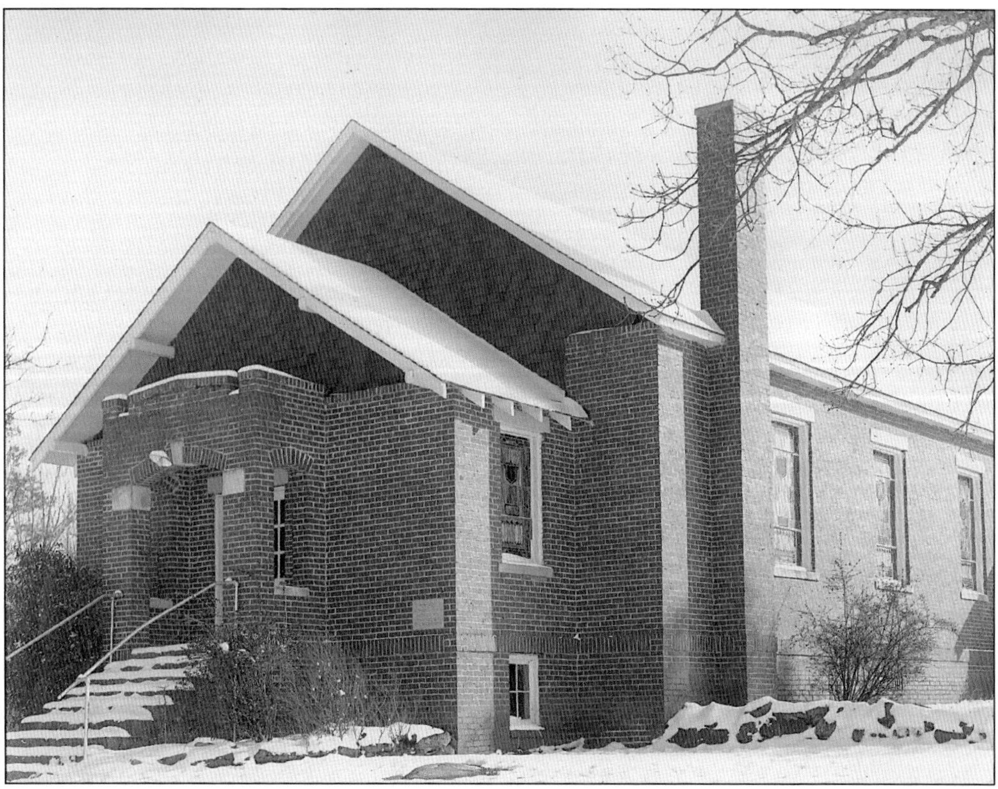

If a family has any documentation of its origins, they will probably have a plat such as this one. Most early Chester County families had some sort of survey or grant that proved their ownership of property. This plat shows land on Tinker's Creek, a branch of Fishing Creek.

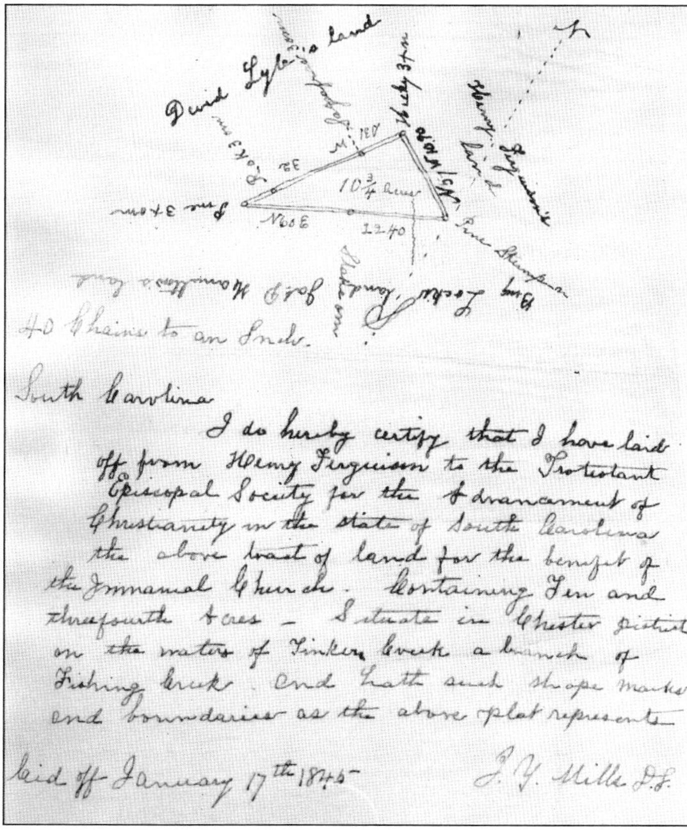

South Carolina

I do hereby certify that I have laid off from Henry Ferguson to the Protestant Episcopal Society for the Advancement of Christianity in the state of South Carolina the above tract of land for the benefit of the Immanual Church. Containing Ten and threefourth Acres - Situate in Chester District on the waters of Tinkers Creek a branch of Fishing Creek. And hath such shape marks and boundaries as the above plat represents

Laid off January 17th 1845 J. Y. Mille D.S.

Horse and buggy or wagon were the major modes of transportation in the first 150 years of Chester County's existence. Below, the Stephensons, residents of northern Chester County, celebrate the United States's bicentennial by taking a buggy ride in remembrance of days gone by.

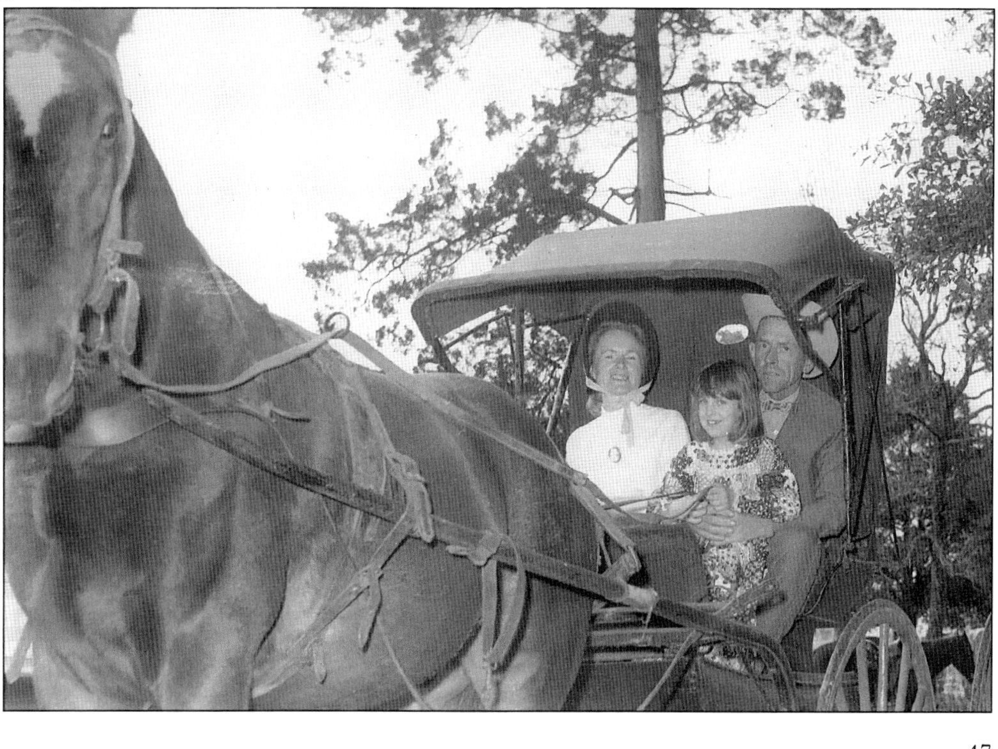

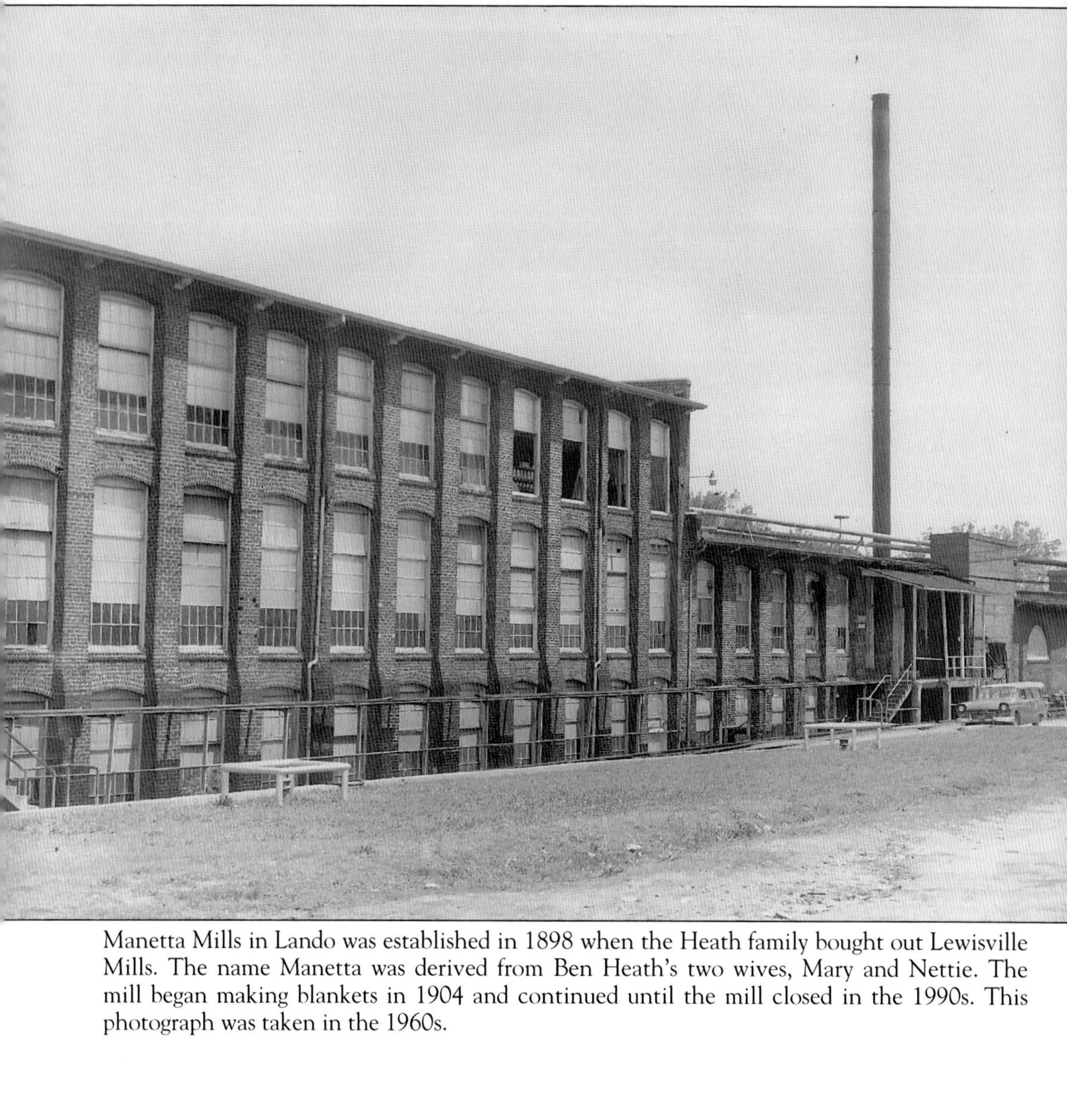

Manetta Mills in Lando was established in 1898 when the Heath family bought out Lewisville Mills. The name Manetta was derived from Ben Heath's two wives, Mary and Nettie. The mill began making blankets in 1904 and continued until the mill closed in the 1990s. This photograph was taken in the 1960s.

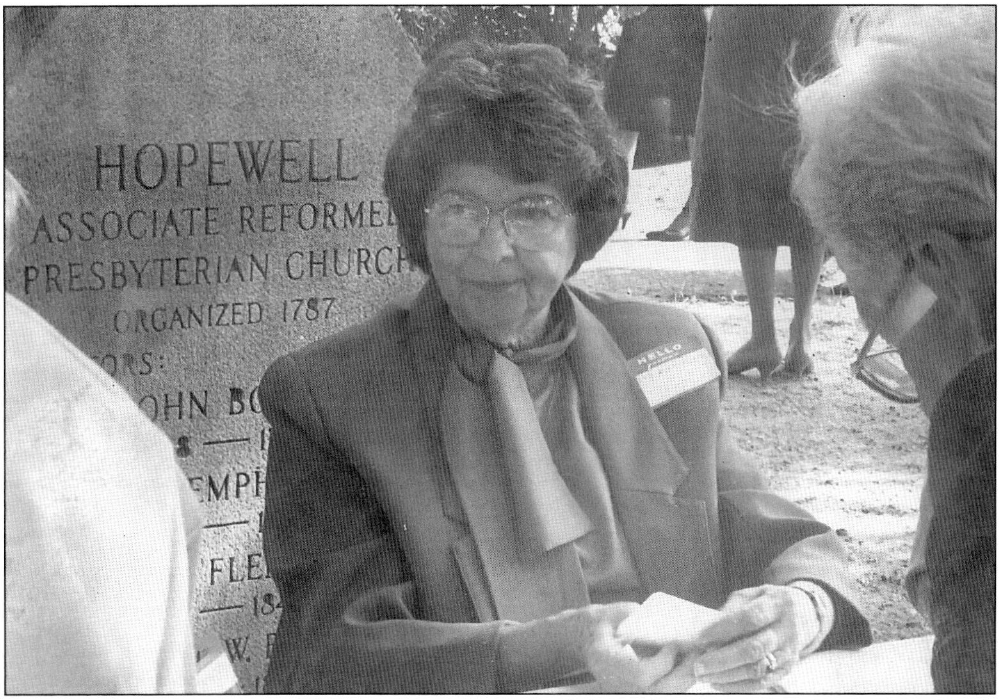

Hopewell Associate Reformed Presbyterian Church celebrated its bicentennial in 1987. Church member Mary Robinson hands out name tags and registers guests at the celebration.

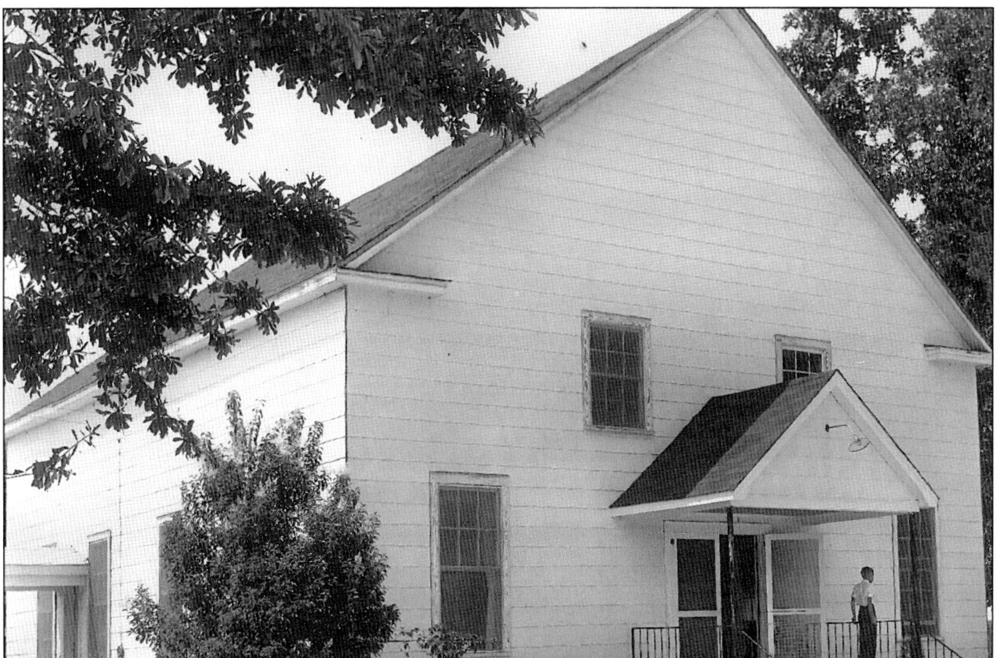

Built in 1851, Mount Prospect Methodist Church near Richburg still has a portion of the slave gallery that was constructed to seat the slaves from neighboring plantations. The church has been remodeled but still retains some of its antebellum elements.

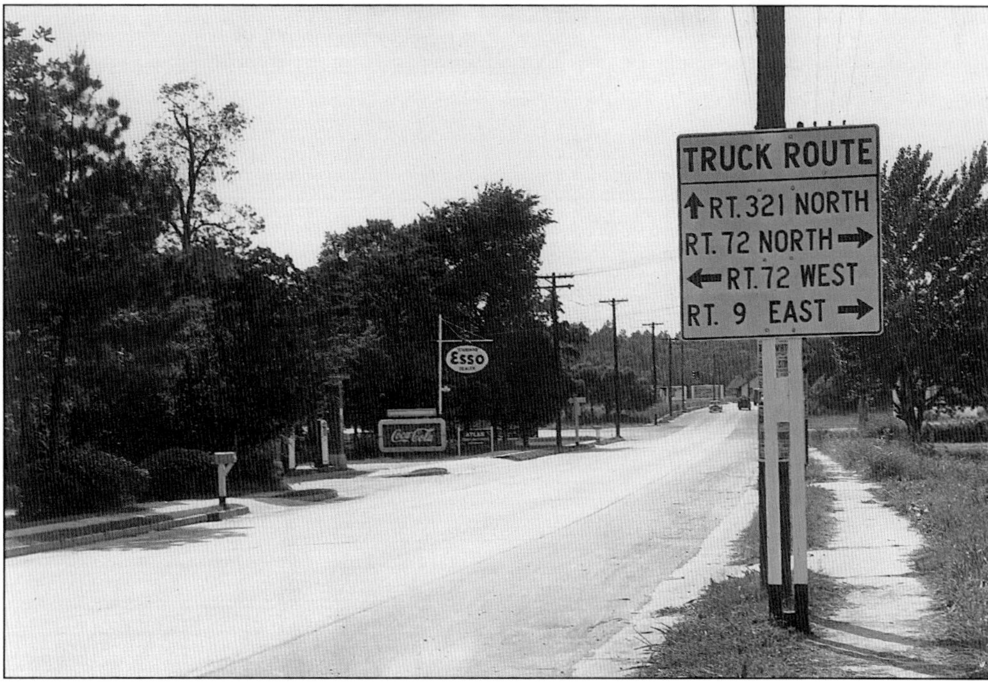

This was the entrance into Chester from the South on U.S. 321 for many years. This photo was taken before the bypass was expanded.

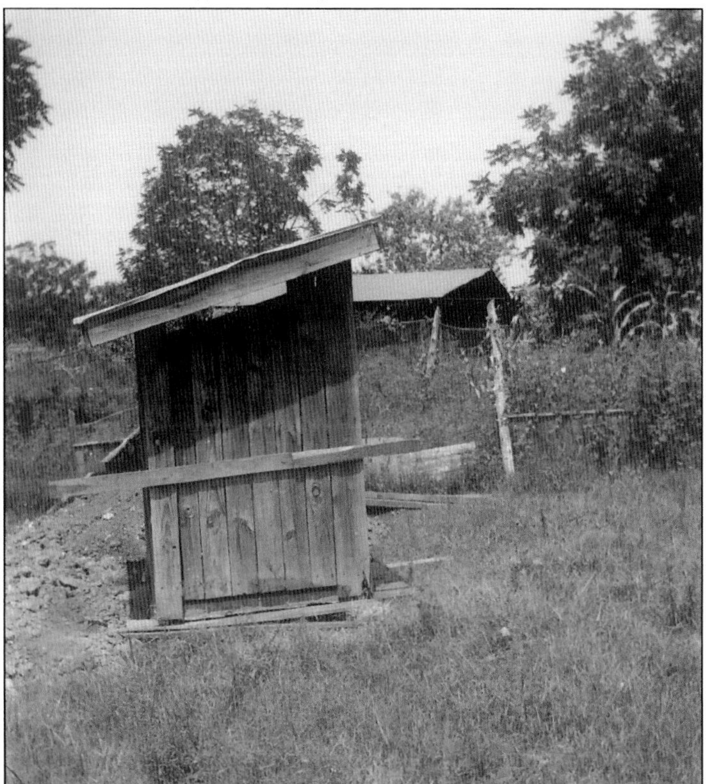

Well into the 1960s, it was not uncommon to see outhouses still in use across the rural sections of the county. This well-built model (seen in this 1948 photograph) is just one example of how outhouses were built.

Three

Towns and Communities

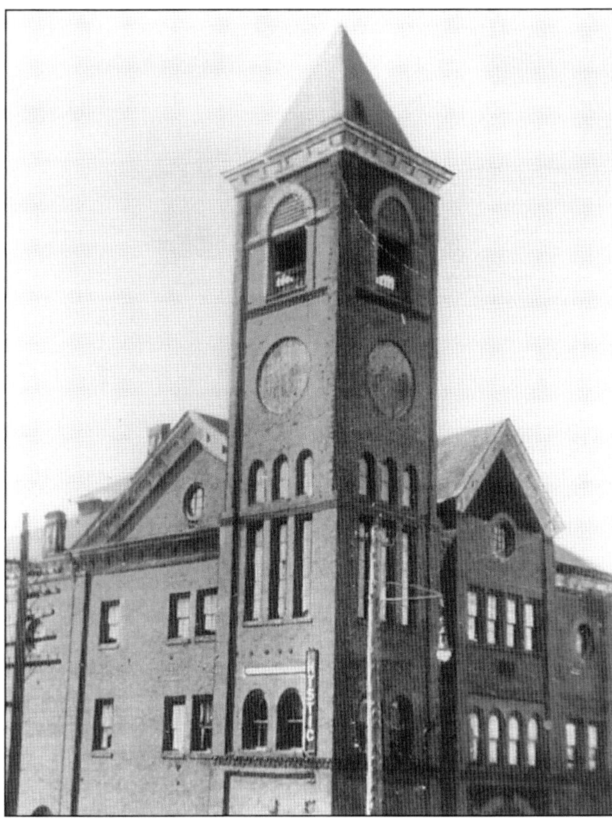

Built as the Opera House in 1890–1891, Chester City Hall is in the 19th-century Romanesque Revival style. Crowning the hill in downtown Chester, City Hall is today a prominent structure. Because Chester was a railroad hub, many of the most popular acts—from plays to vaudeville to opera—graced the stage and brought people from many different areas to the small but bustling city. The auditorium, which took up the second and third stories of the building, was used for community events as well, while the first floor was reserved for city offices. In 1929, the building burned, destroying the tower and the Opera House portion. When rebuilt, the tower was shortened, some of the gables were changed, and the auditorium was eliminated. The building now serves as city offices.

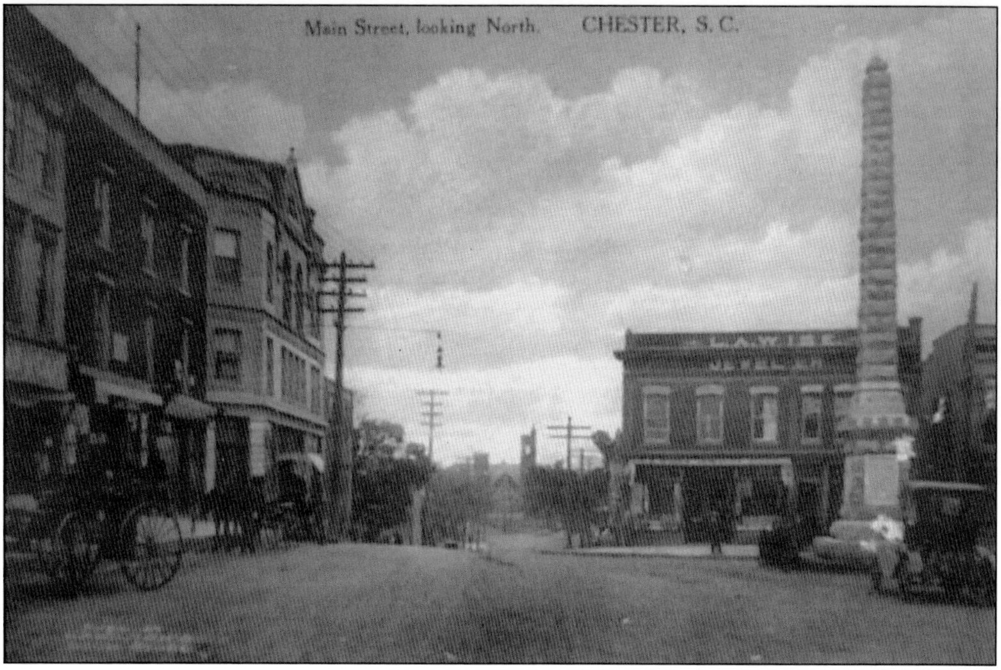

This photograph depicts a scene looking down Main Street in Chester in the early 1920s. Note the dirt streets and the relative lack of automobiles. Just to the right of center is the J.A. Wise Jewelry Store. This building housed a jewelry store for more than 100 years.

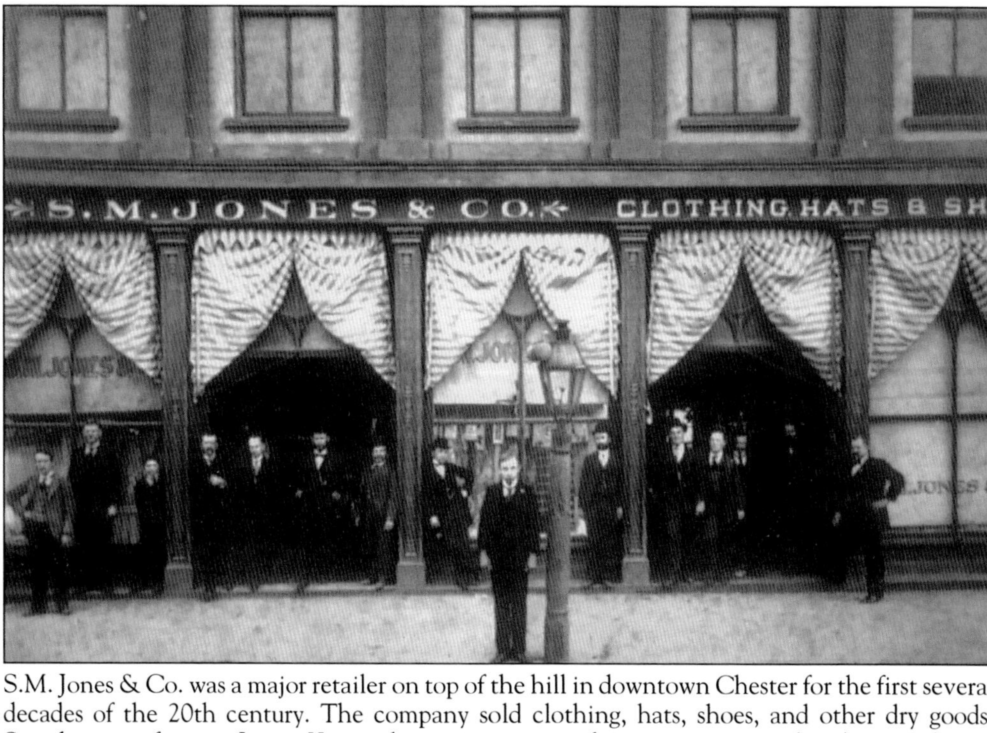

S.M. Jones & Co. was a major retailer on top of the hill in downtown Chester for the first several decades of the 20th century. The company sold clothing, hats, shoes, and other dry goods. Standing out front is James Knox, the store manager for many years, with other employees standing behind him.

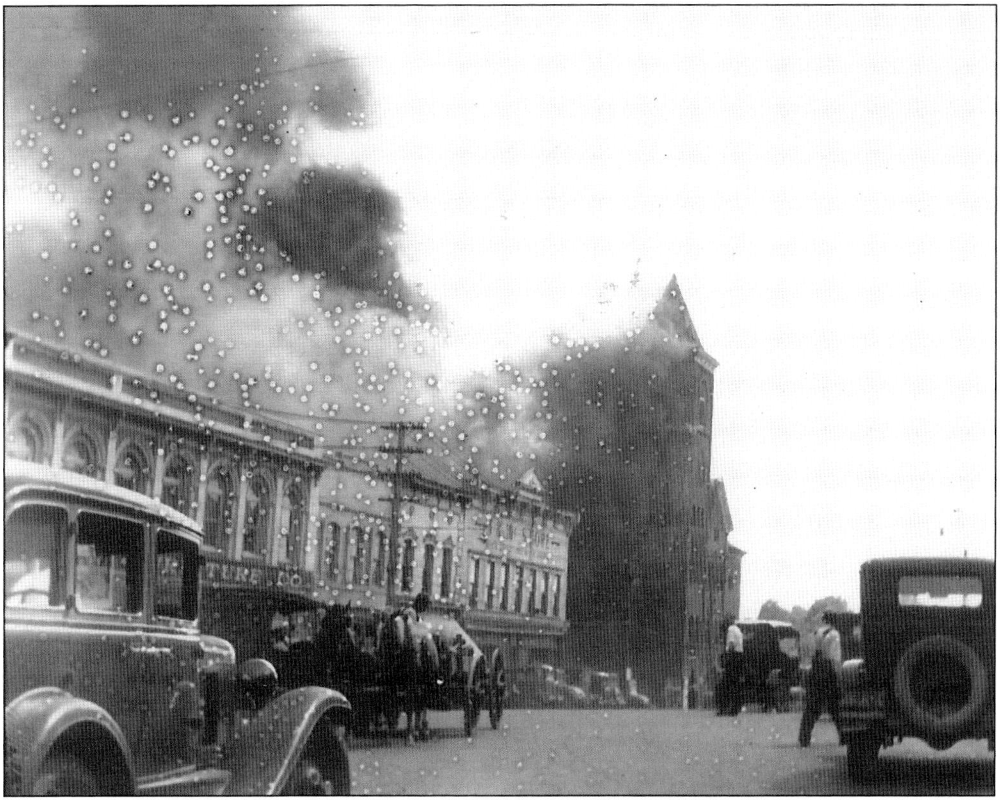

The Opera House burned in 1929, and this photograph shows smoke rising from the tower and the sensation it caused as people flocked to watch the Chester Fire Department put out the devastating fire. The Opera House/City Hall served as the crowning architectural element of Chester's unique downtown hill, and folks watched to see if the structure could be saved. The wind was blowing toward the north and, therefore, much of the tower was destroyed.

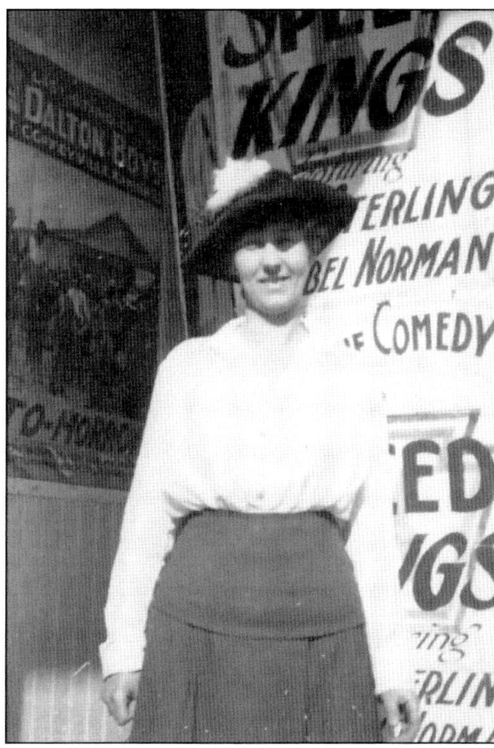

This unidentified lady is attending a performance at the Chester Opera House, c. 1900.

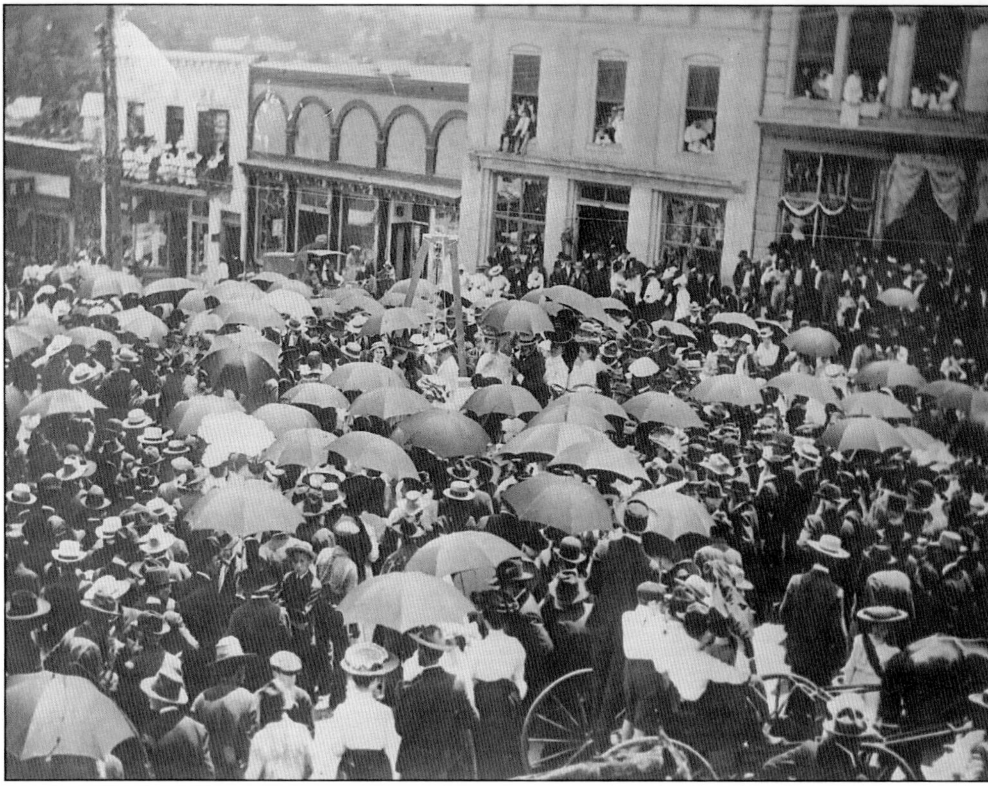

The laying of the cornerstone for the Confederate Monument in downtown Chester was a big event in 1905. Above, people from all over the county gathered on top of the hill, stood on buggies, sat on balconies, or hung out of windows. Notice the block and tackle near the center of the photograph and the groups of ladies gathered at center. The monument was erected by the Chester Chapter of the United Daughters of the Confederacy. Below is a photo of the monument at its completion. Note the Chester Ice Co. wagon at center.

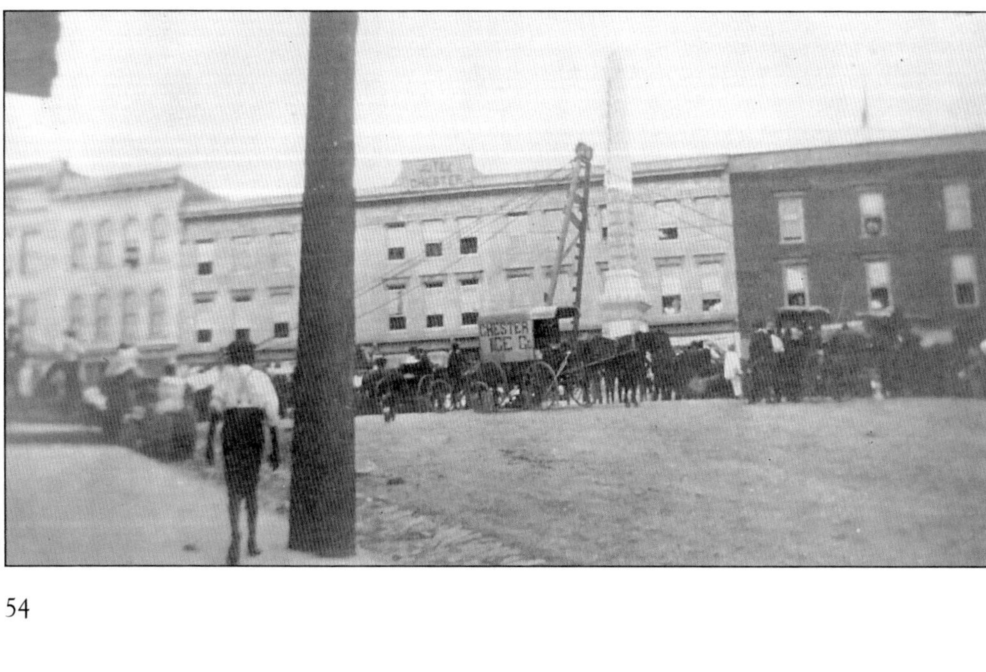

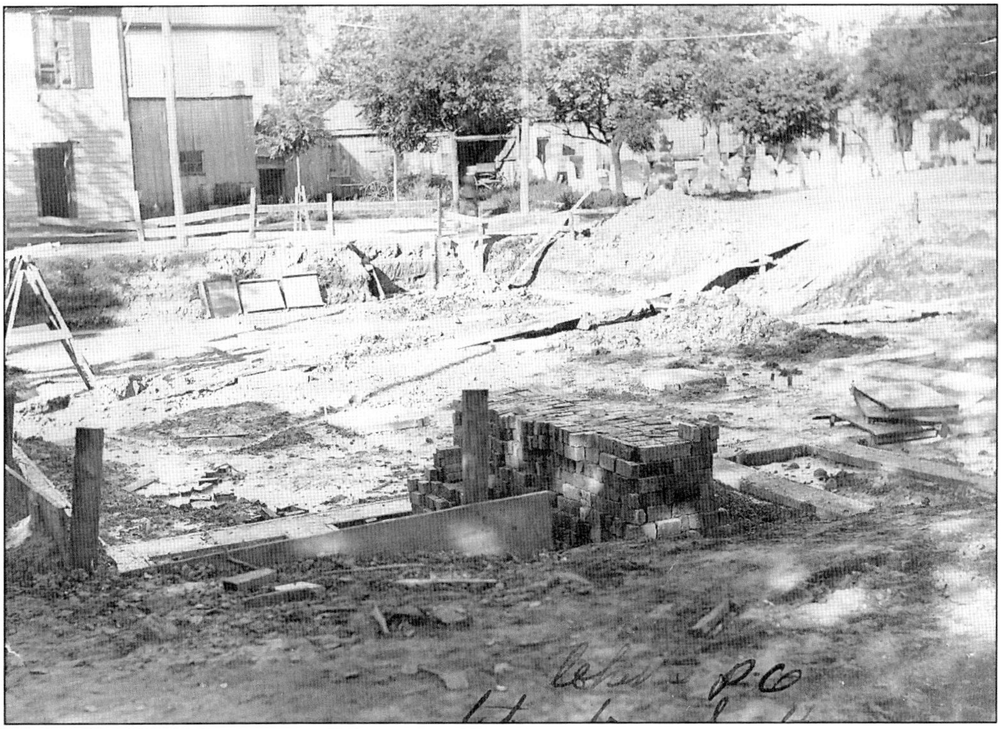

The federal government purchased land on the corner of Main and Wylie Streets in 190,7 and by 1908, work on the Federal-style building, which became the Chester Post Office, had begun. Above, work on the foundation of the building can be seen, and below, final work is being completed. The building was first occupied in July 1909. Prior to the 1908 structure, the post office was housed in various buildings on Main Street and at one time in the courthouse.

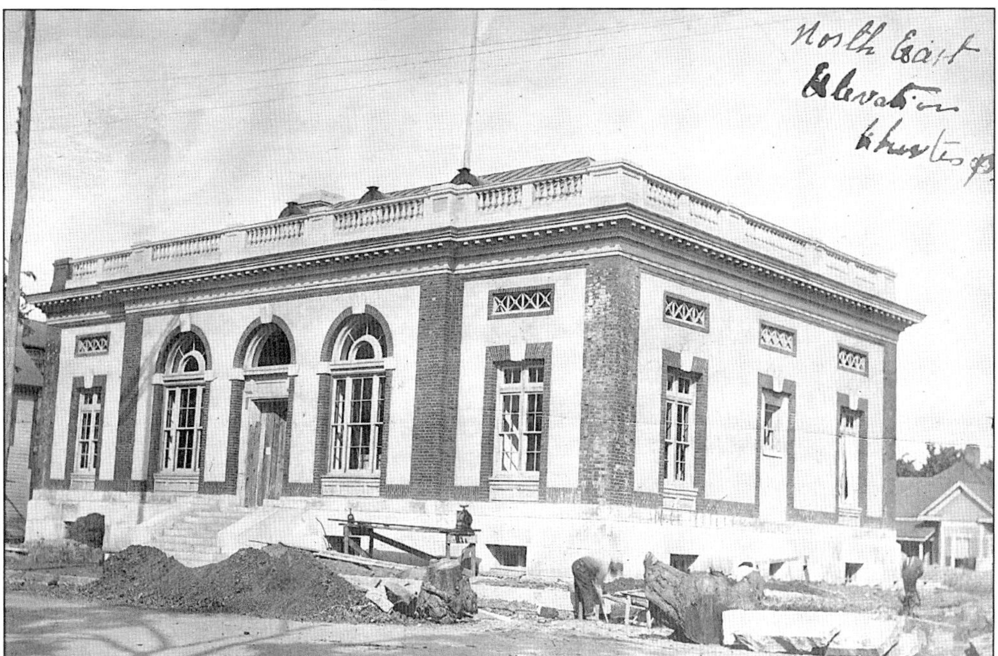

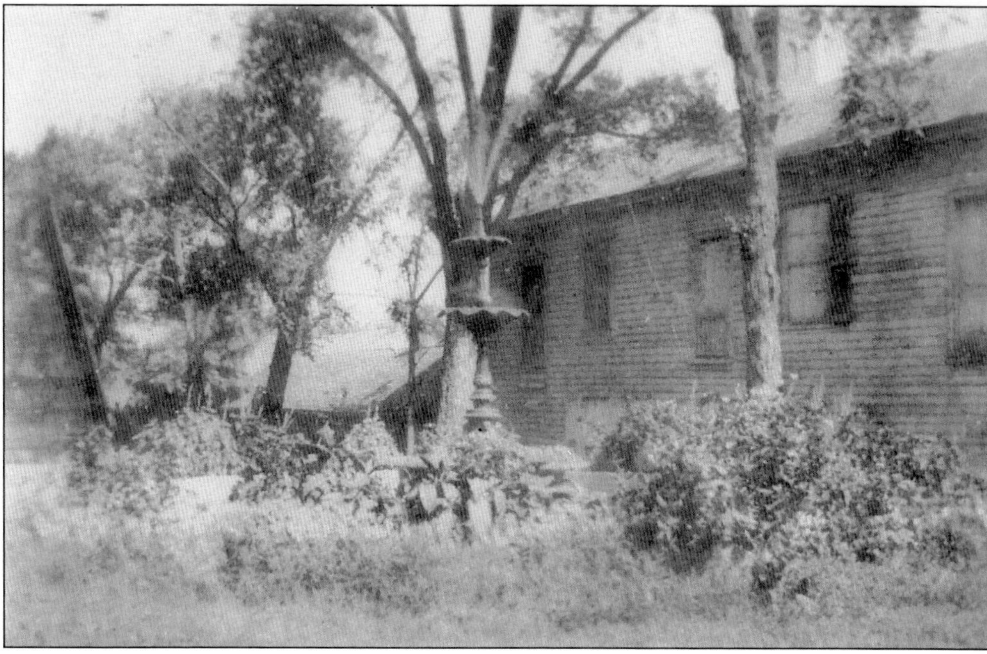

At some point in the 1910s to the early 1920s, there was a fountain on the lawn of the Chester County Courthouse. There are photographs taken around 1913, like the one below, that show no fountain and photographs after 1925, when a World War I monument was erected on the lawn, that also show no fountain. But the photograph above shows the tiered fountain on the right side of the front of the courthouse.

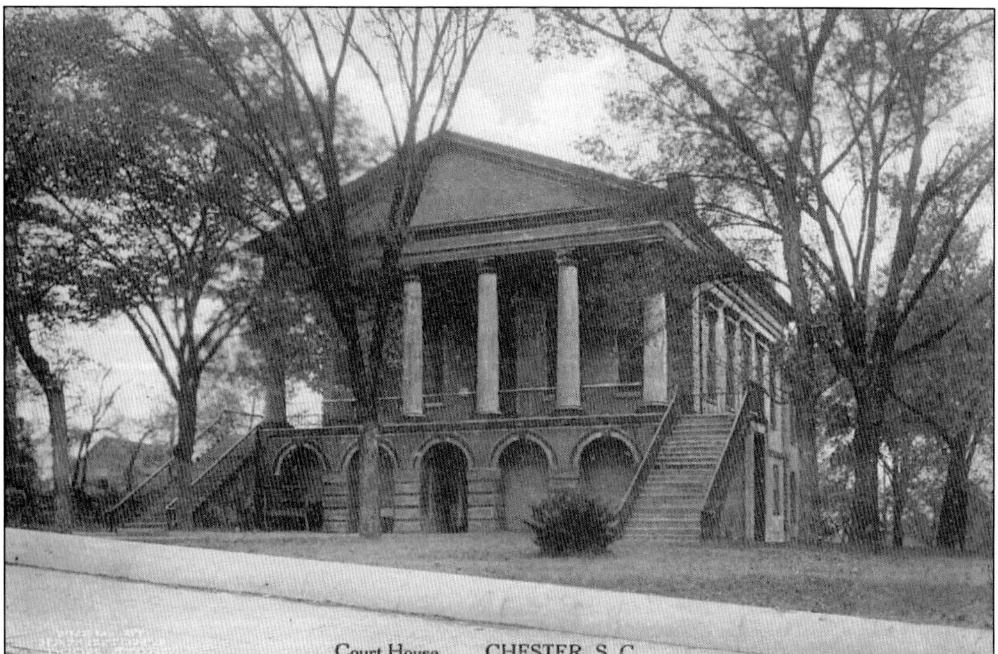

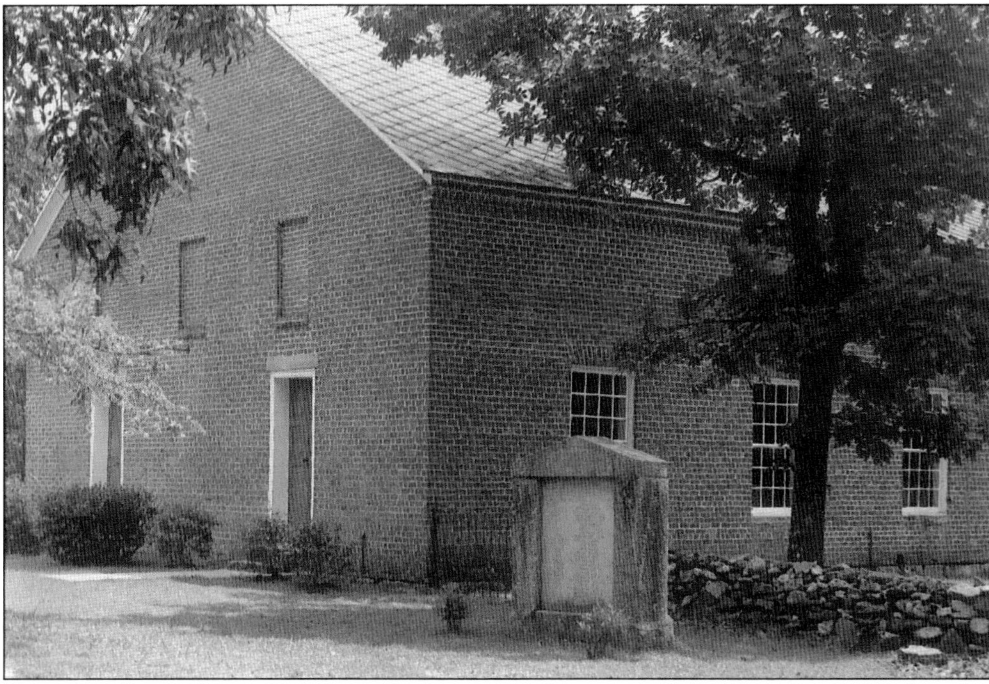

The first communities in what was to become Chester County sprung up around churches. Two of the oldest churches still in existence in the county are Old Catholic Presbyterian Church, above, (southeast of Chester, just off S.C. 97) and Fishing Creek Presbyterian Church, below, (northeastern Chester County, several miles off S.C. 72). Both were established prior to the Revolutionary War.

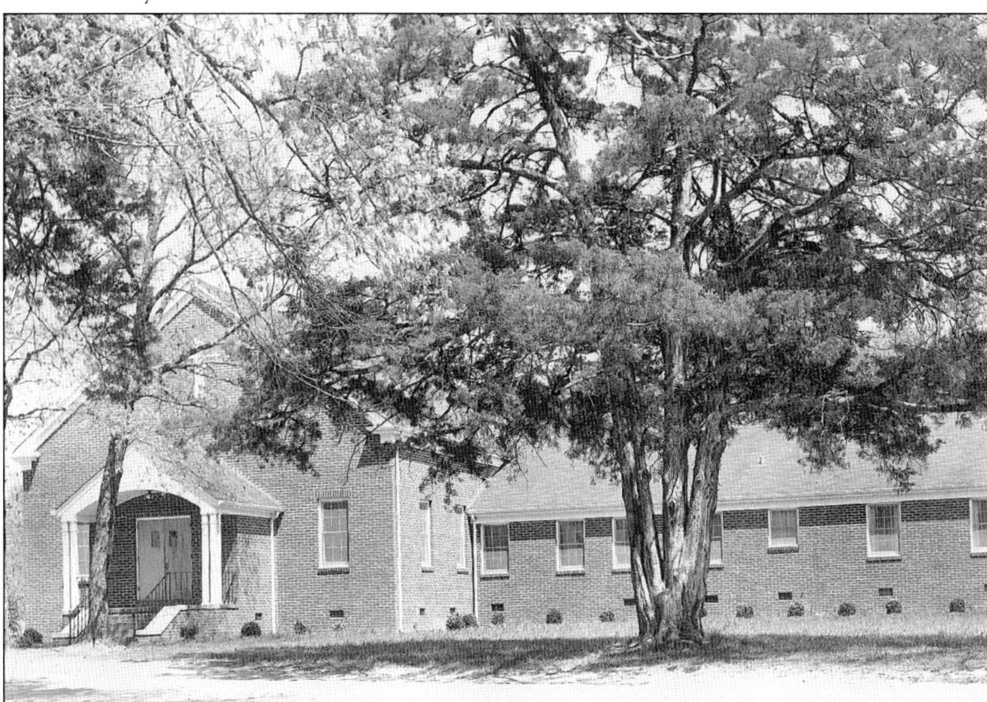

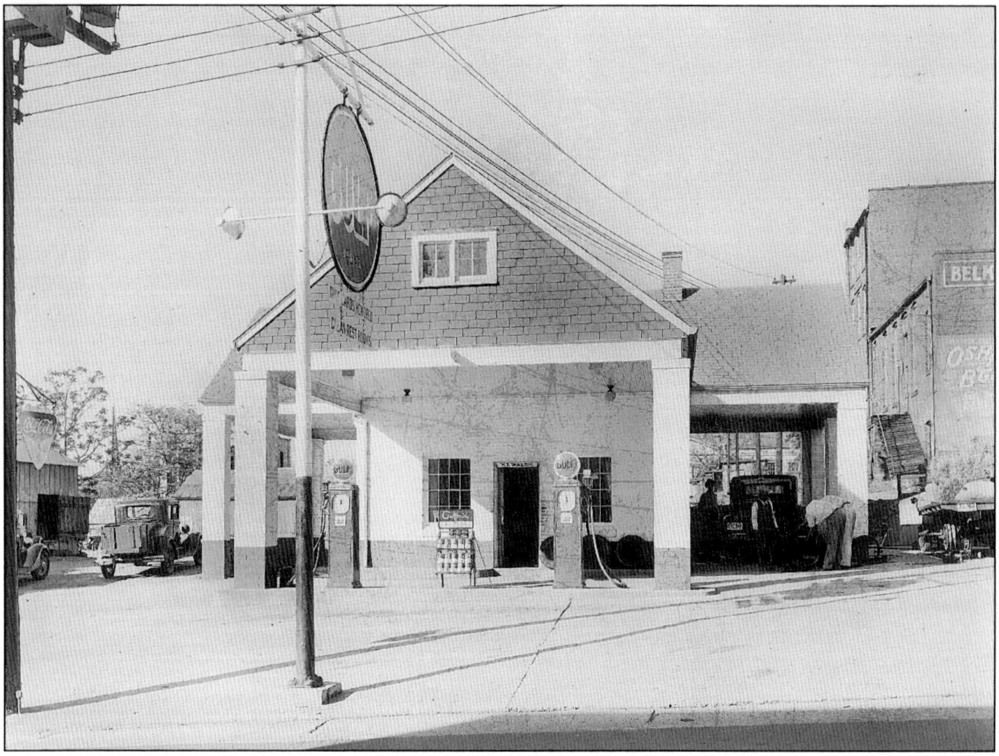

Located on Center Street in Chester, H.T. (Hack) Walsh's Gulf station, pictured here c. 1937, was a place to get a cold drink and a tank of gas and to have your car repaired. Several stations have occupied this building over the years.

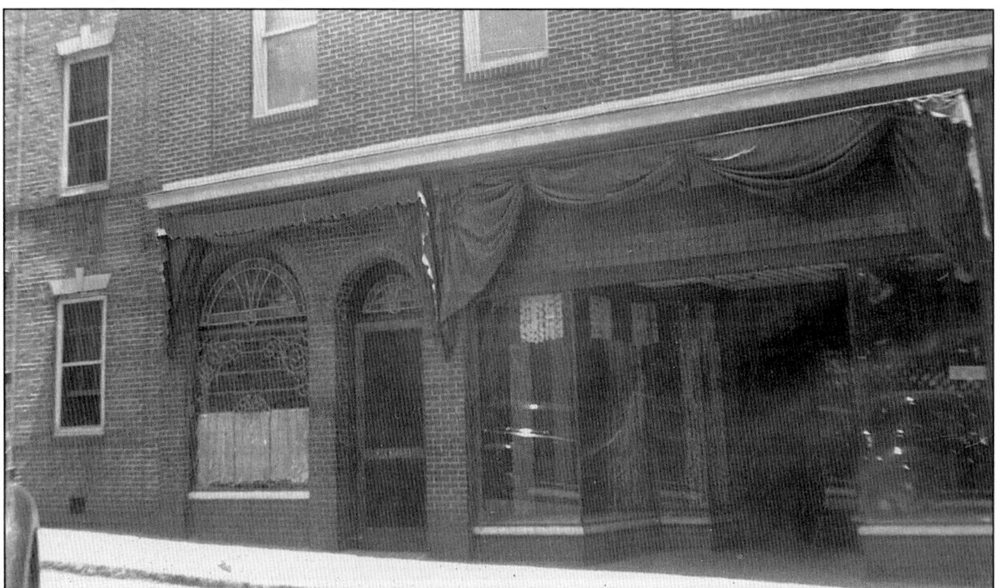
This building on Wylie Street has served as a funeral home, an insurance office, and a non-profit agency among other things over the years. In the mid-1930s, the building was Barron's Funeral Home.

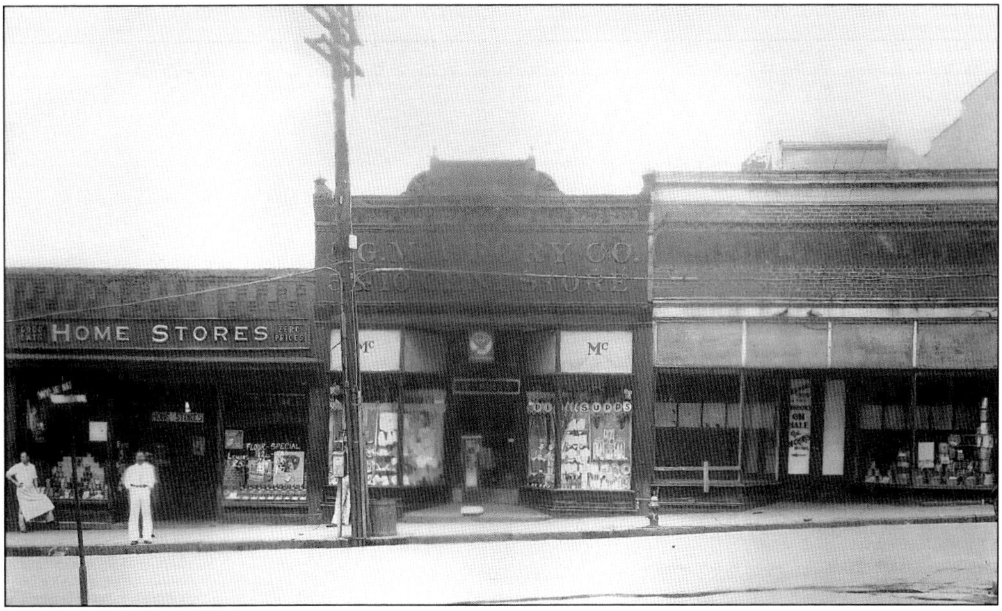

McCrorey's Dime Store opened in the early 1920s in downtown Chester in the building pictured above at 131 Gadsden Street. Around 1938, the owner of McCrorey's purchased the buildings flanking the original store but could not purchase the building out of which they were operating. They were allowed to lease the space, tear down all three buildings, and build the structure pictured below. It was one of the largest retail establishments in town from the late 1930s through the early 1970s. McCrorey's closed in 1974, and the building now houses a restaurant/gift shop called Russell & Company.

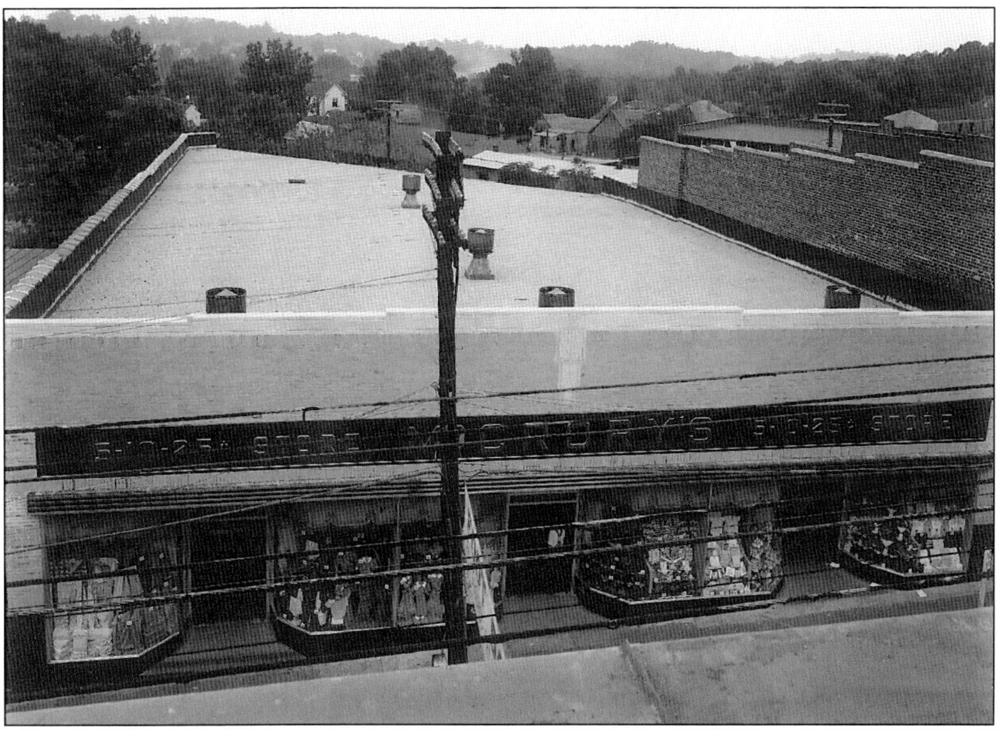

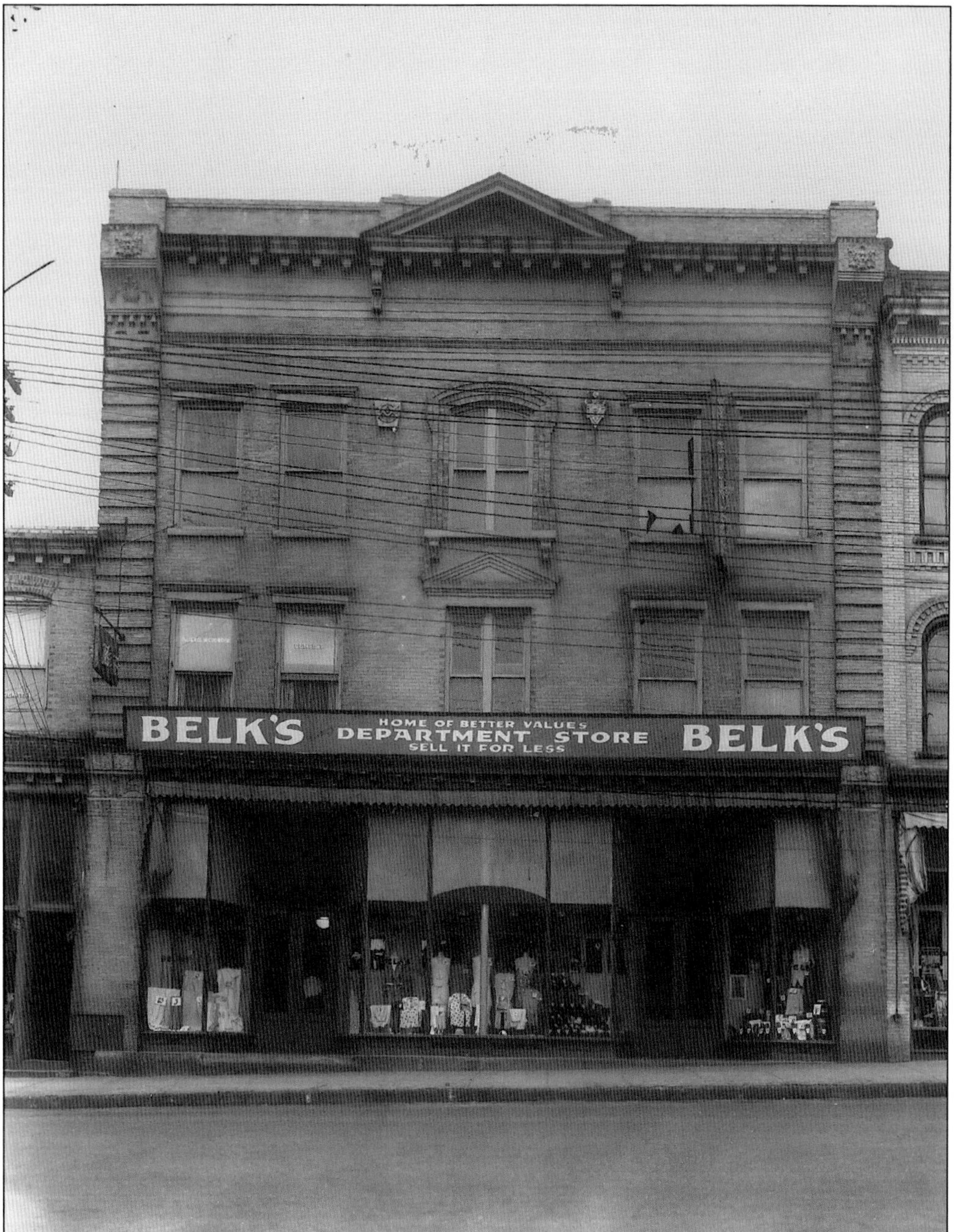

Belk's Department Store opened in Chester in 1893; it was the second of the Belk brothers' stores. This store on top of the hill was destroyed by fire in January of 1942. The company rebuilt in the same location after WW II. This photograph was taken in the 1920s.

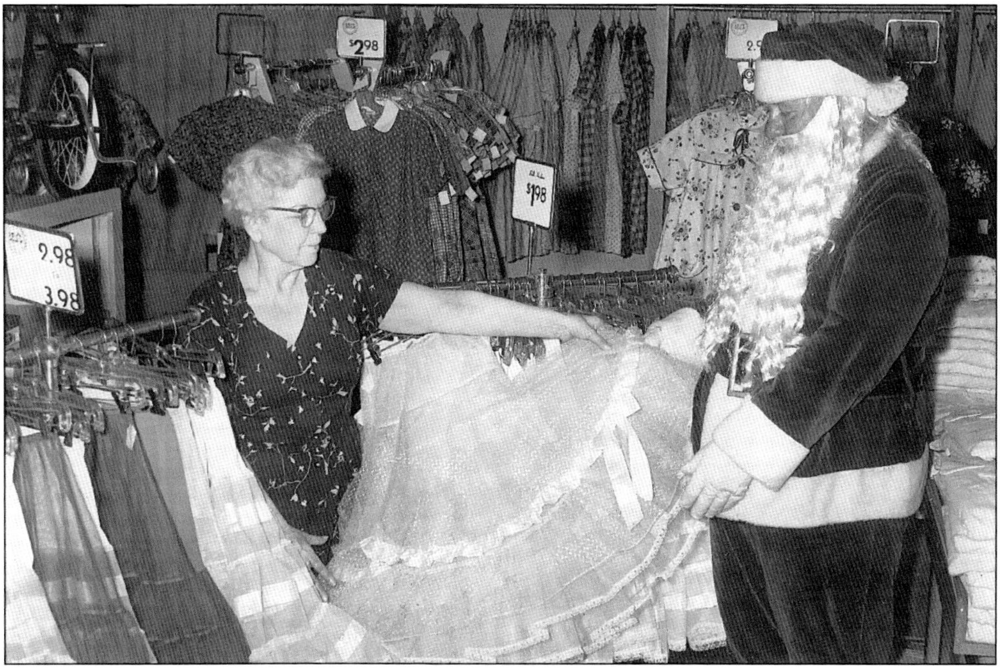

Santa did his shopping at Belk in Chester in the early 1950s. These photographs were used for ads in the local newspaper. Showing Santa gift selections are Anne and Sidney Walker, longtime employees of the store.

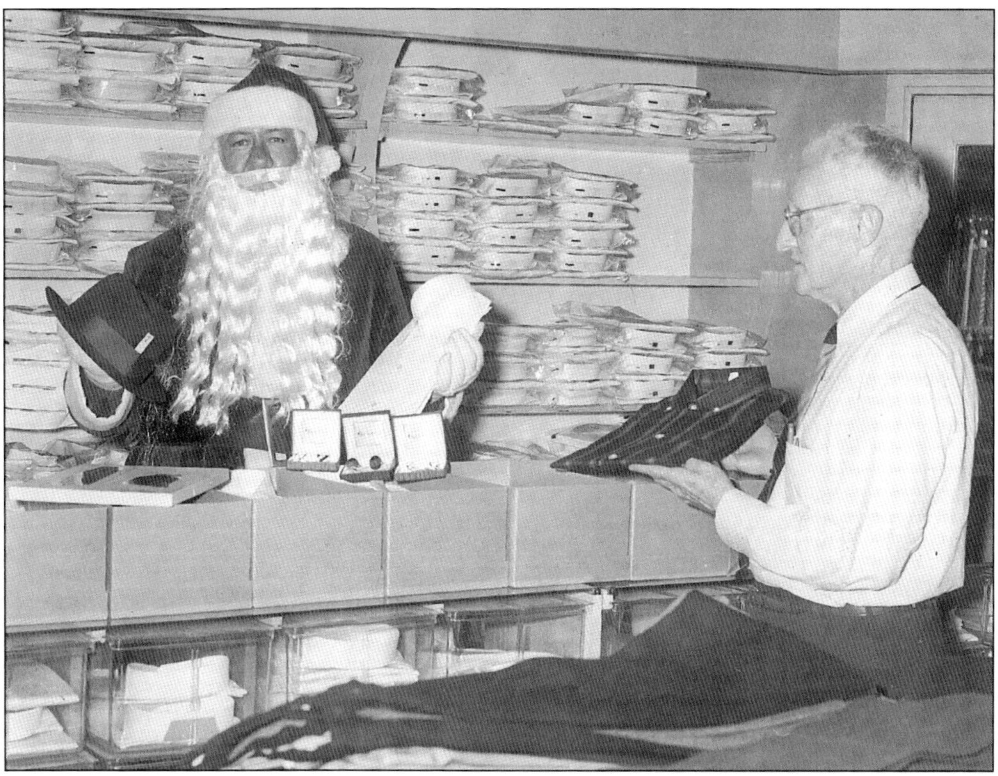

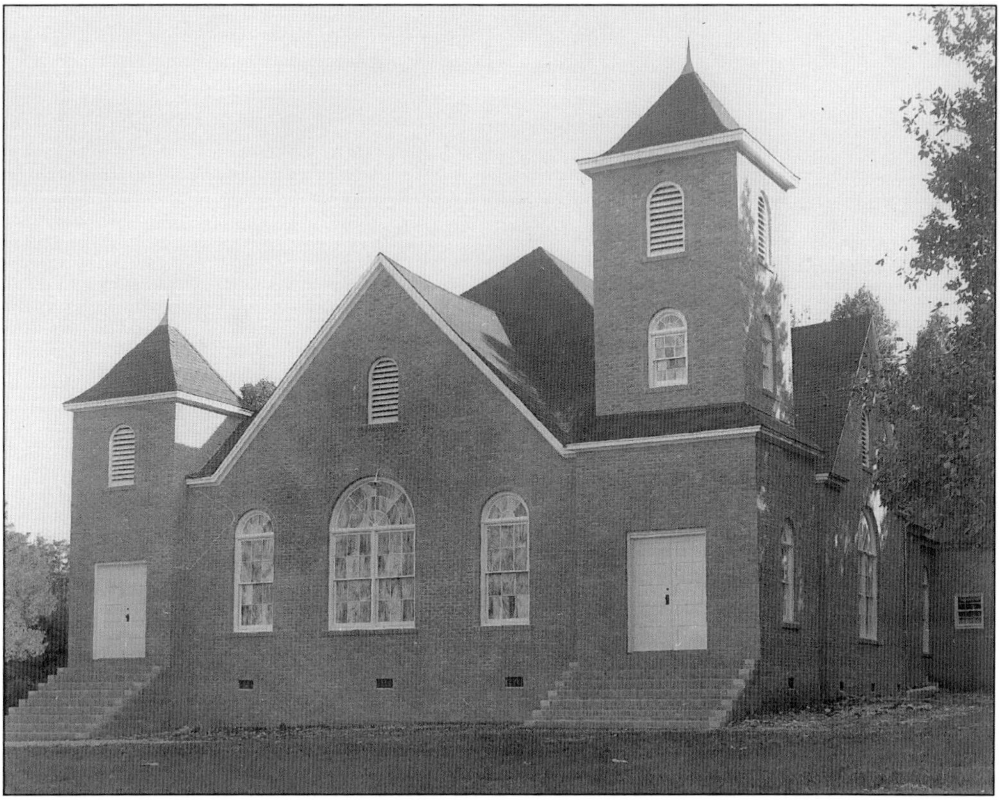

Black Rock Baptist Church was established about 1853 when some African Americans who had been baptized in a white church wanted a church of their own. Leroy Featherstone, a slave at the church's inception, became their minister and served for 67 years. He baptized more than 4,000 people. This building was constructed in 1920 after a fire destroyed the first building.

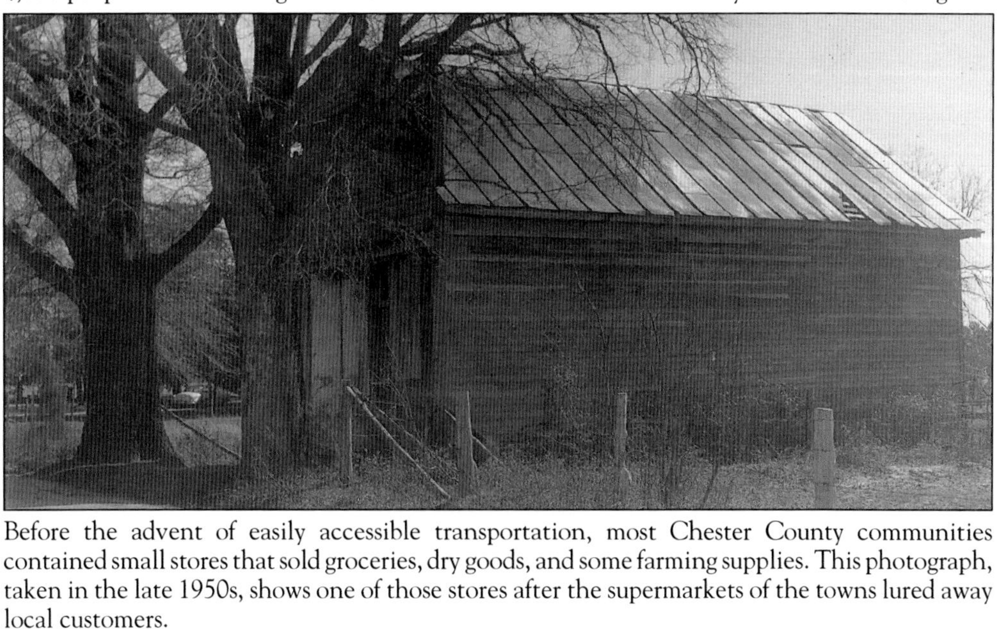

Before the advent of easily accessible transportation, most Chester County communities contained small stores that sold groceries, dry goods, and some farming supplies. This photograph, taken in the late 1950s, shows one of those stores after the supermarkets of the towns lured away local customers.

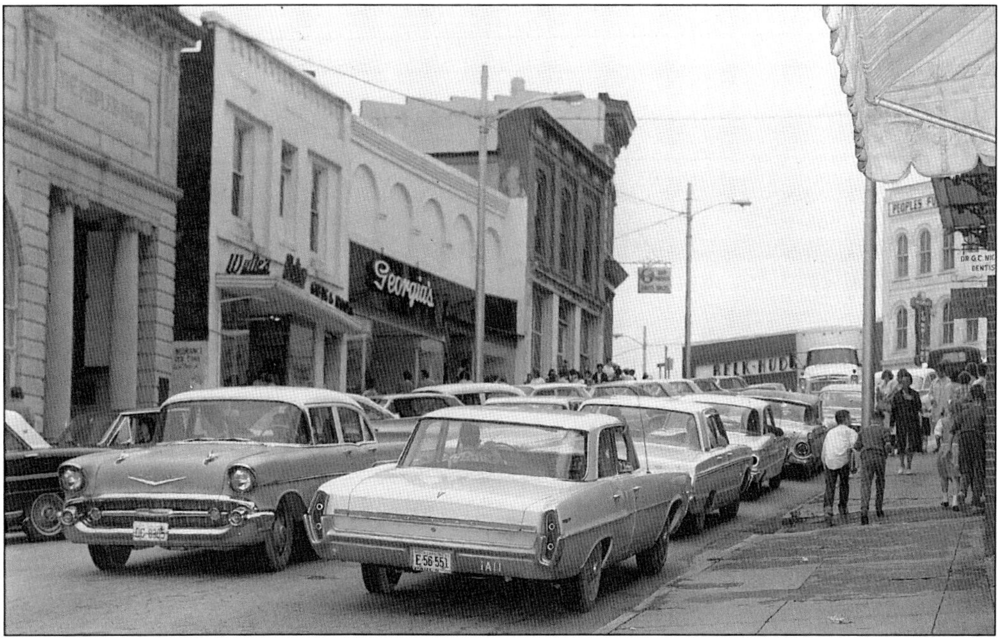

The ravages of urban sprawl had not hit the streets of Downtown Chester in the mid-1960s. The 1970s brought the malls and shopping centers to the by-pass. This scene of Gadsden Street was typical for a Saturday when most people in the primarily rural county came to town to do their shopping.

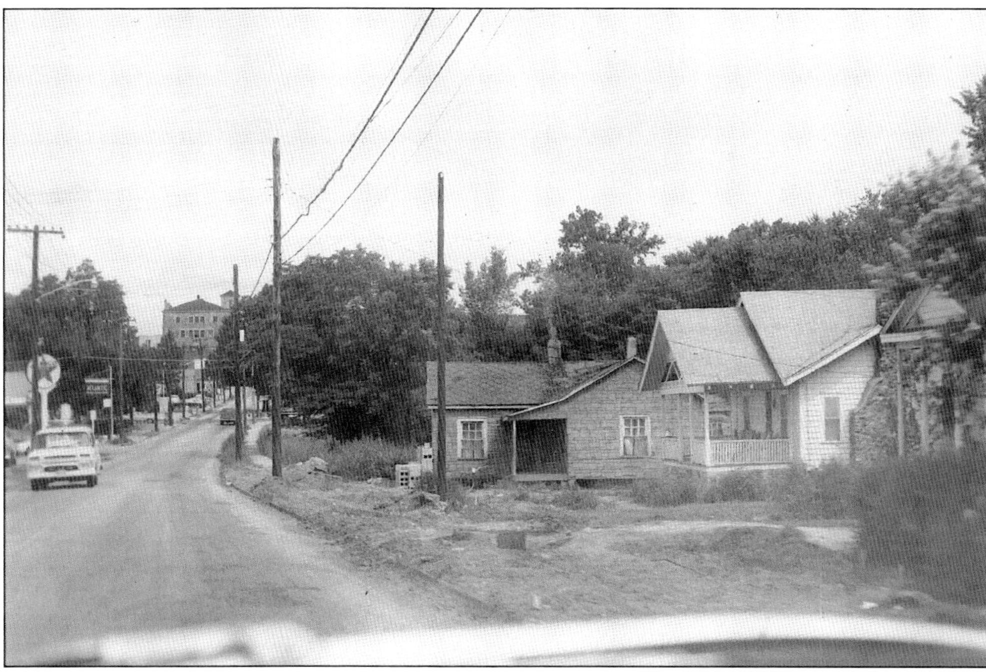

Shown here is Columbia Street in the early 1960s before portions of the street were widened. This photograph was taken from where the fire station currently is located, approximately where Chester High School was once located.

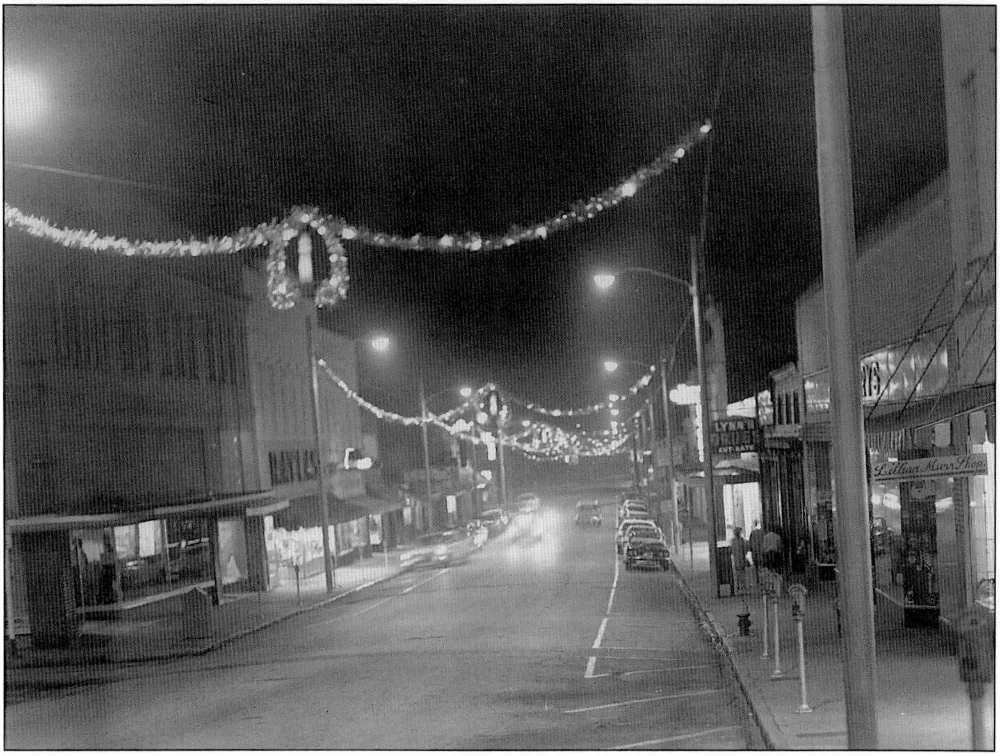

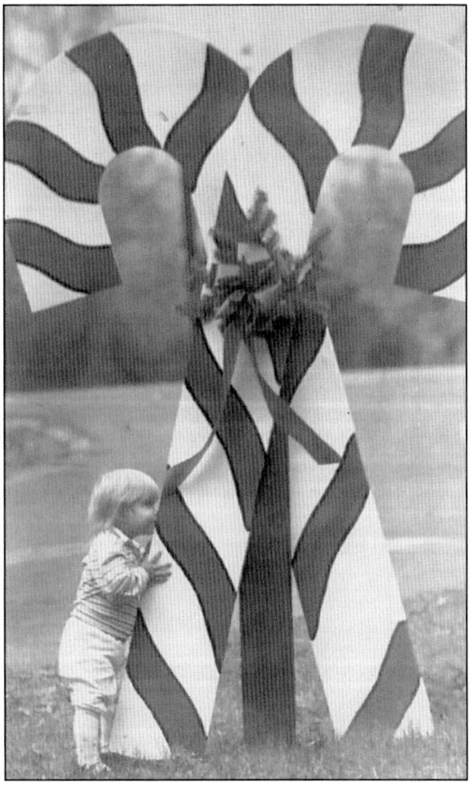

For decades, a favorite pastime of Chester city and county residents has been to ride downtown in the evenings near Christmas and look at the Christmas lights. For years the lights were strung across Gadsden and Main Streets. This photograph was taken in the mid to late 1960s.

In the 1980s, Great Falls used large wooden cut-outs as Christmas decorations downtown. This adorable little girl decides to see how they taste.

Valley Lunch was located in the Valley at 152 Gadsden Street in downtown Chester. It was open at this location in the 1950s. In the 1940s, the restaurant was located in an old streetcar in the alleyway now known as Merchant's Walk, right next door to 152 Gadsden. Don't you wish that milkshakes were still 25¢?

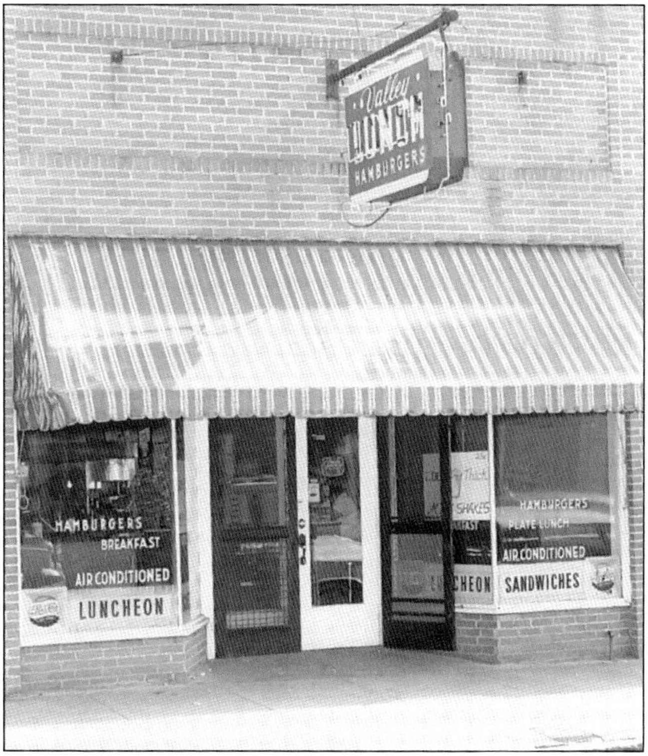

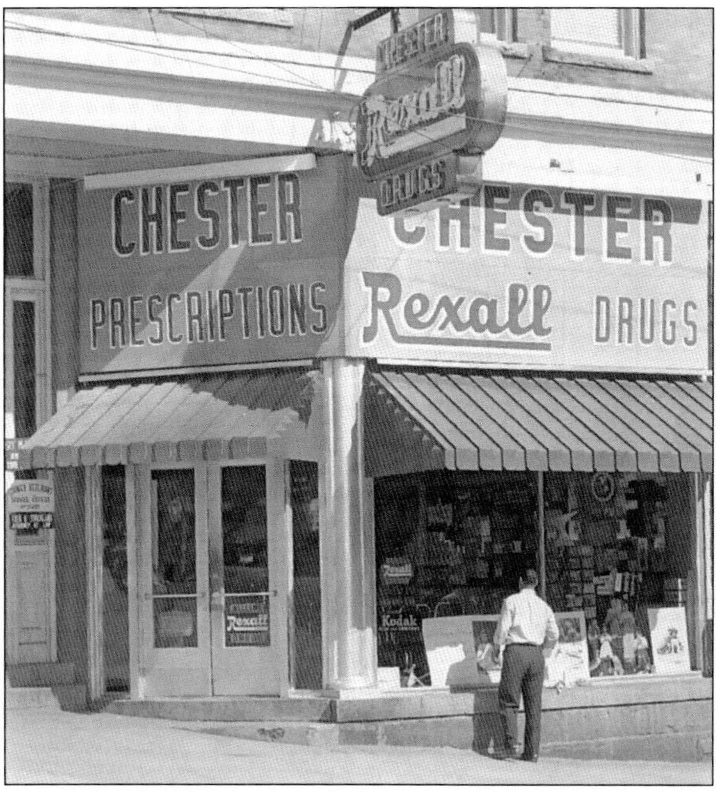

Chester Drug was a fixture for many years on top of the hill in downtown Chester. Located at 134 Main Street, the store had a window (pictured here) filled with advertising and displays in the early 1950s. Chester Drug closed down in the early 1980s, and since that time, several restaurants have been housed in that space. The most recent one is Summit Food & Spirits.

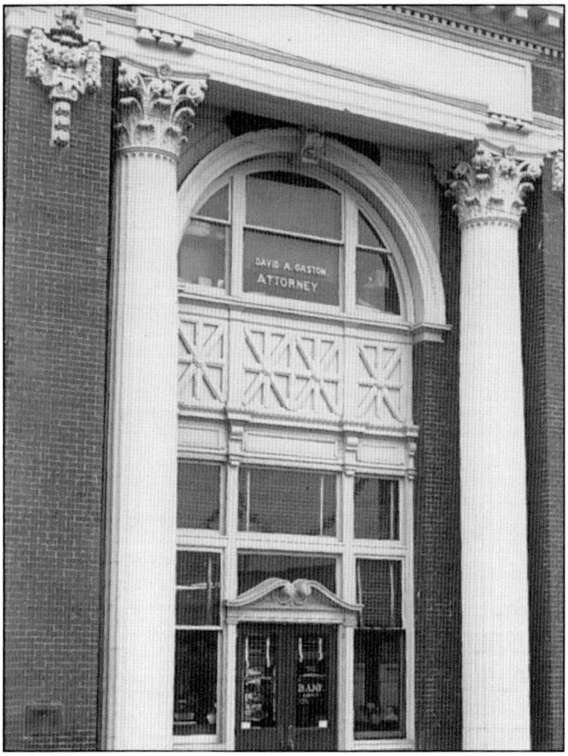

Organized in 1899, the Commercial Bank moved to this building on the corner of Gadsden and Wylie Streets in Chester in 1913. The bank was bought out in 1972.

Elliott's Market was a grocery store downtown and one of several in Chester before the advent of the supermarket. Located at 161 Gadsden Street, the store drew people from all over the area on a weekly basis to do their grocery shopping. The store closed in the early 1970s.

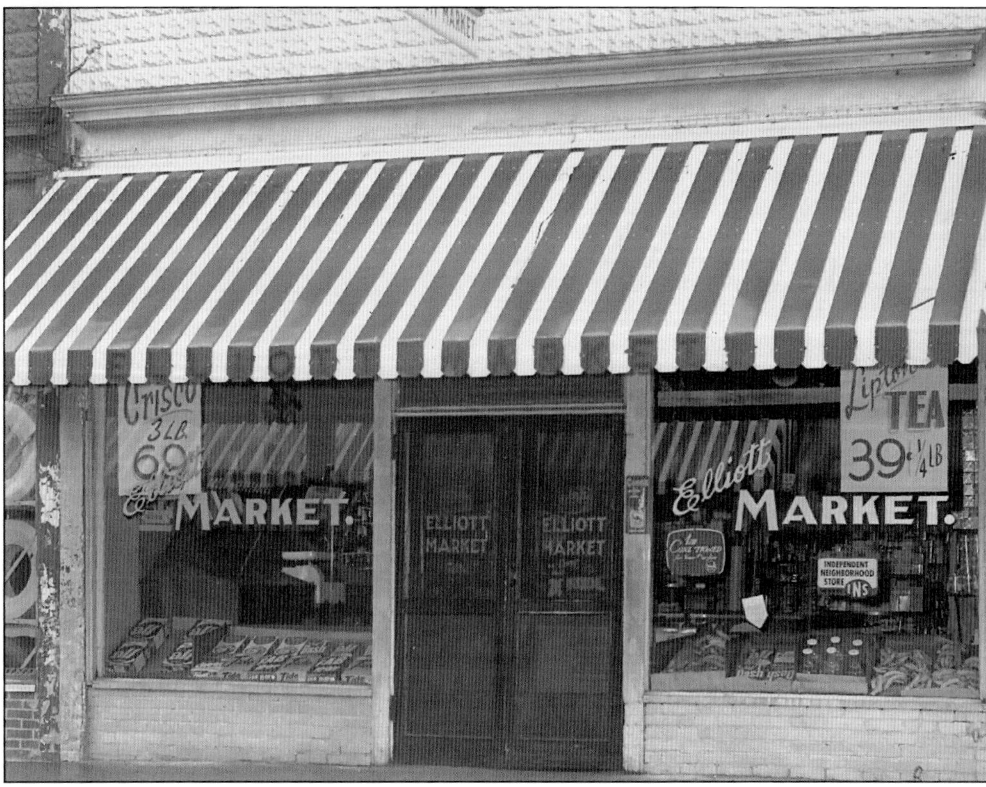

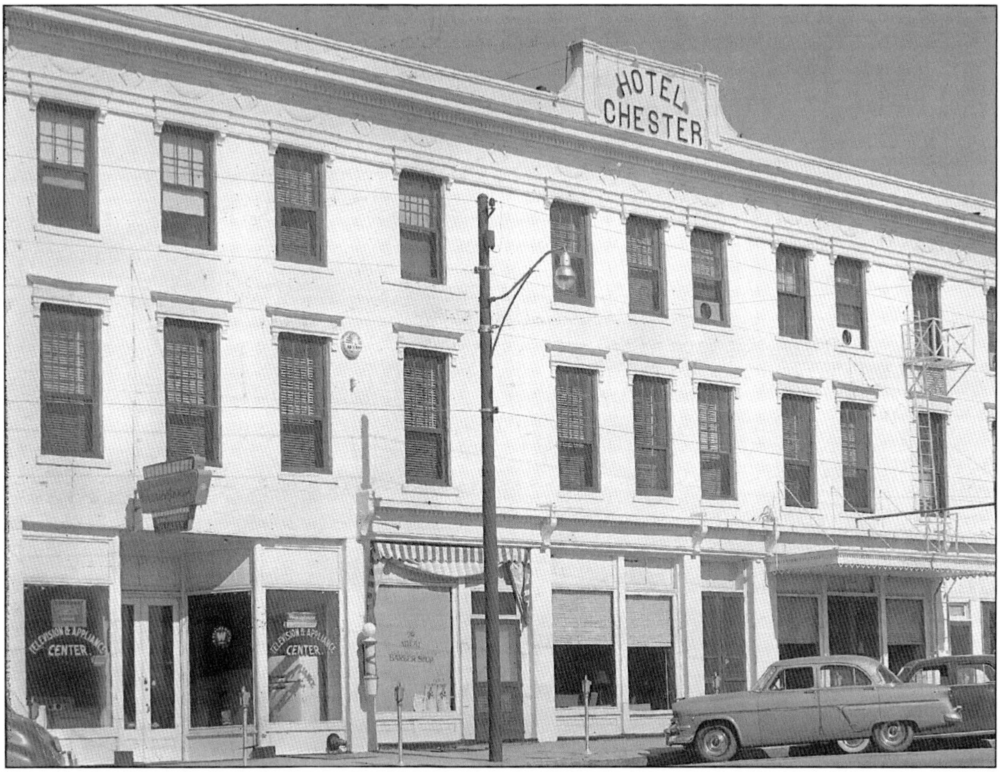

Hotel Chester served as a hotel under various names from 1855 until the early 1960s. The front portion was built in 1855 by Samuel McAliley, a Chester businessman and politician. McAliley was the sole dissenting voice during the first vote of the Secession Convention of 1860. This photo was taken in the mid-1950s.

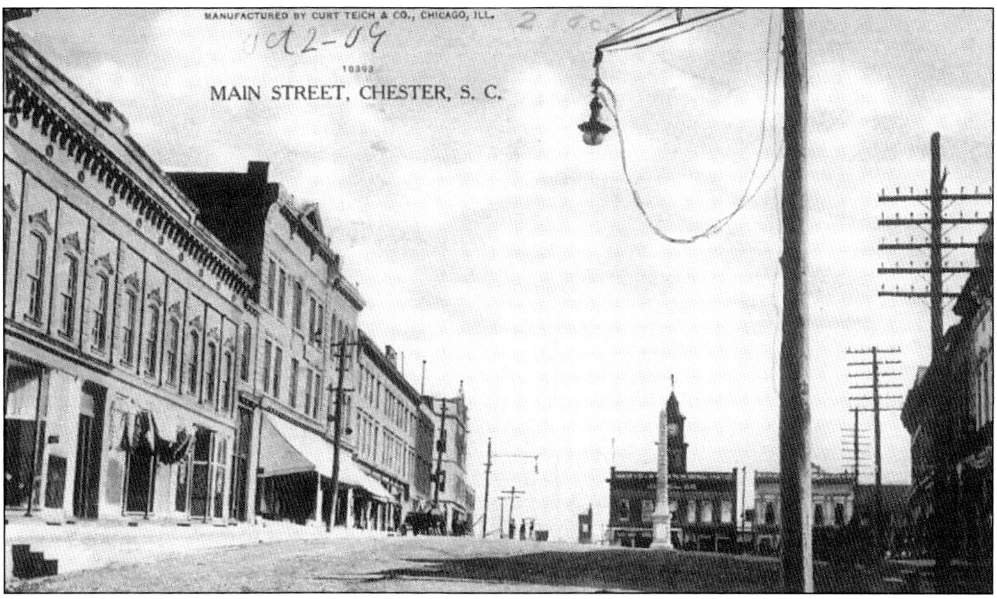

Main Street looking north has changed little in the past century. This photograph, made into a postcard, was taken around 1909.

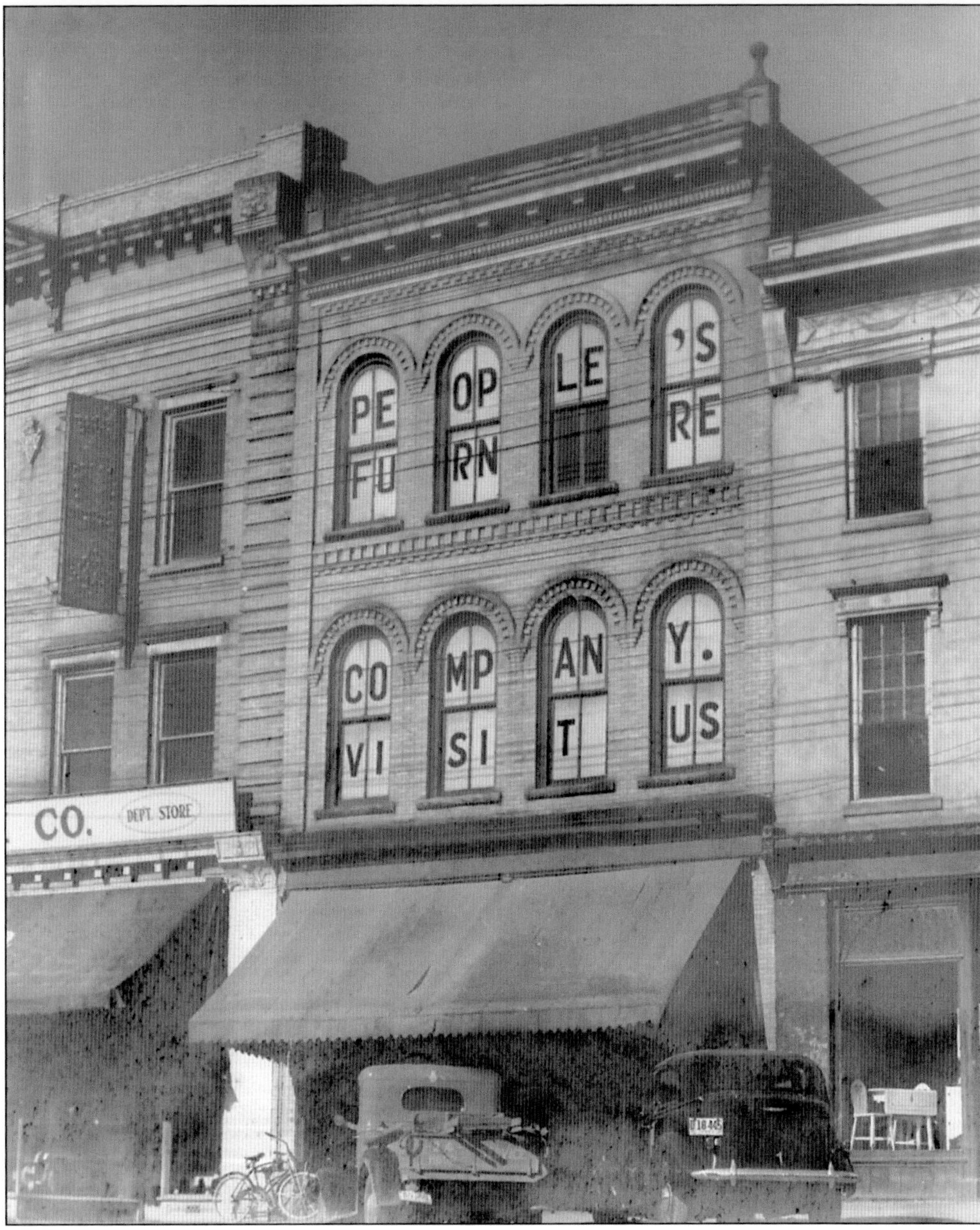

This photograph of People's Furniture Company building was taken in 1937. This furniture store, located at 114 Main Street, has been in business for more than 75 years.

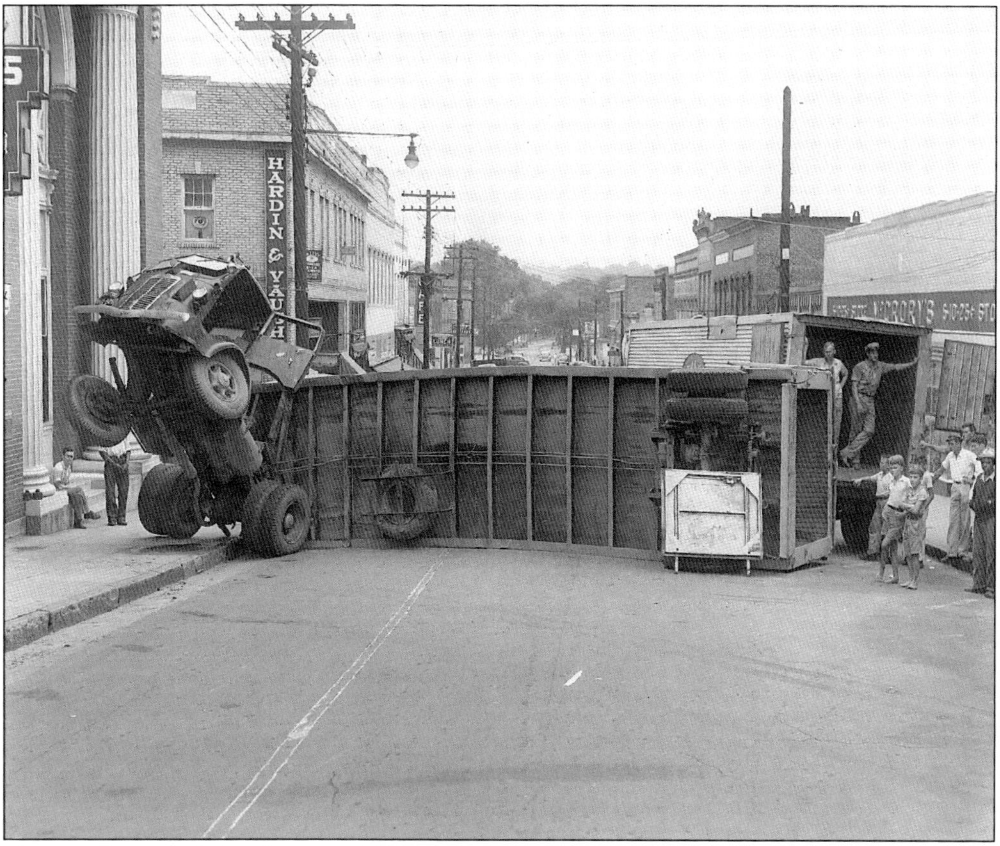

This wreck on Gadsden Street on July 14, 1943 caused a sensation and held up traffic for hours on the main street through downtown Chester's business district.

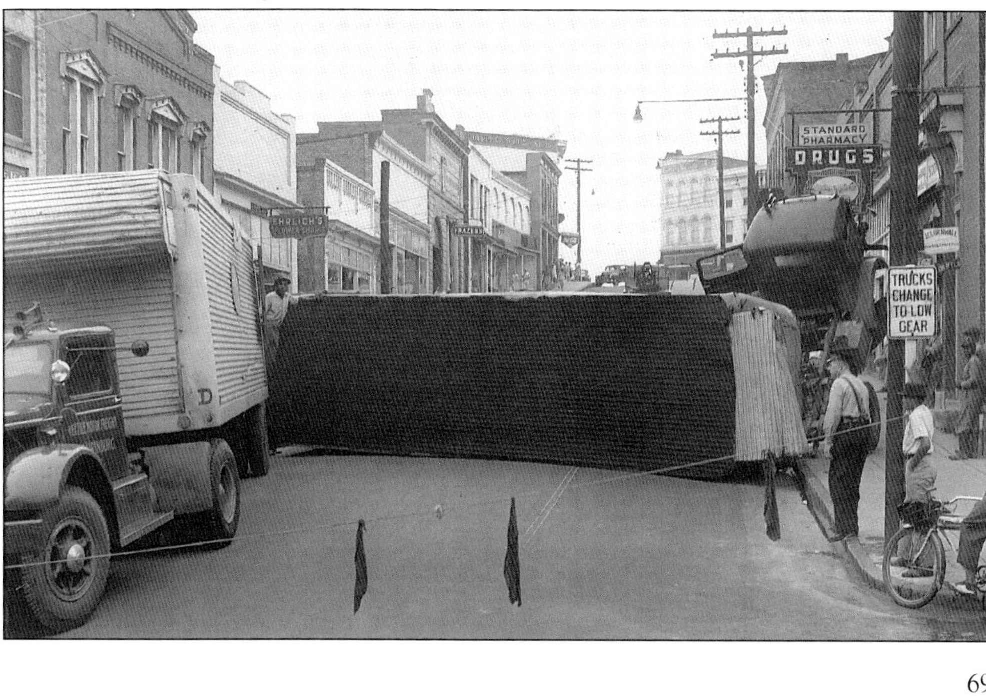

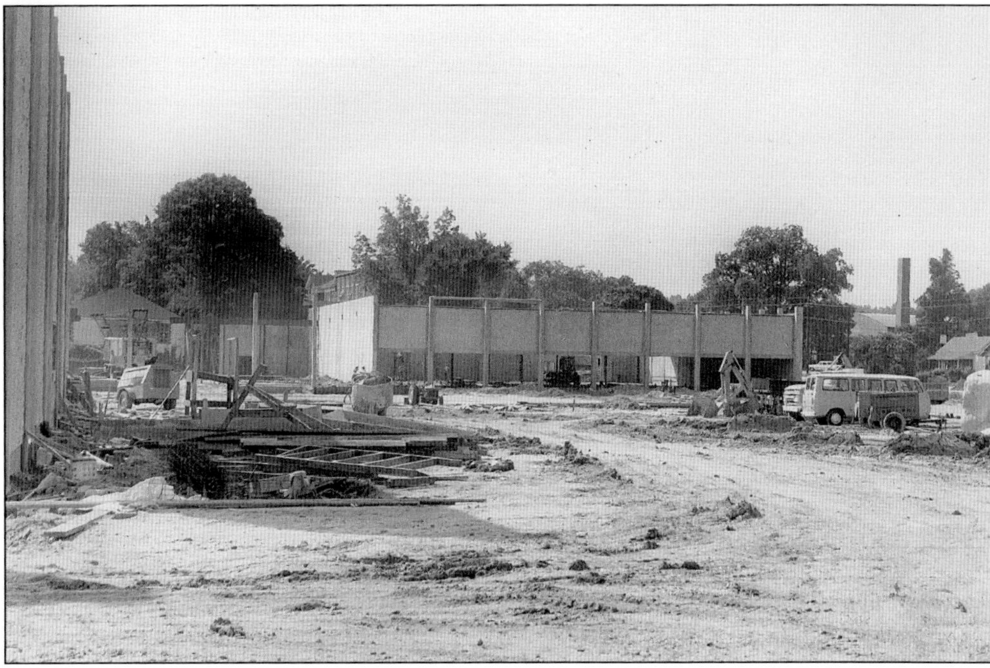

The face of downtown Chester changed in 1970 and 1971 when the first shopping center, initially named People's Plaza and later changed to Cestrian Square, was constructed. Above, is what would become Big Star grocery store and below is the nearly completed construction of The People's Bank. Behind the building above is the back of Brockman High School.

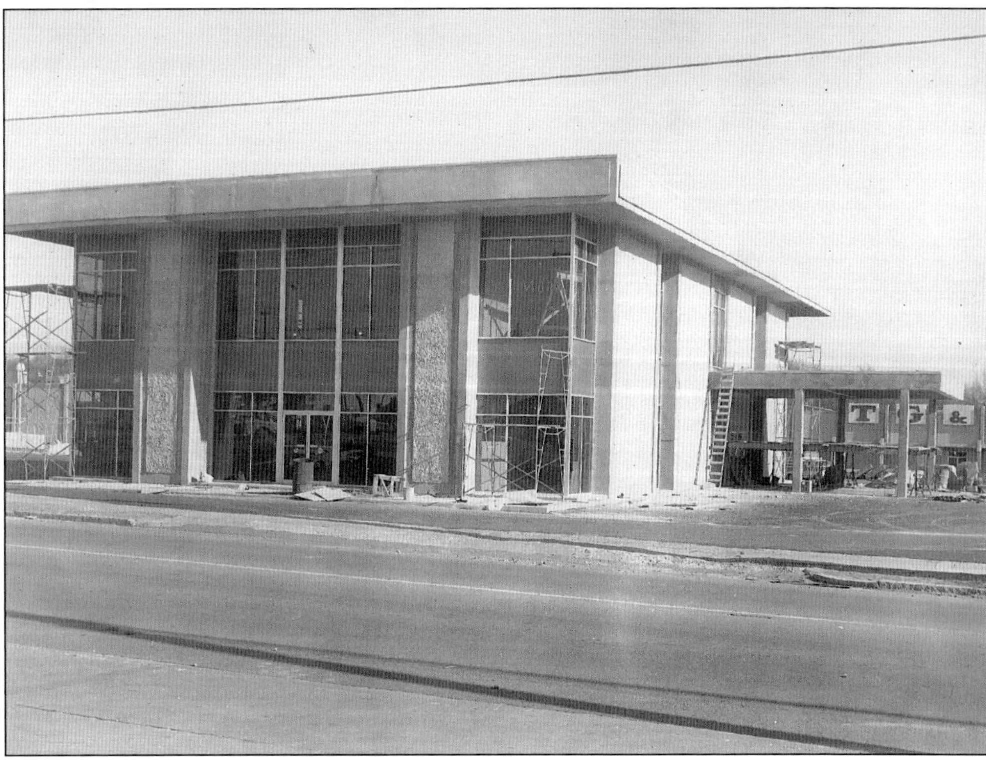

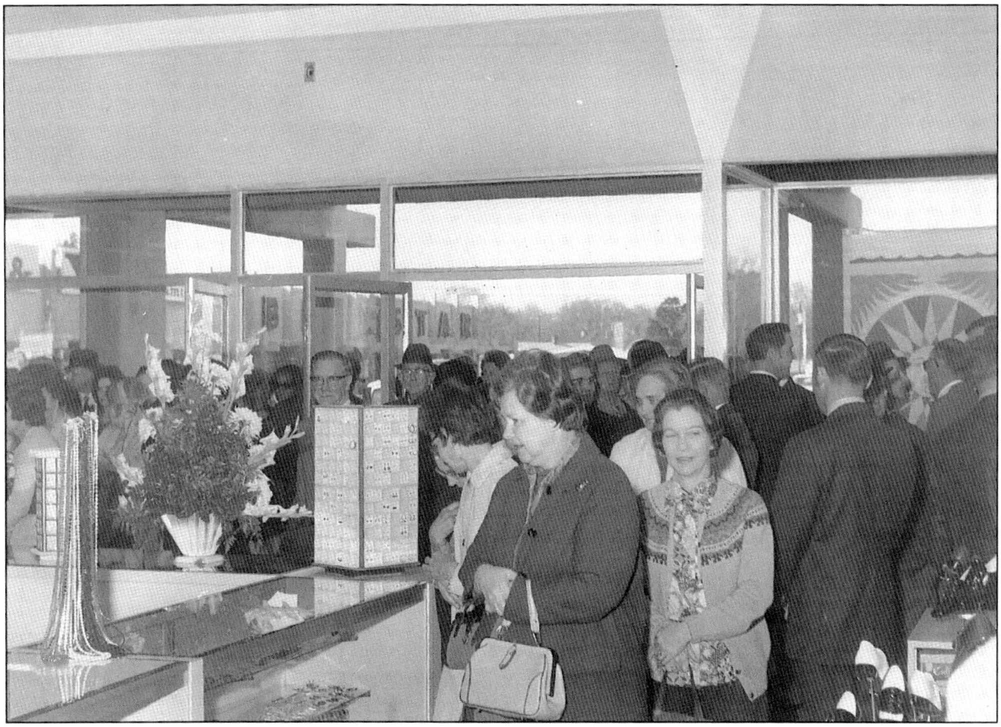

When People's Plaza opened in 1971, B.C. Moore and Sons was one of the anchor tenants. This crowd gathered for the ribbon cutting. Just over the earring stand is Mayor Ed Dawson, who participated in the ceremony.

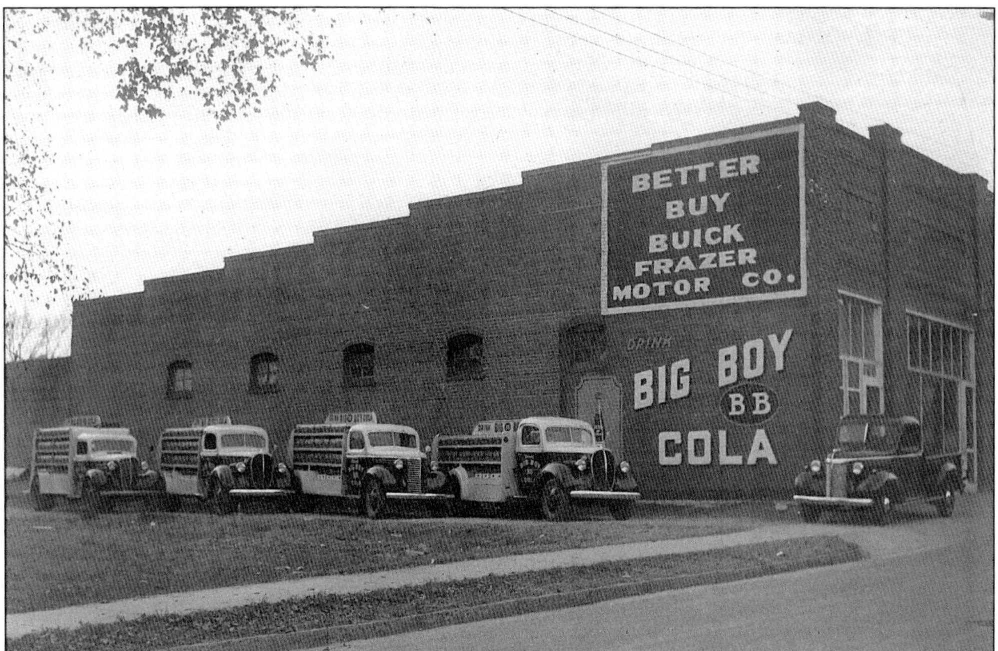

The Big Boy Cola Bottlers was a business on Columbia Street in downtown Chester. This photograph of the building and delivery trucks was taken in November 1939.

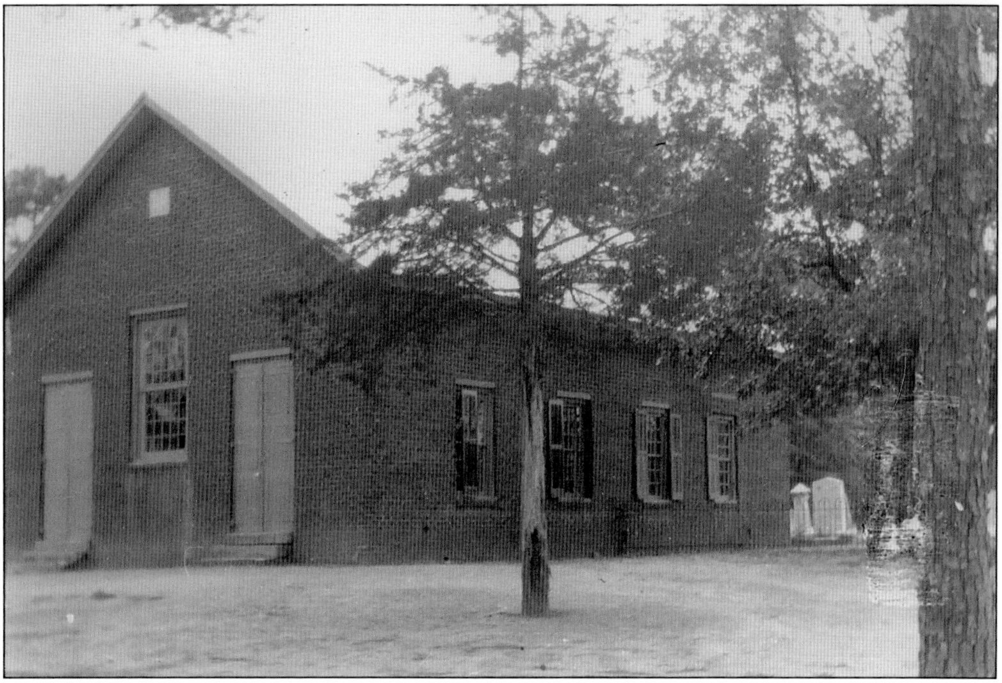

Woodward Baptist Church was established in 1789, and this building, which is the present sanctuary, was built in 1830. Mrs. Jefferson Davis, her children, and party spent the night at the church in April 1865 on their flight from Richmond.

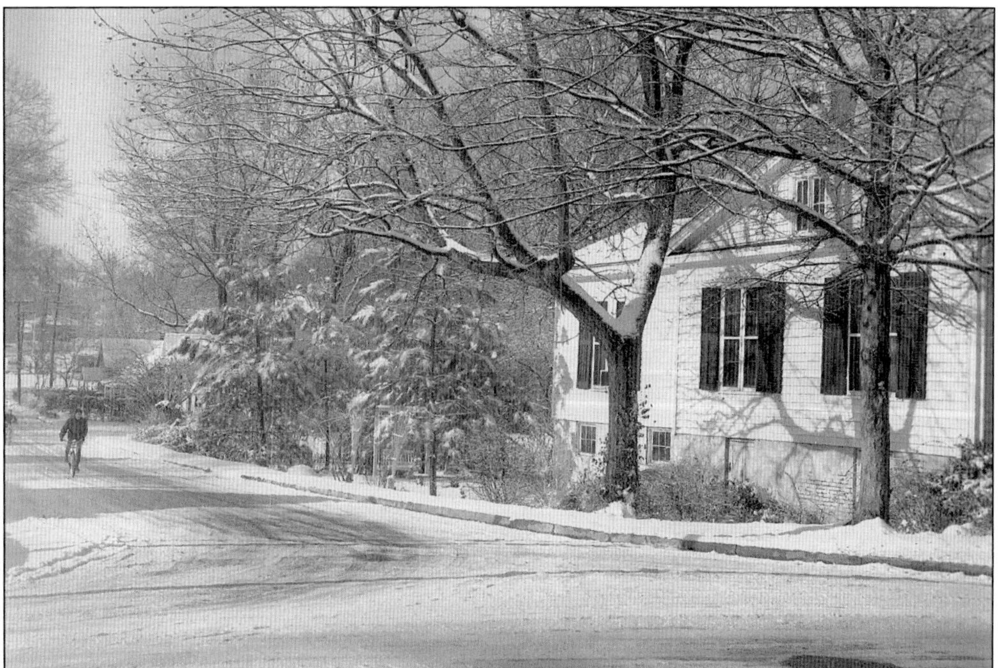

Snow has almost always been a special event in Chester County. This lovely scene at the corner of Walker and Wylie Streets was captured during a January snow in 1966.

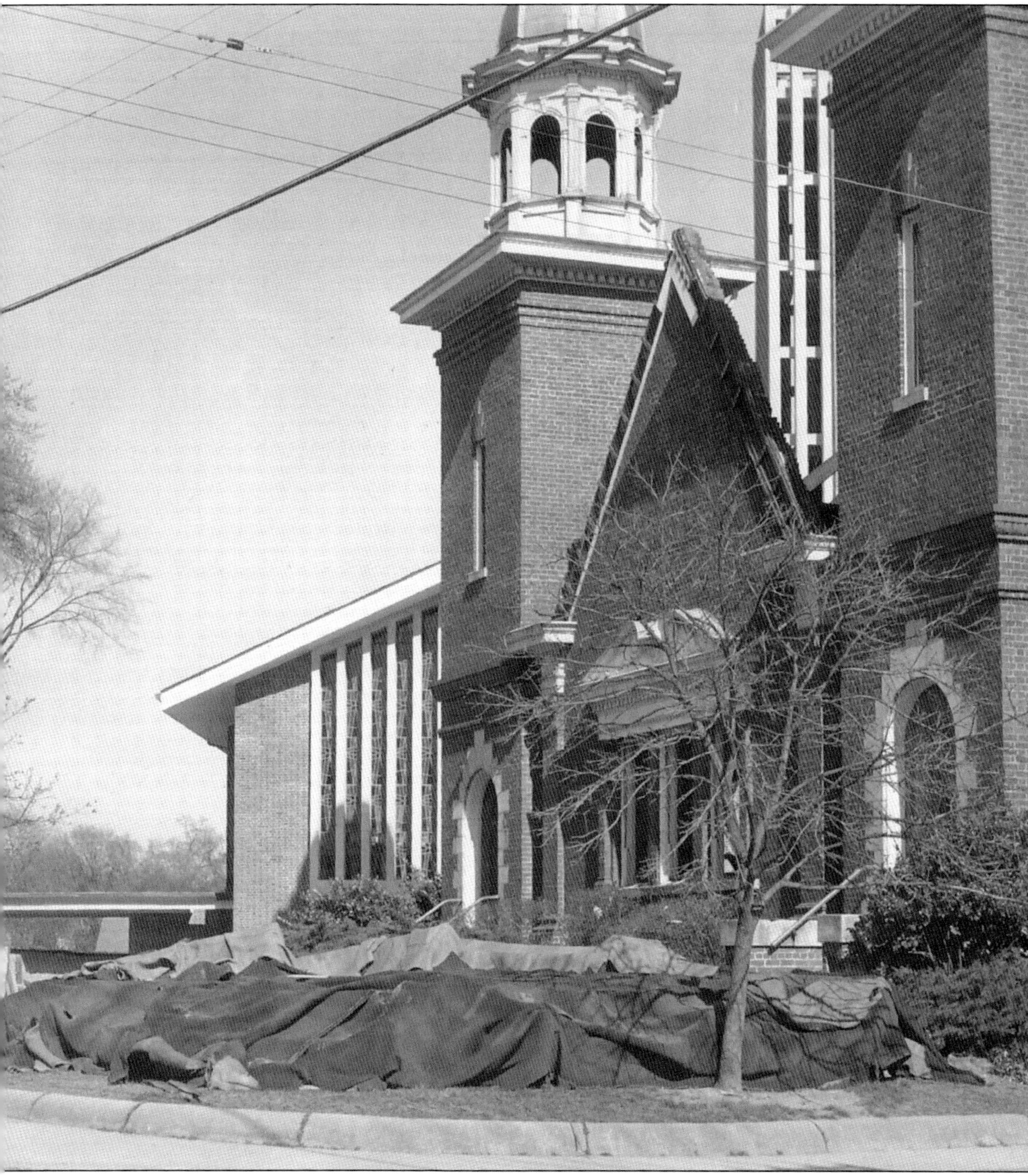

The first church built in Chester was the Baptist Church located on the same site that it is now—Church Street. It was a wooden structure that was built about 1836. In the 1950s, the Baptist sanctuary, which was built in 1885, was torn down to make room for the new sanctuary. This photo shows the sharp contrast between the old and the new.

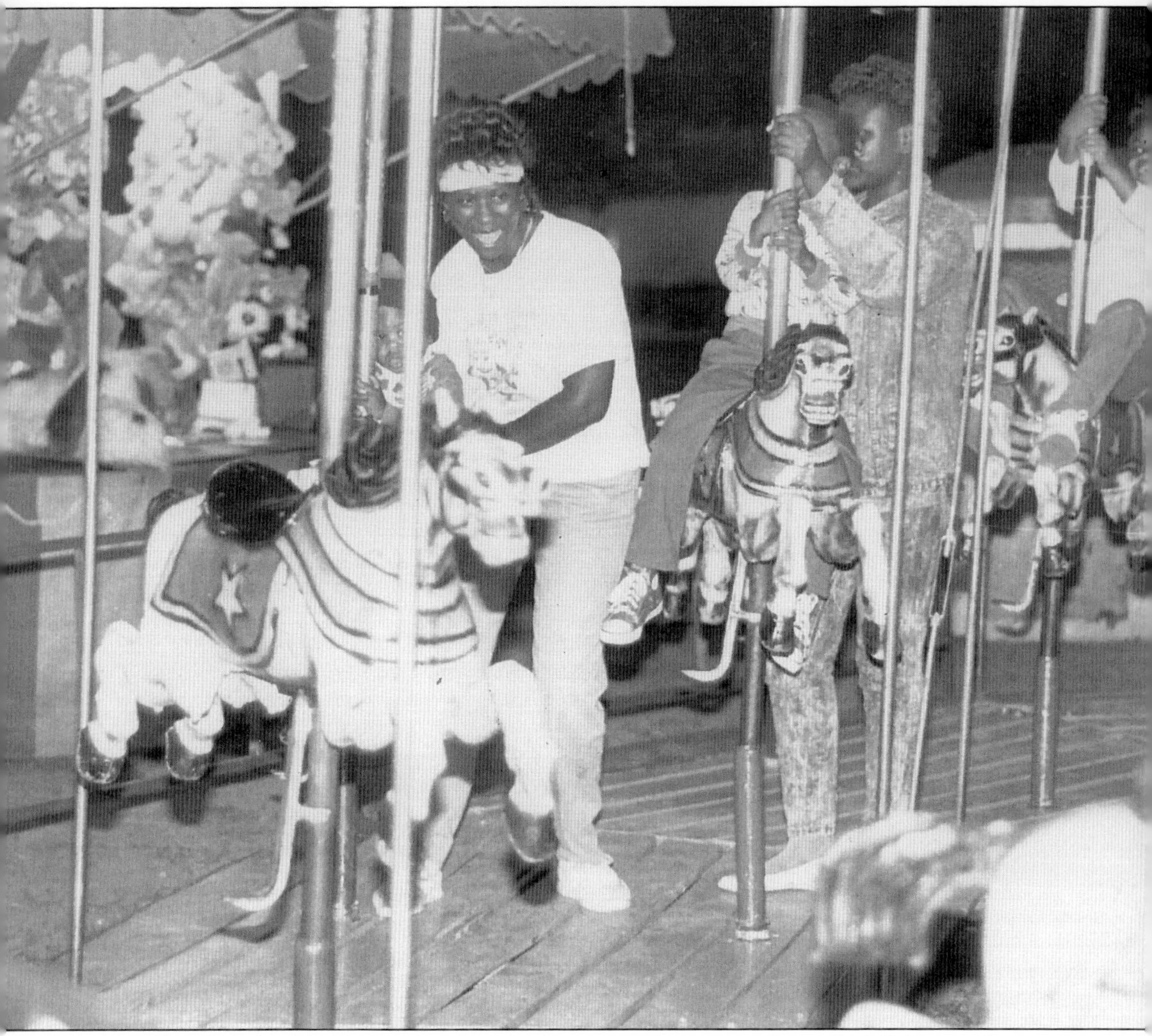

For decades, the Chester Fair was a most anticipated event in the early fall. Not only was it an opportunity for people to display their home-grown vegetables, their cattle, and other animals but also a chance for the children, both young and old, to enjoy rides and carnival activities. This scene from 1989 shows from one of the last fairs held in the county.

Four

People

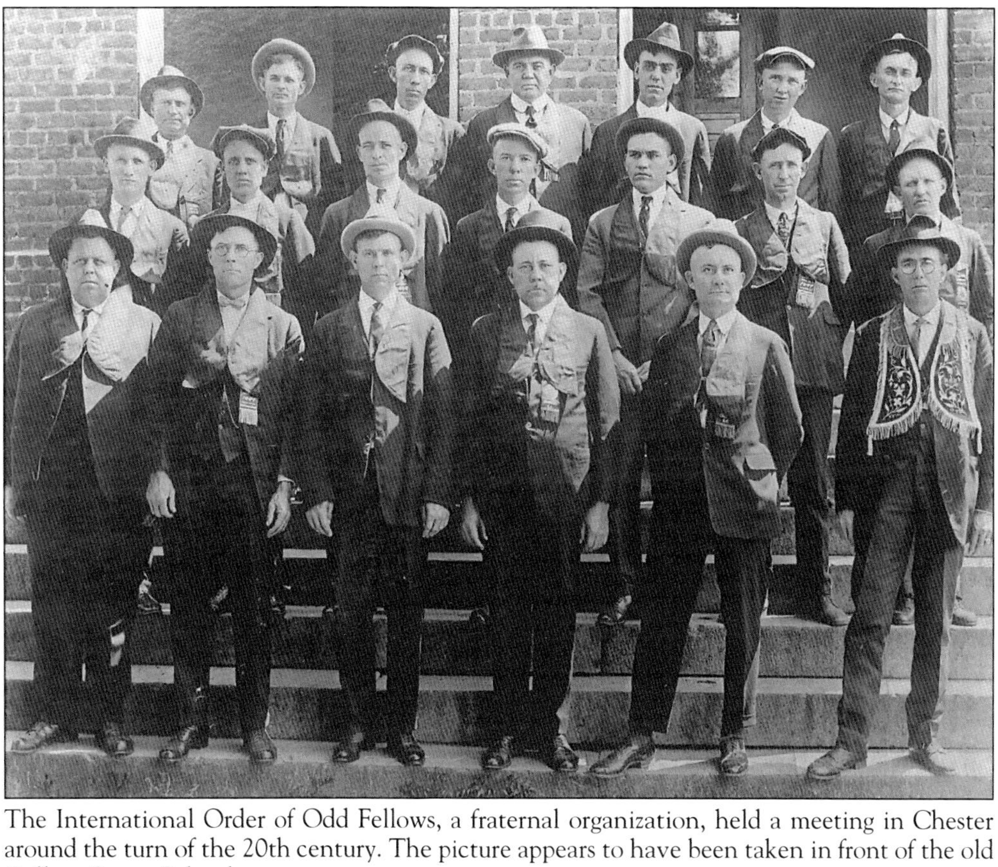

The International Order of Odd Fellows, a fraternal organization, held a meeting in Chester around the turn of the 20th century. The picture appears to have been taken in front of the old College Street School.

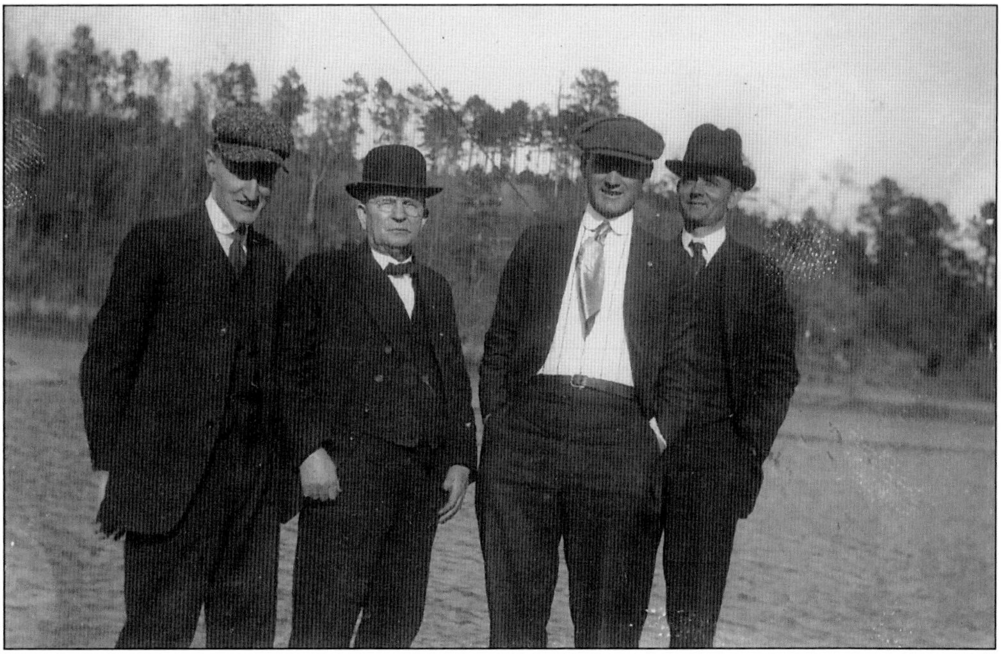

This handsome group of early-20th-century men poses for a portrait in a rural portion of Chester County. The three-piece suit was a popular fashion statement for men around 1920 when this photo was taken.

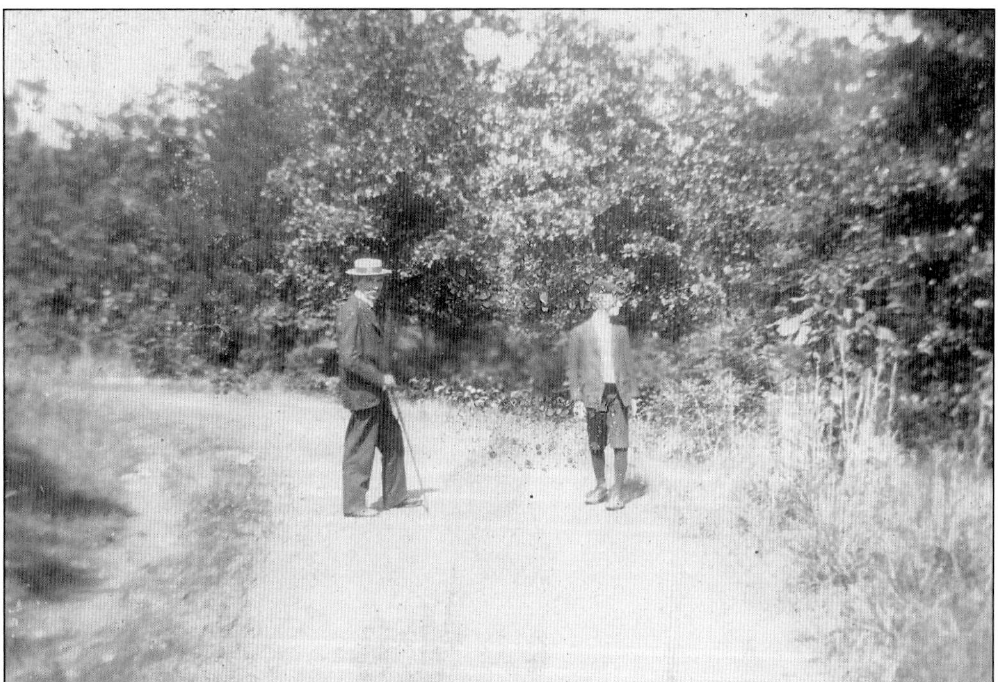

Two dapper young men in the 1910s walk down a dirt road in Chester County. Walking was still the most convenient mode of transportation, especially for young men.

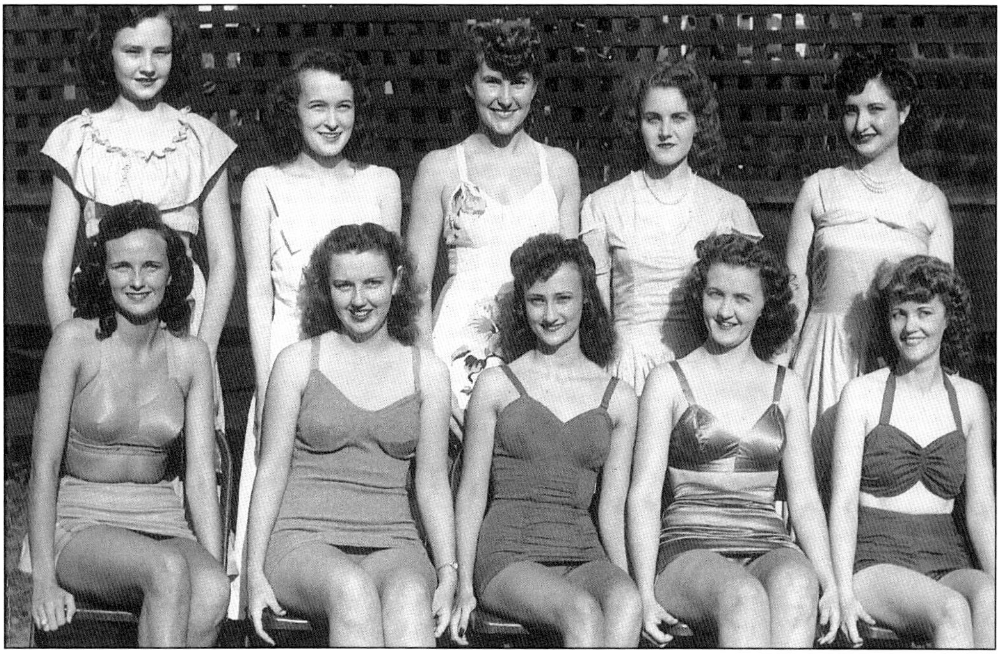

This group of bathing beauties, participants in a local beauty contest in the1940s, pose for a portrait. They are, from left to right, as follows: (front row) Loree Caston, Peggy Helms, Harriett Wolfe, Mildred Black, and Kathleen McNinch; (back row) Betty Jean Grant, Betty Rose Roddey, Vivian Bishop, Margaret Varnadore, and Nell Hatchey.

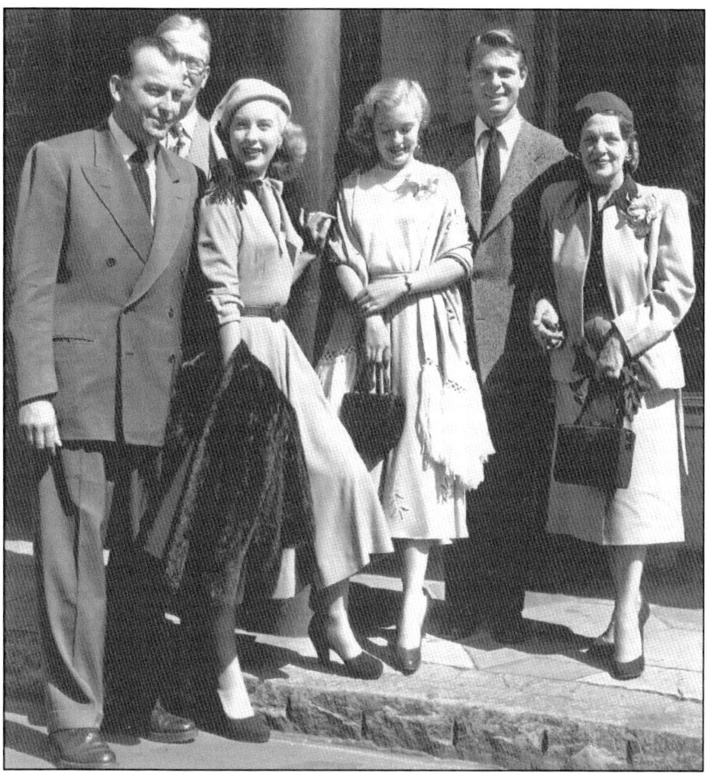

A group of Chester citizens pose beside Hardin & Vaughn, a retail clothing store in downtown Chester in the early 1950s.

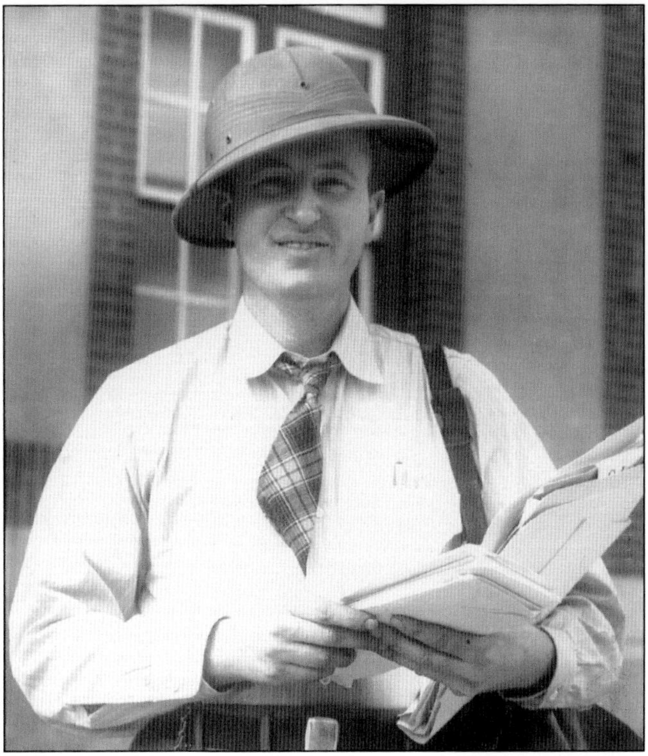

H. Wallace Tinsley was a postal carrier for many years. Here, he is pictured in front of the post office about to go on his route, *c.* 1940s.

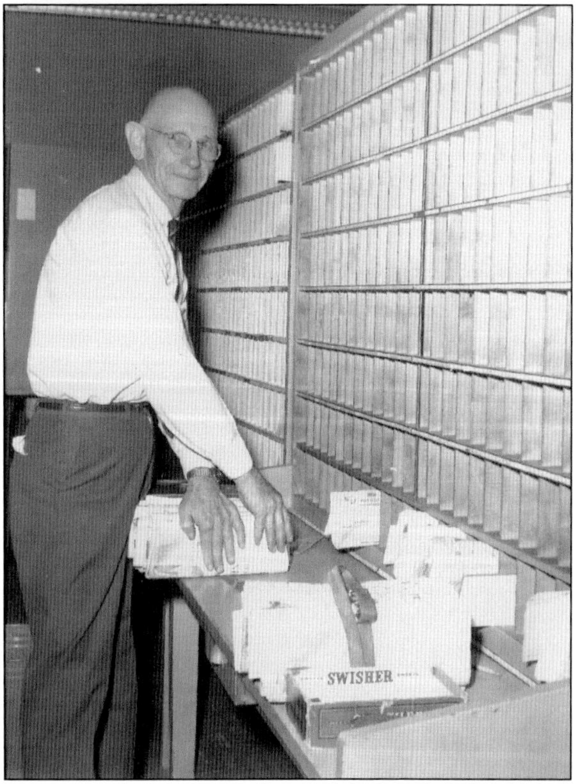

Tom Anderson, a longtime employee of the U.S. Postal Service, sorts mail at the Saluda Street post office. This picture was taken upon his retirement in the 1960s.

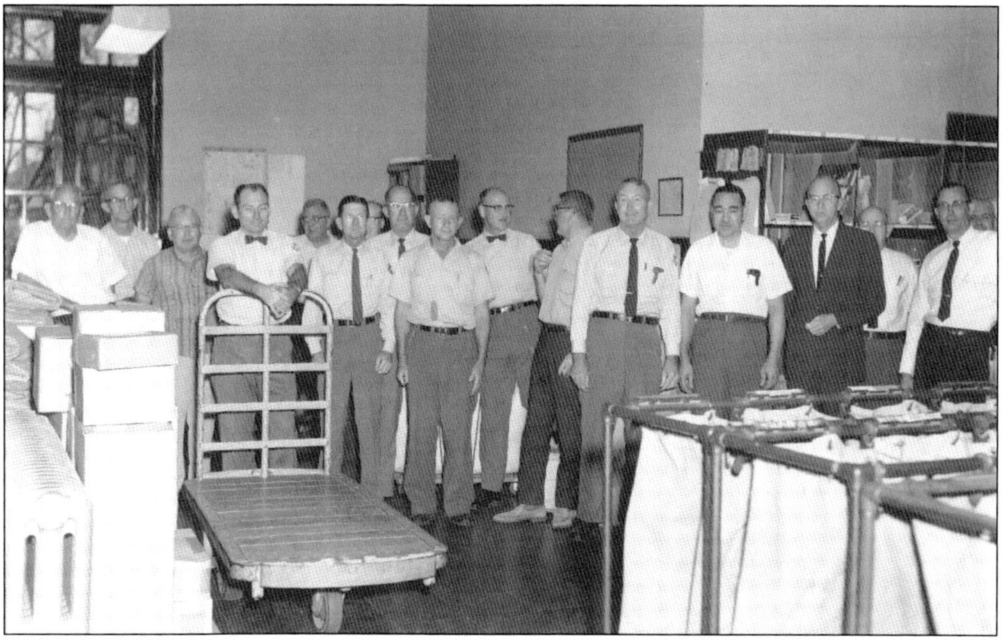

This group of postal workers pose for a photograph in the old post office at the corner of Main and Wylie. They are, from left to right, as follows: Herman Carter, Bob Hollis, Robert Crawford, James (Stick) E. Kennedy, Pete Wylie, Abe Horton, Bob Huey, Bob Dunbar, J.G. Franklin, Bob McKown, Joe Giltner, Guy Faulk, Floyd McClurkin, Haynes Wilkes, Walker Huggins, Heyward Gourley, and Sam Grant.

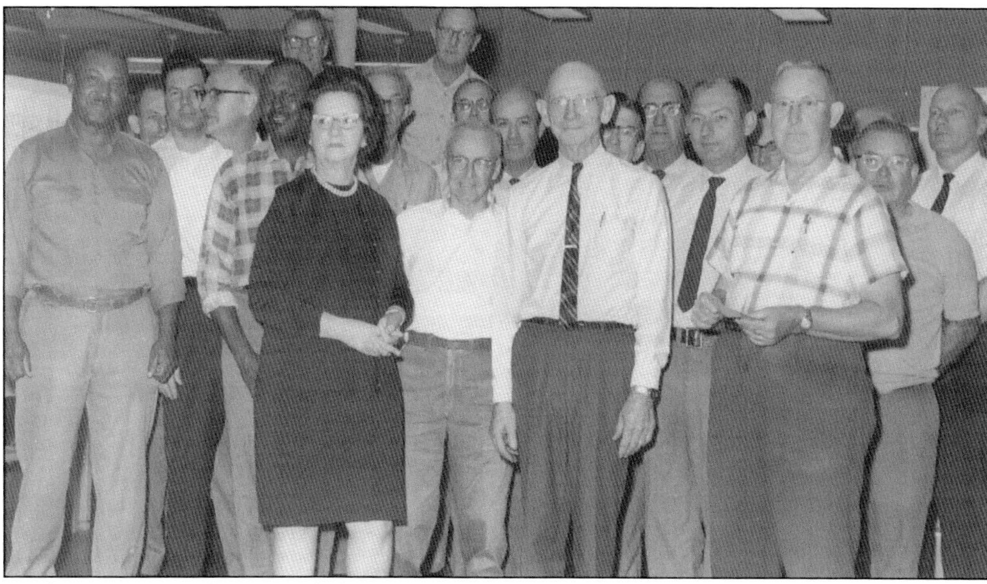

At the new post office on Saluda Street, which opened in 1964, a group of postal employees posed for this picture. They are, from left to right, as follows: Bernard Nelson, Robert Dover, Marion Cash, Bob McKown, Bill Crosby, Joe Giltner, Lola Thompson, Bob Hollis, William Dennis, Heyward Gourley, Ambrose Wylie, Robert Huey, Tom Anderson, W.H. (Abe) Horton, Bob Dunbar, James (Stick) Kennedy, James Marion Conrad, Robert Crawford, Sam Grant, and Killough White.

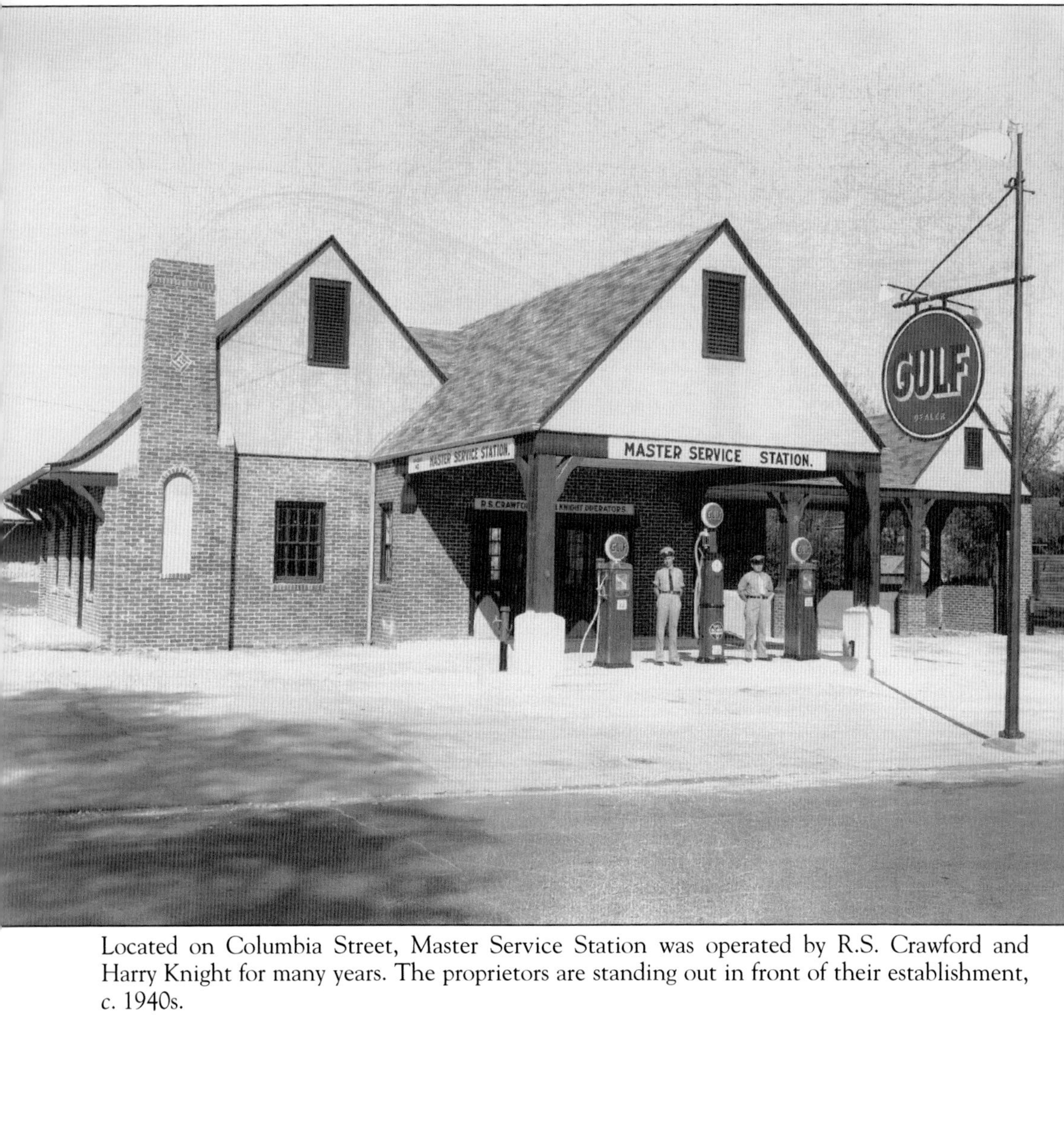

Located on Columbia Street, Master Service Station was operated by R.S. Crawford and Harry Knight for many years. The proprietors are standing out in front of their establishment, c. 1940s.

John Lyles (Johnny) Young was a service station attendant during the 1940s. This service station was located on Gadsden Street.

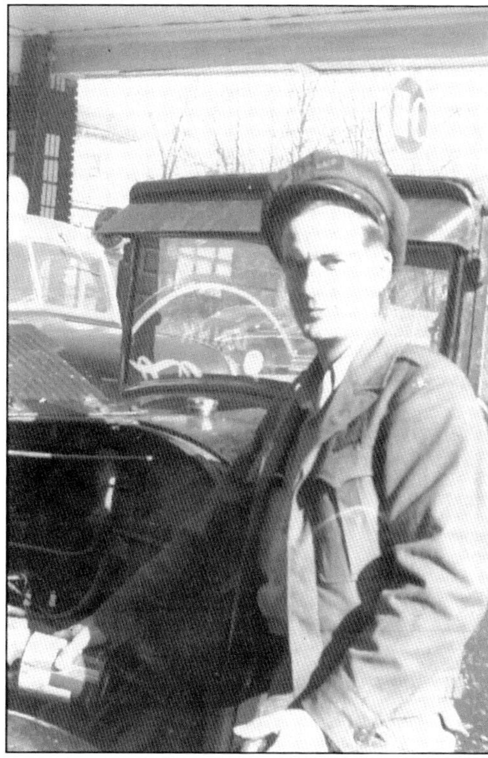

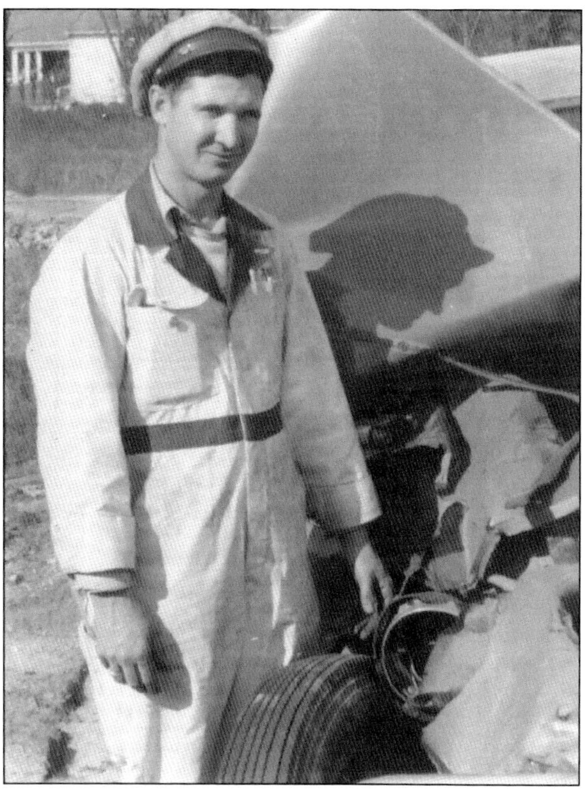

Paul Hullander, who owned an auto and tire service, stands next to a wrecked vehicle.

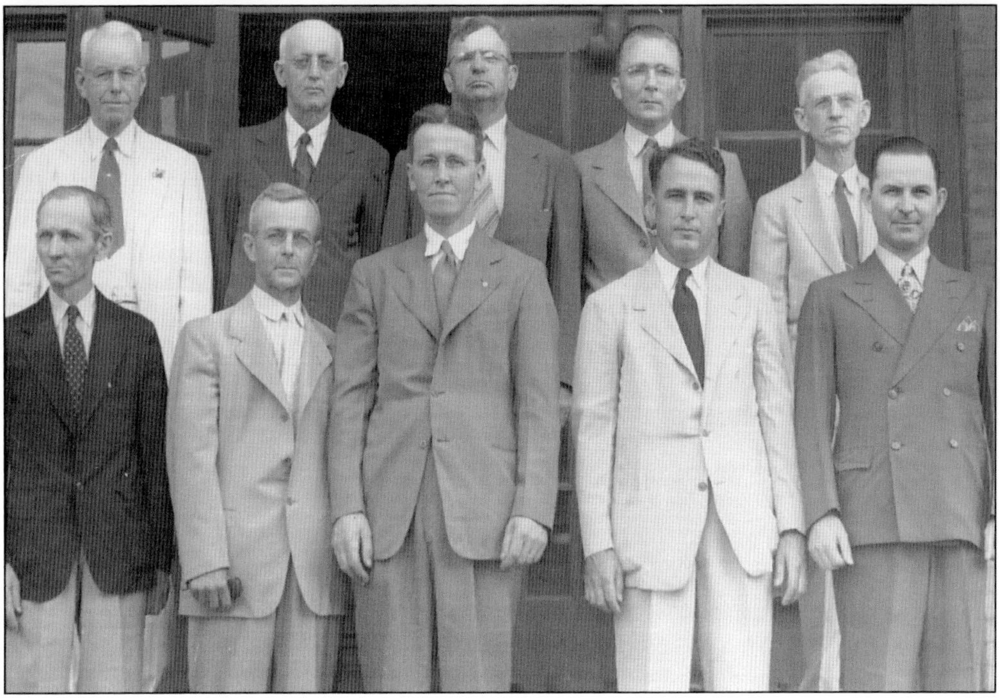

This is the Chester mayor and city council, *c.* 1944. They are, from left to right, as follows: (front row) W.W. Pegram; Dr. Lyles Hamilton; Mayor Fred J. Powell Sr.; Ted Davis; and Charlie McTeer; (back row) J.H. McLure, clerk and treasurer (1918–1945); John Bell; Sam Gough; Joe Sanders; and Colvin Cornwell.

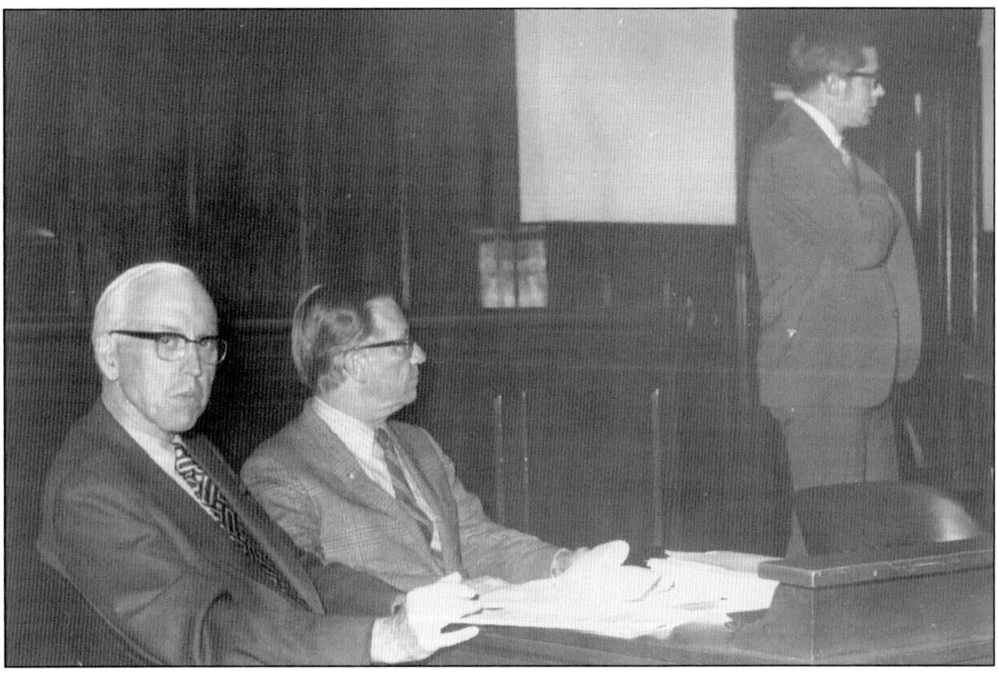

At a public meeting held at the Chester County Courtroom, (from left to right) S. Lewis Bell, Mayor Ed Dawson, and an unidentified man talk to the crowd that has gathered.

Billie Etters and Maude Ruth Clark pose for a publicity photograph for the annual Chester County Guernsey Festival in the mid-1940s. The majority of the dairies in the county kept Guernsey cows, and Chester County was at one time known as the Wonderful Guernsey Center of Dixie.

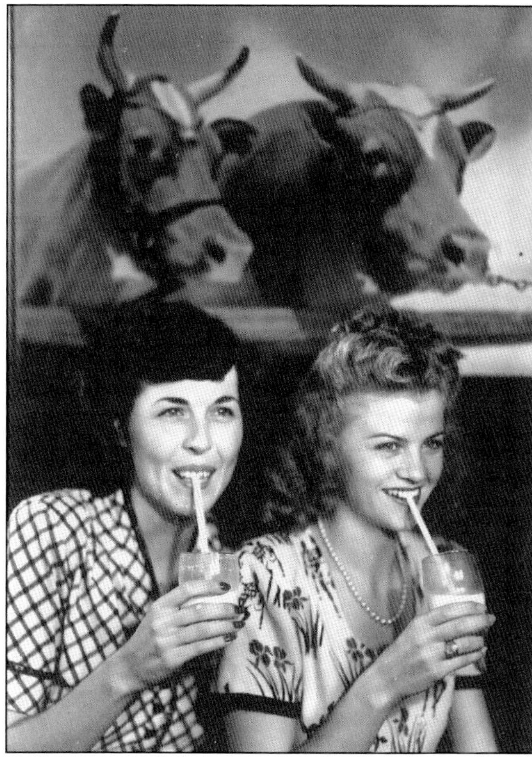

Elliot White Springs loved the beautiful girls of the area, and each year beauty contests were held for the counties in which Springs Cotton Mills had plants. Chester Day was held at Springs Park, near Great Falls, each year. Pictured here, from left to right, are Harriett Wolfe, Seppie Grant (Robbins), and Frances Prince (Worthy) as they take a few minutes during the contest to talk with Springs.

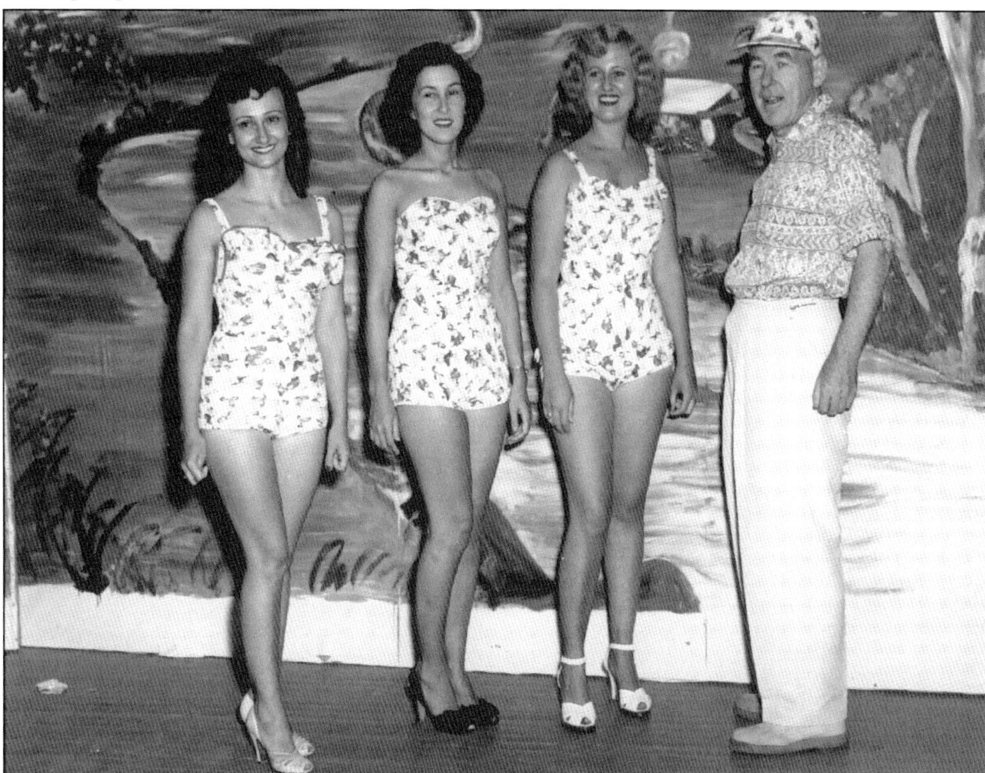

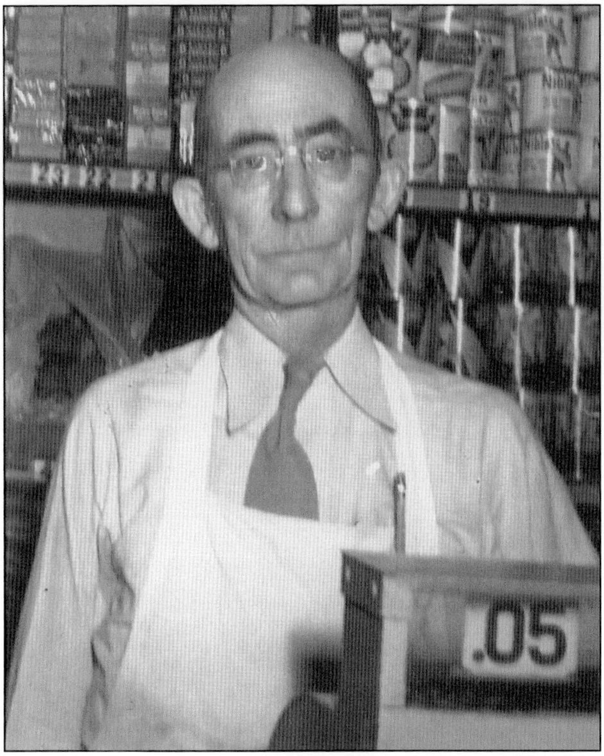

J.S. Jackson, the manager of the A&P Store in downtown Chester for many years, stands behind his cash register in front of fully stocked shelves, *c.* 1950.

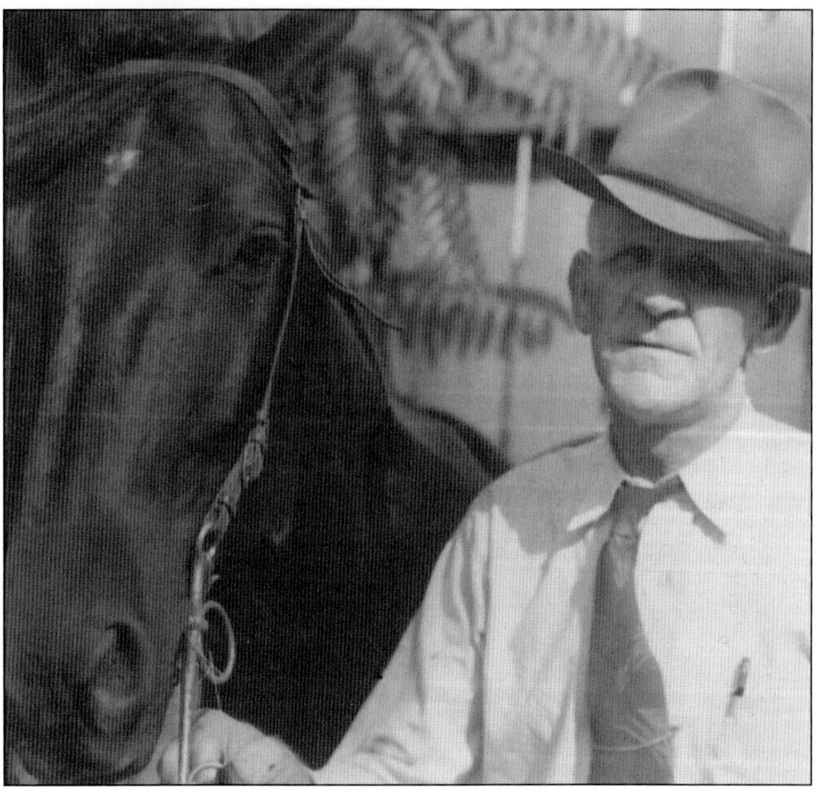

Mr. Moore, whose livery stable was behind the Frazer Stables on Columbia Street, stands with one of his charges outside the stable in the late 1940s.

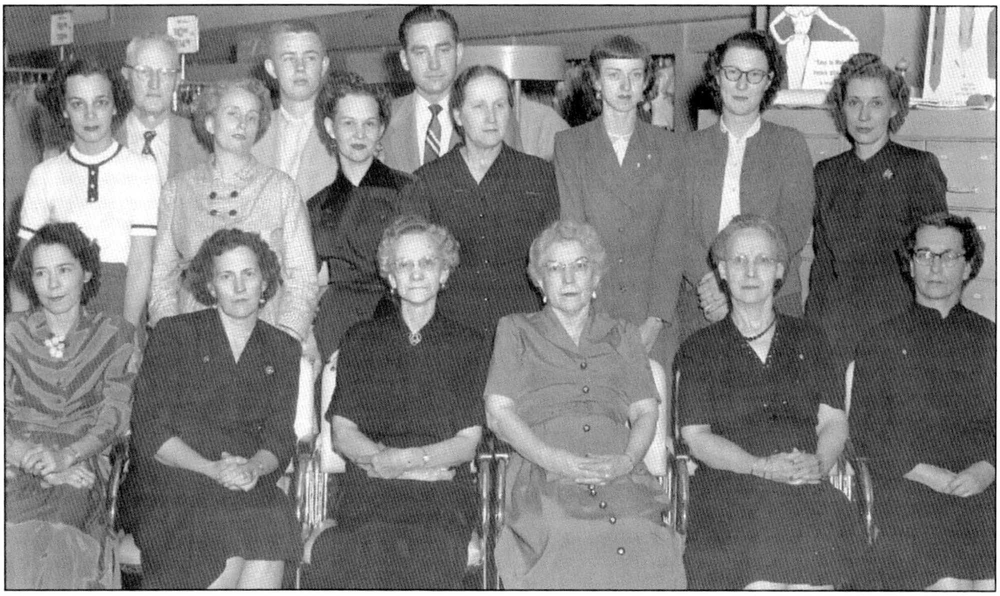

A group of Belk employees posed for this photograph about 1950 in the store on Main Street on top of the hill in Chester. They are, from left to right, as follows: (front row) Eloise McKeown, Sue Hudson, Laura Belle Cochran, Anne Walker, Margaret Gladden and Mrs. ? Crenshaw; (middle row) Miss ? Hoyle, Mildred Mattox, Martha Hudson, Mrs. ? Anderson, Dot Bennett Price, Viola Boulware, and Lib Proctor Grant; (back row) Sidney Walker, Jim McKeown, and Wesley Davis, the assistant manager.

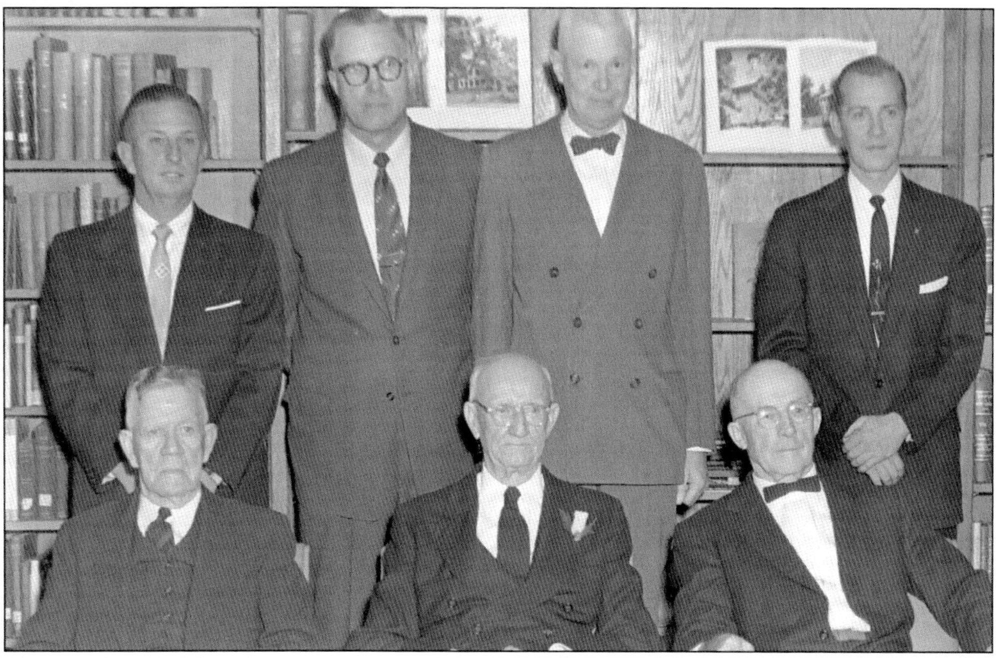

This unidentified board or commission from the 1950s posed for this picture in the Chester County Library when it was located in the War Memorial Building. Seated, from left to right, are Dr. George Hennis, Henry White, and an unidentified person. Standing, from left to right, are Harry Heath, Wylie White, Paul Hemphill, and Phelps Brooks.

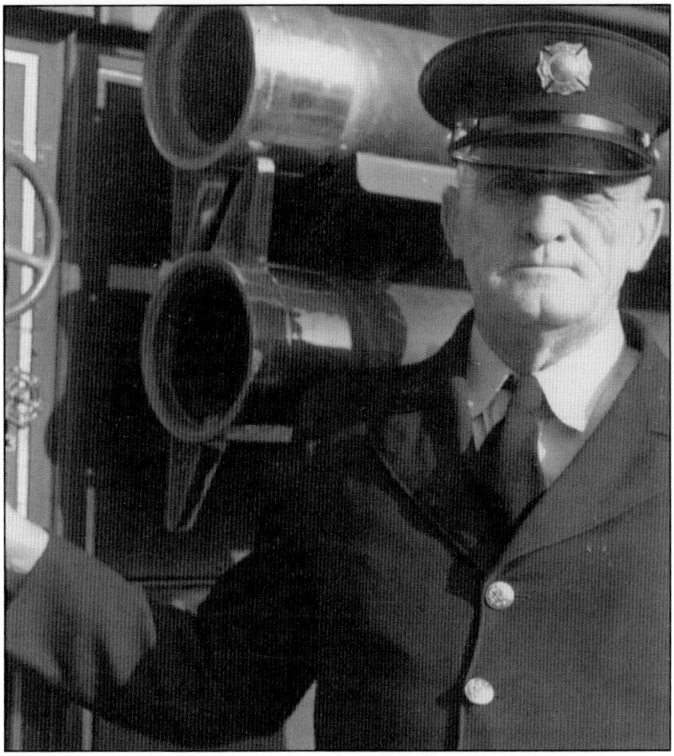

Sam T. Weir was the chief of police and fire chief from 1933 to 1947. He is shown with the department's fire engine in this picture, which was taken at the time of his retirement.

The Chester County Sheriff's Department poses for a photograph on the back steps of the Chester County Courthouse in the 1960s. They are, from left to right, (first row) Harvey Morgan, Jim Holley, Wilson McDaniel, unidentified, and Jerry King; (middle row) "Pop" Hayes, unidentified, and Joe Bagley; (back row) James Brice Waters and Marcus Ray.

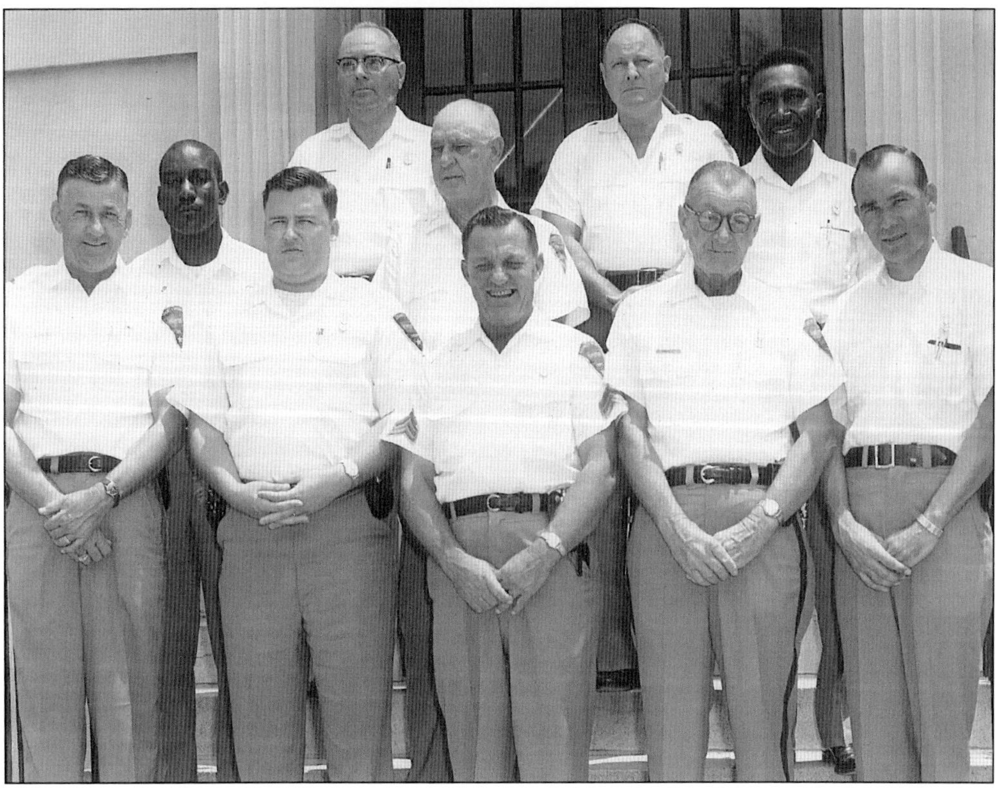

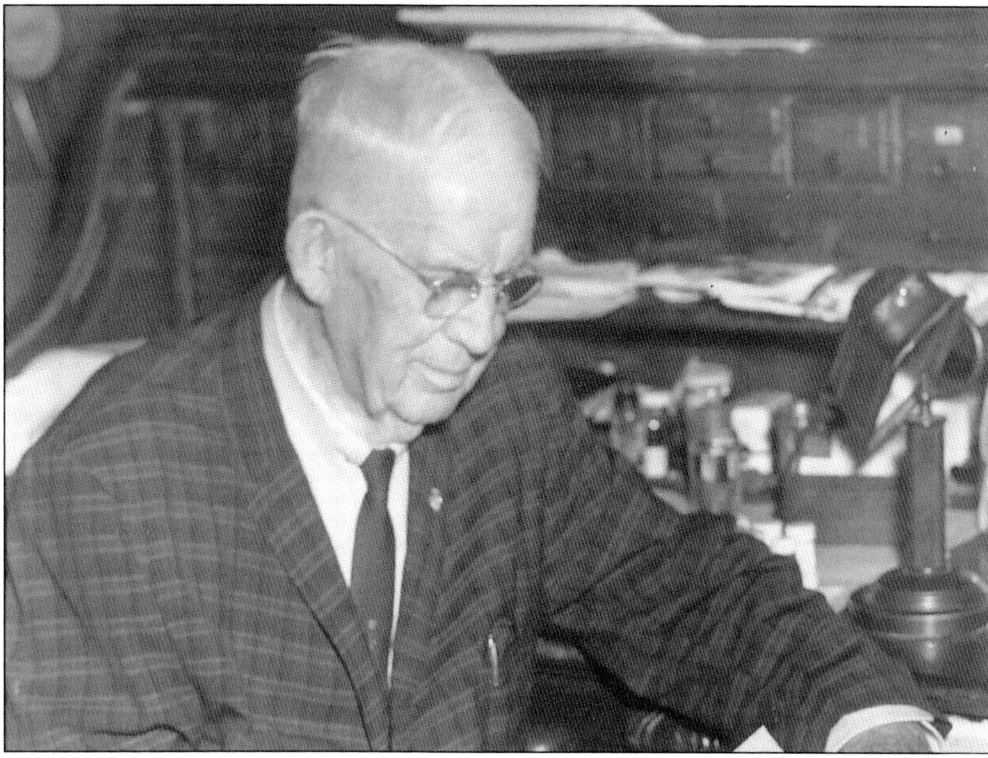

Dr. William R. Wallace practiced medicine in Chester County for 65 years from 1909 to 1974, and he was the oldest practicing doctor in the state of South Carolina (at age 92). Wallace was born in the Rossville community, graduated from Presbyterian College in 1903, and decided to be a doctor after seeing an advertisement about the Medical College of Virginia from which he graduated. Wallace started out using a horse and buggy and bought his first car, a Reo, for $350 in 1910. House calls were $2, and he was often paid in vegetables, butter, or feed for his horse. During his career, Wallace estimated delivering 3,500 babies, although his wife always estimated more. Wallace died on April 29, 1976.

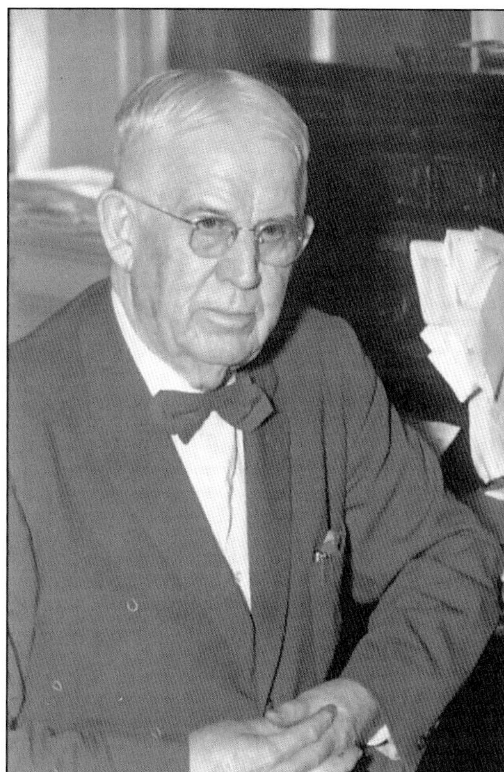

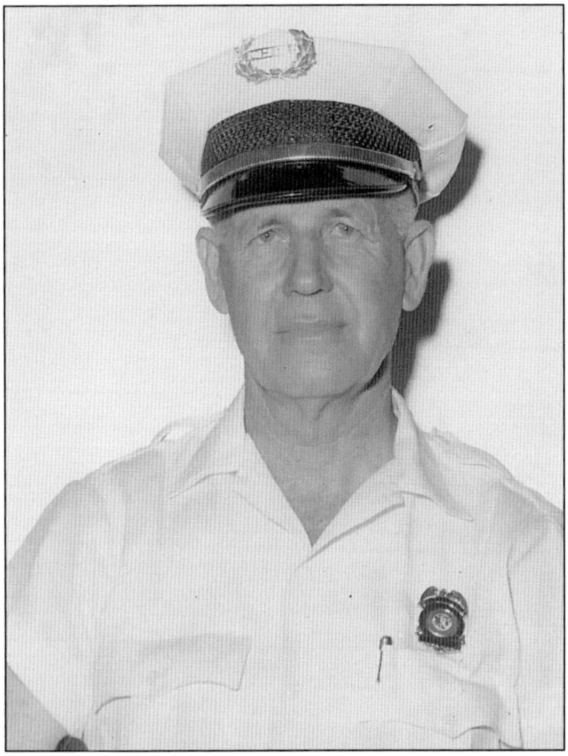

Chief John Stone served as Chester's police chief for many years. Just after WW II, he became a patrolman for the force, and in the 1960s, he became chief. He remained in that position until he retired in the 1970s.

When Chief John Stone retired, city manager Stinson "Red" White, left, and Ed Lee with the City Police Department, center, presented him with his service revolver.

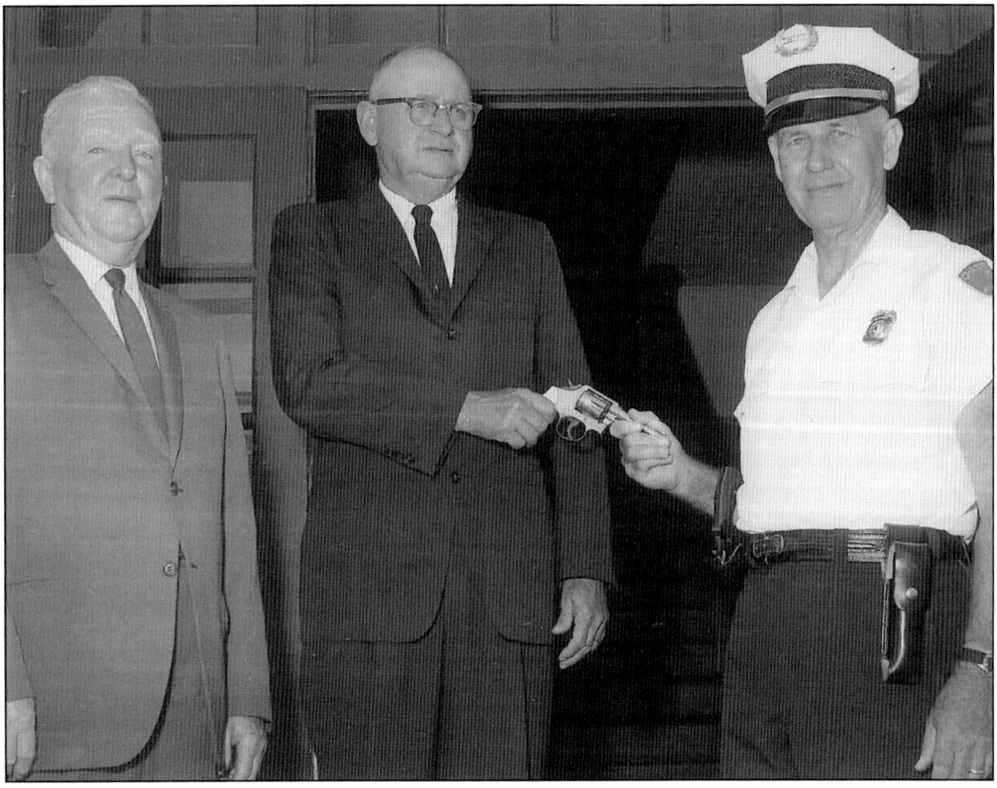

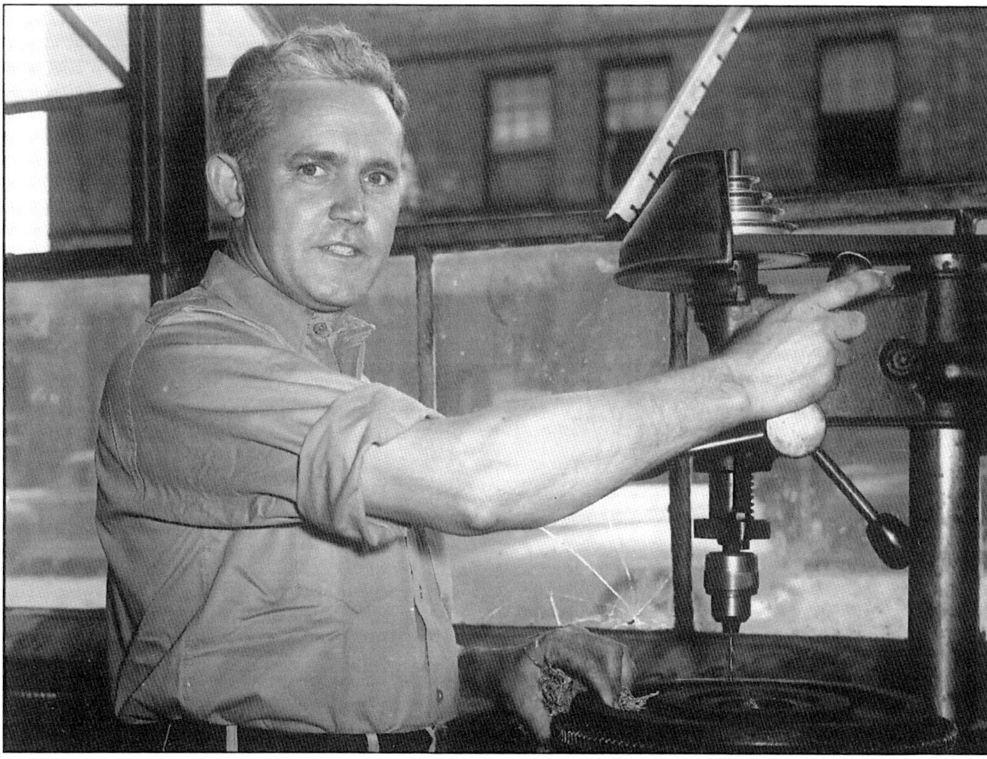

Glenn Conrad operates a drill press at W.T. Betts & Sons where he did mechanical work. W.T. Betts & Sons sold farm equipment, trucks, tires, and appliances and was located on Hudson Street for many years.

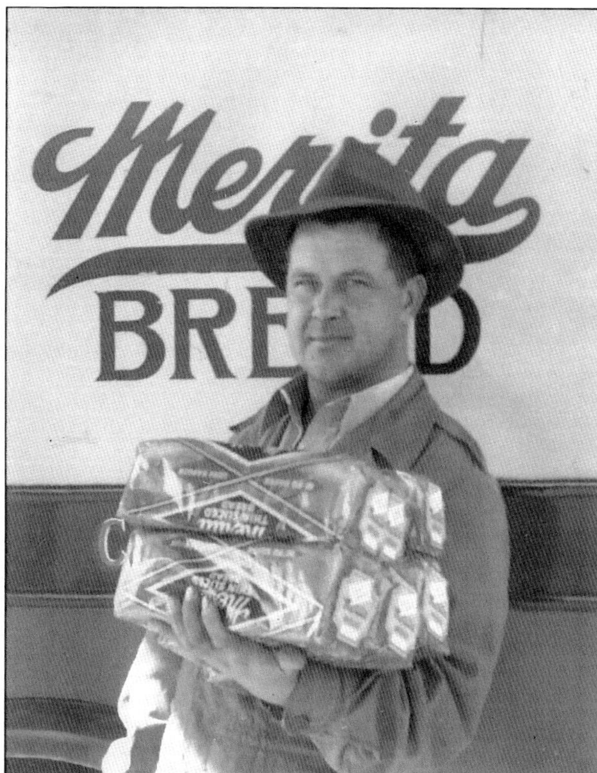

Mack McColl delivers Merita Bread in Chester about 1950.

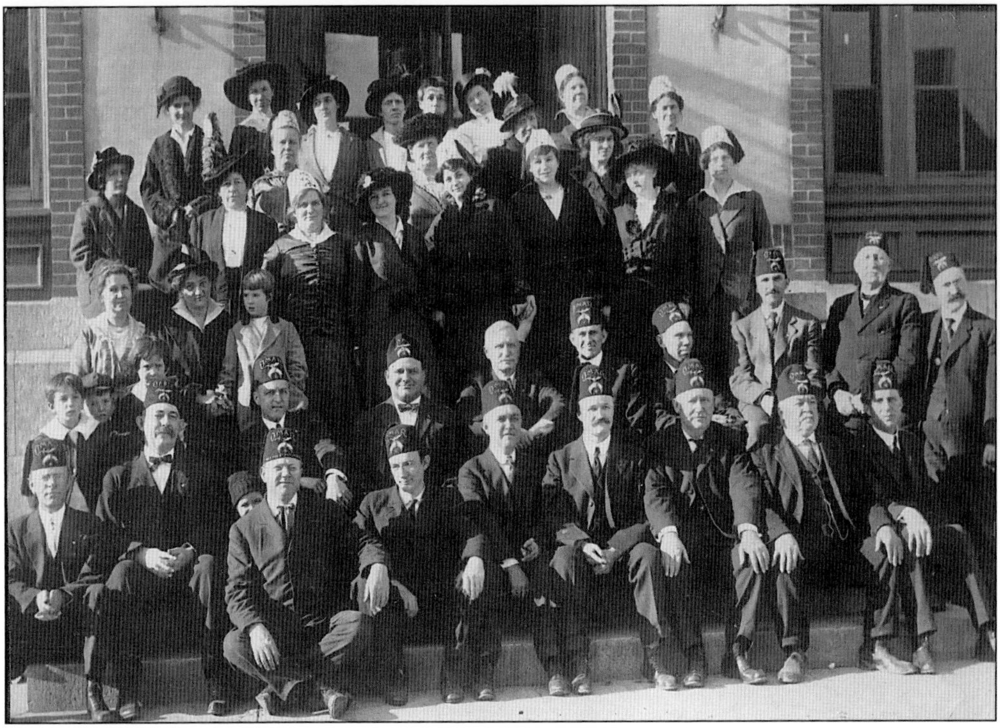

This group of Shriners pose on the steps of the Chester Post Office at the corner of Main and Wylie Streets, *c.* 1910.

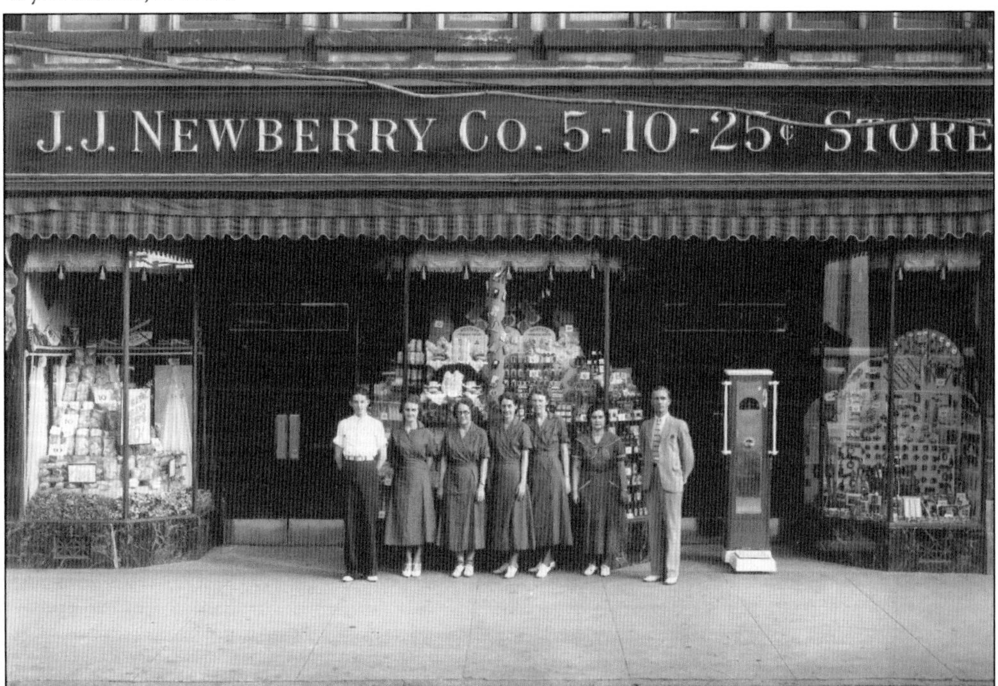

J. J. Newberry's was a popular dime store located on top of the hill in downtown Chester at 113 Main Street. The manager and employees, *c.* 1930s, pose in front of the store.

Springs Cotton Mills was a major part of people's lives in Chester County for many years. There were numerous activities that centered around the people who worked at Springs. These three beauties were part of the Miss Springmaid contest in the late 1940s. Note the television sets, which were prizes in the contest.

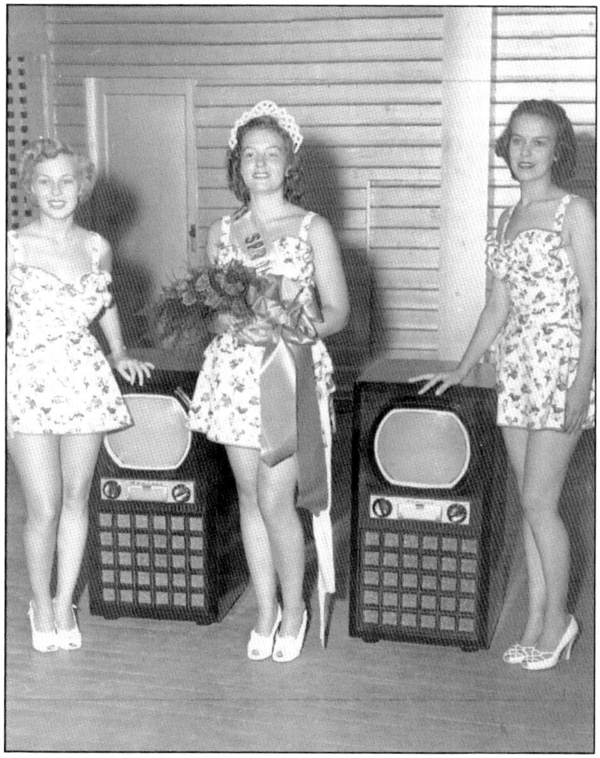

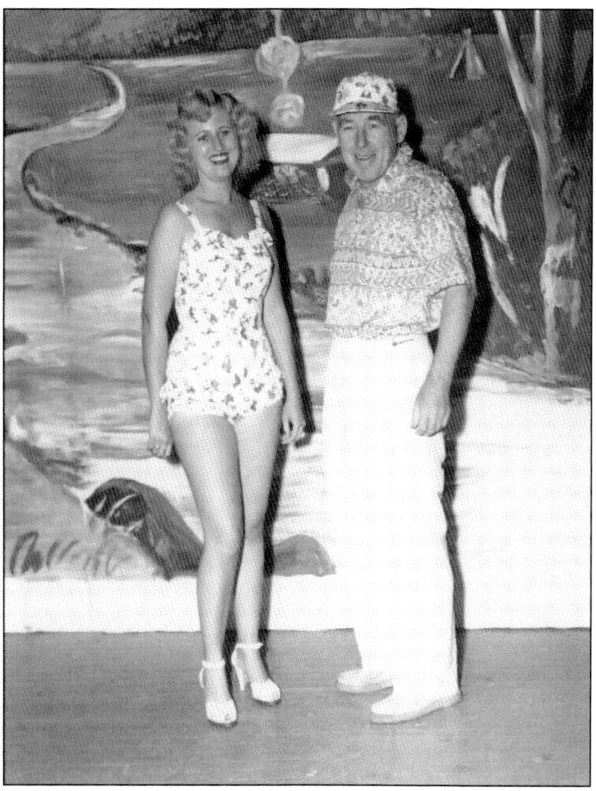

Elliott White Springs, CEO of Springs Cotton Mills, poses with a contestant in the Miss Springmaid contest in the late 1940s.

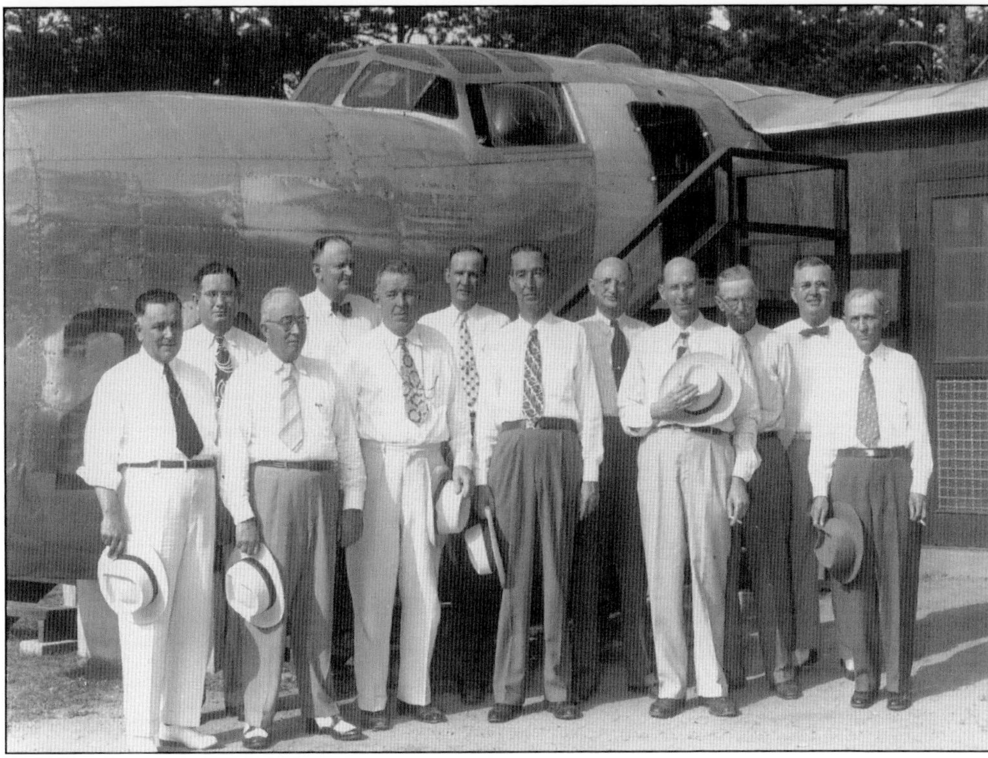

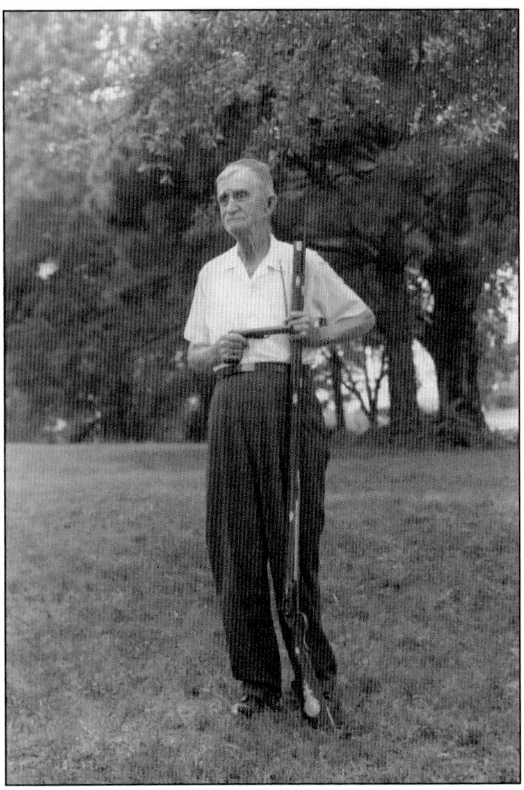

Springs Park was a recreational facility for Springs Mills employees located just across the Catawba River from Great Falls. This group of gentlemen stand in front of displays at the park in the early 1950s.

W.T. Castles shows off his great grandfather Thomas Bennett's craftsmanship by displaying a rifle and pistol made by Bennett who lived during the first half of the 19th century. These guns are now displayed in the Chester County Historical Society Museum.

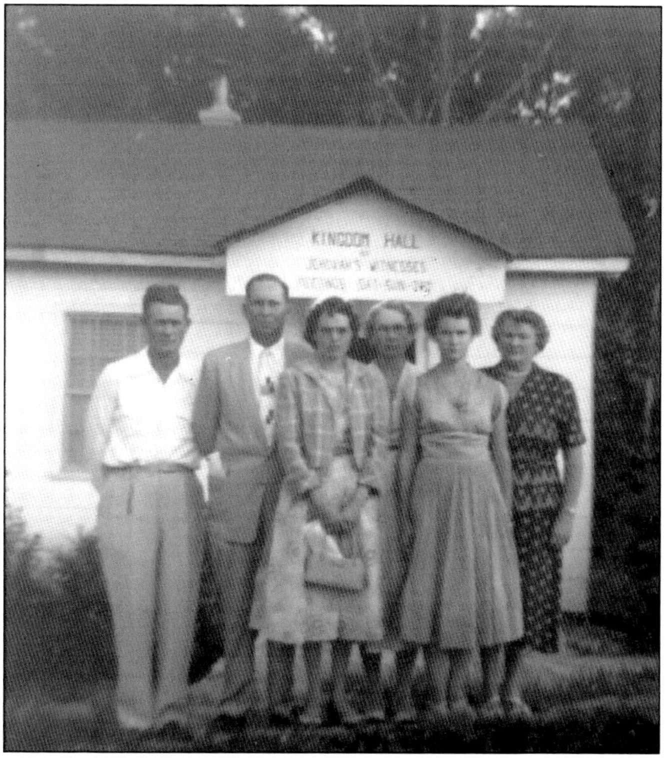

Members of the Kingdom Hall of Jehovah's Witnesses pose in front of their meeting house in the 1950s.

Some Christian denominations believe that members can handle snakes and, with God's protection, be led safely through the experience. In this photograph, a Mr. Tinker and an unidentified man hold poisonous snakes in a service in the 1950s.

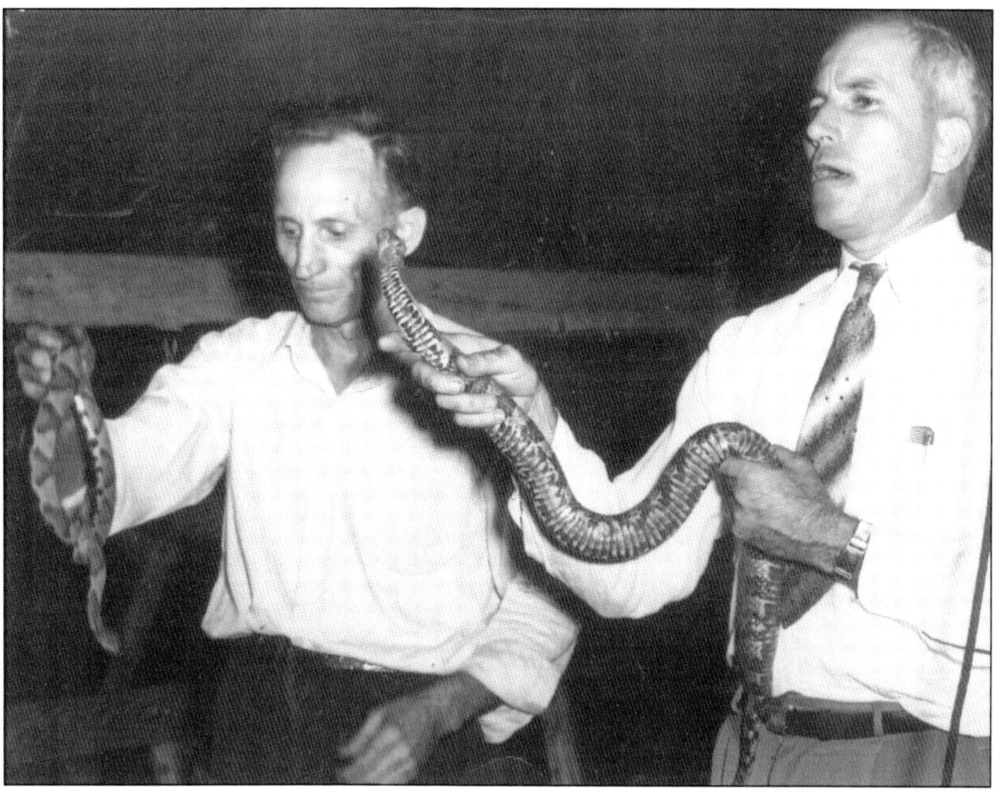

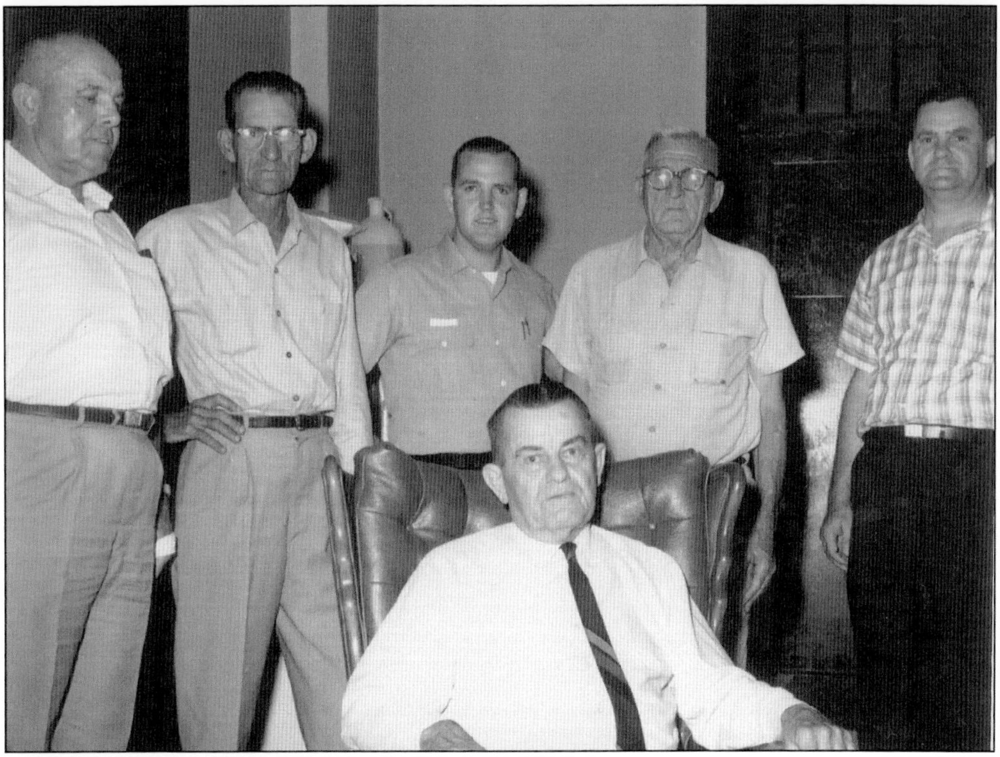

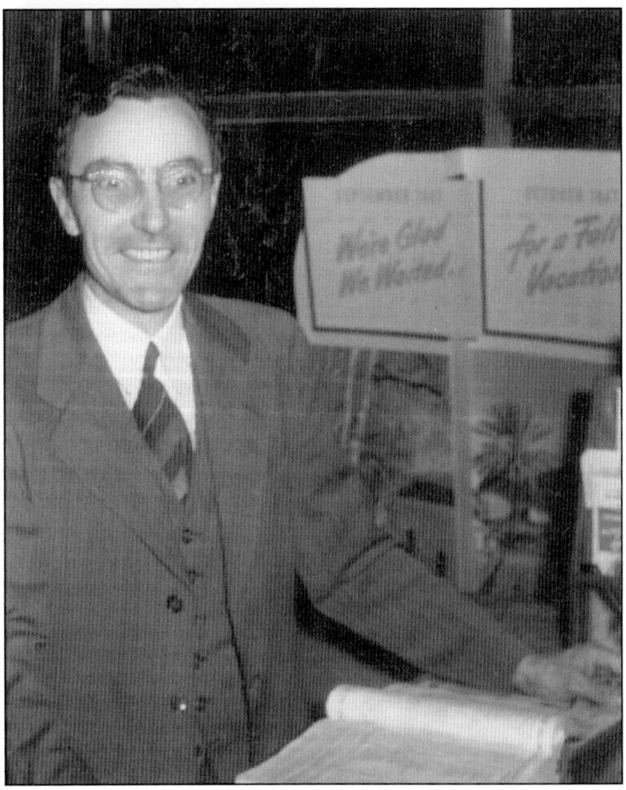

When Hood Worthy retired as Chester's city manager after serving from 1945 to 1966, the Fire Department bought him a recliner. Hood Worthy is seated in the chair and behind him, from left to right, are Eph Weir, Bob Nichols, Dewey Guyton, Tom Roddey, and Glenn Bickett.

Born in Ireland, Eddie Davis moved to Chester as a young man. He ran the Chester bus station and later ran a hot dog stand on Hudson Street. The last establishment he ran was on Center Street where the Chester County Library is now.

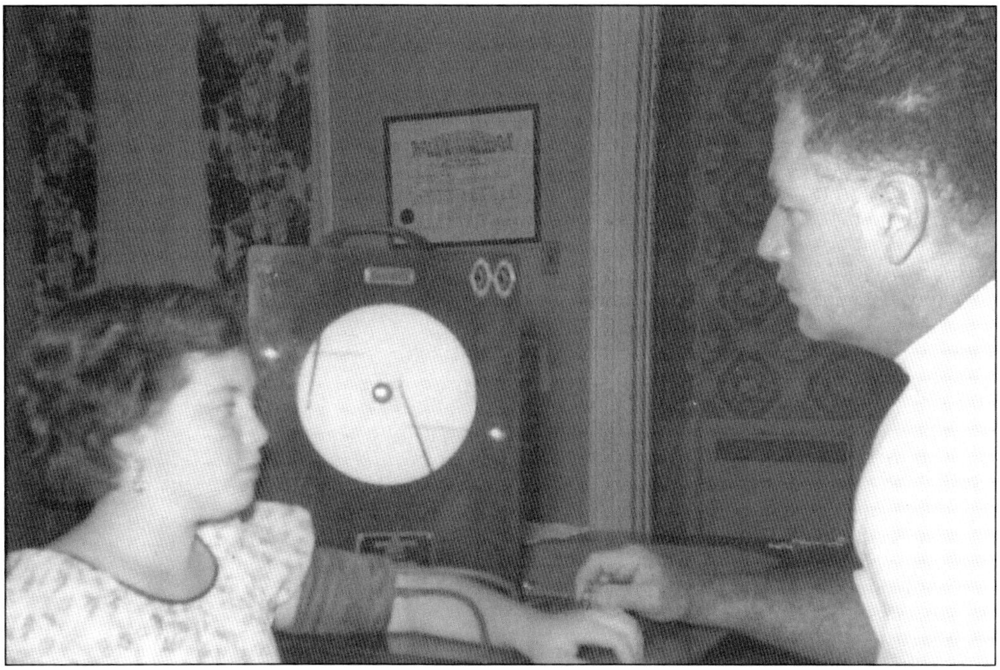

Dr. Raymond Gosh was a chiropractor and had his home and office on Pinckney Street. Here he takes the blood pressure of a little girl with the latest equipment of the 1950s.

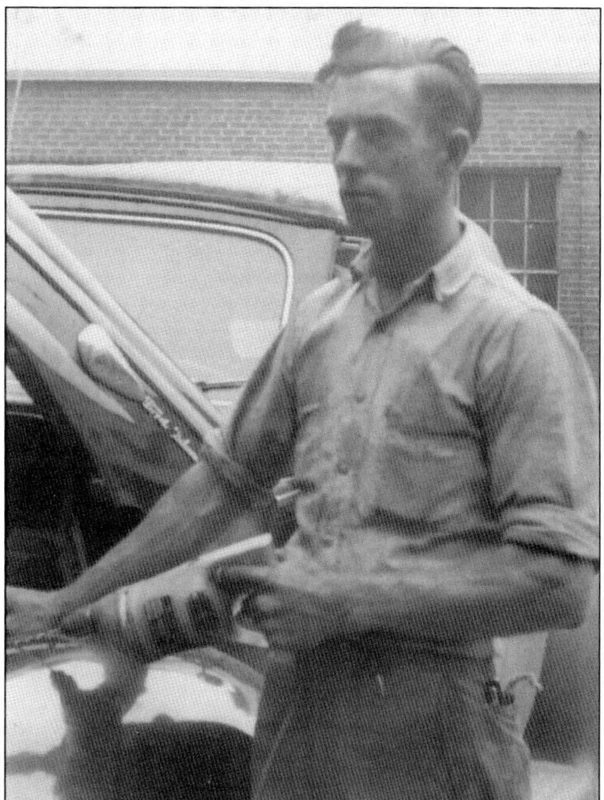

Red Weir works on a car at the Ford place on Columbia Street in the 1940s. Fords were sold there under various owners and names including Durant Taylor, Cox Ford, Carroll Motors, and Gwin Automotive.

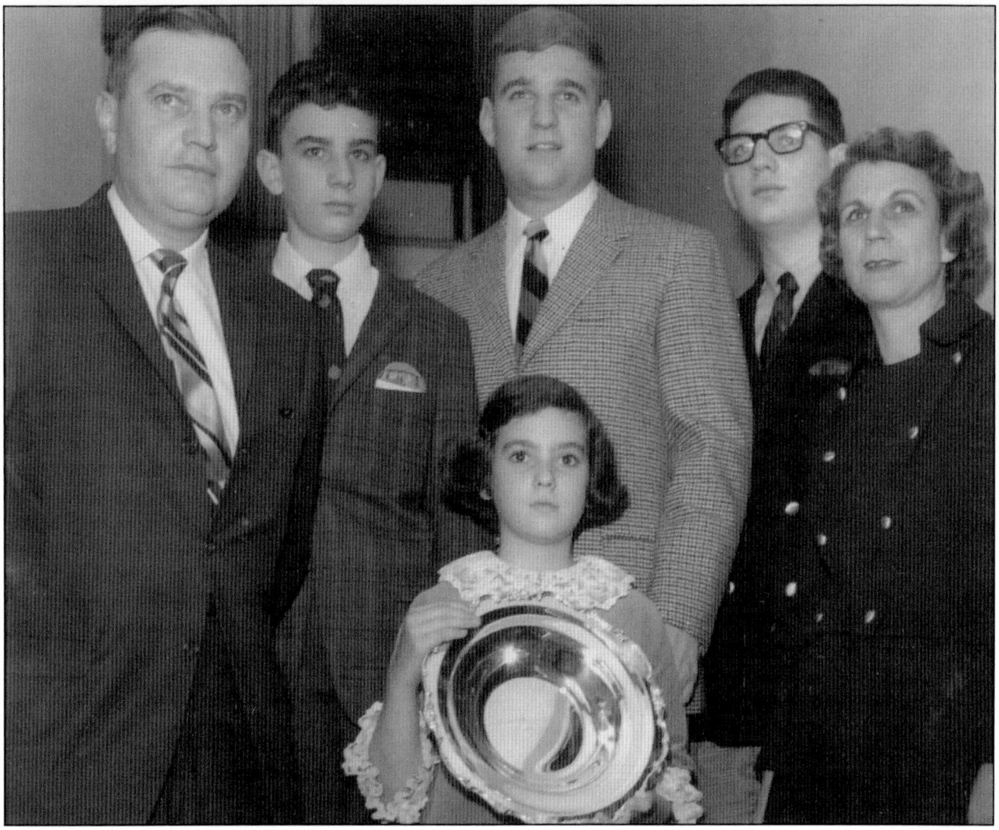

The Dr. Malcolm Marion Jr. family was Family of the Year in 1968. They are, clockwise from the left, Dr. Marion; Doug, 13; Malcolm III, 18; Bill, 15; Ann; and little Ann, 10.

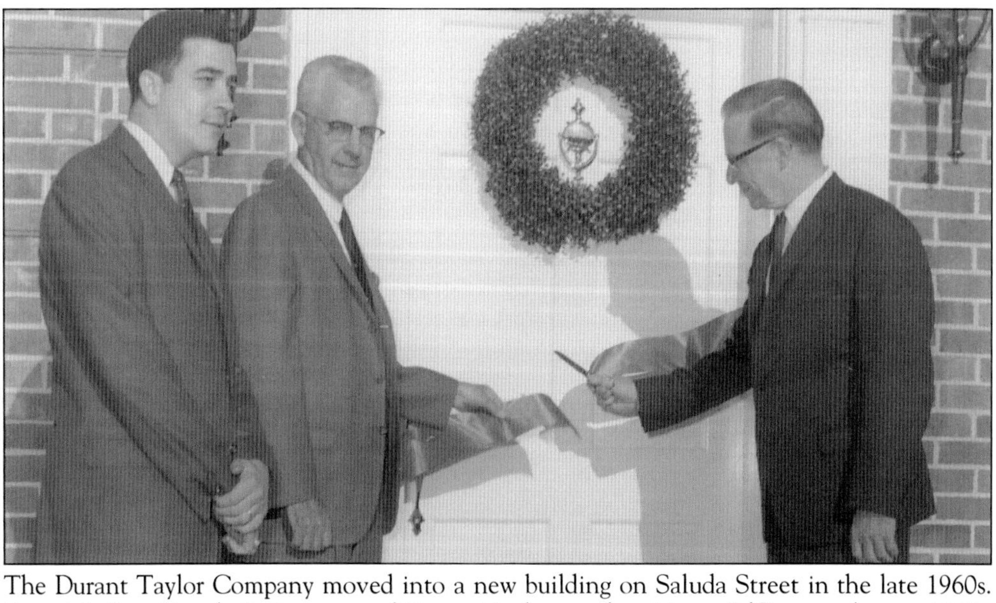

The Durant Taylor Company moved into a new building on Saluda Street in the late 1960s. From left, Rev. Dwight L. Pearson and Durant Taylor watch as Mayor Ed Dawson (mayor 1967–1975) cuts the ribbon on the facility.

James T. Funderburk served as mayor of Chester from 1975 to 1983. He was most noted for bringing zoning to the city.

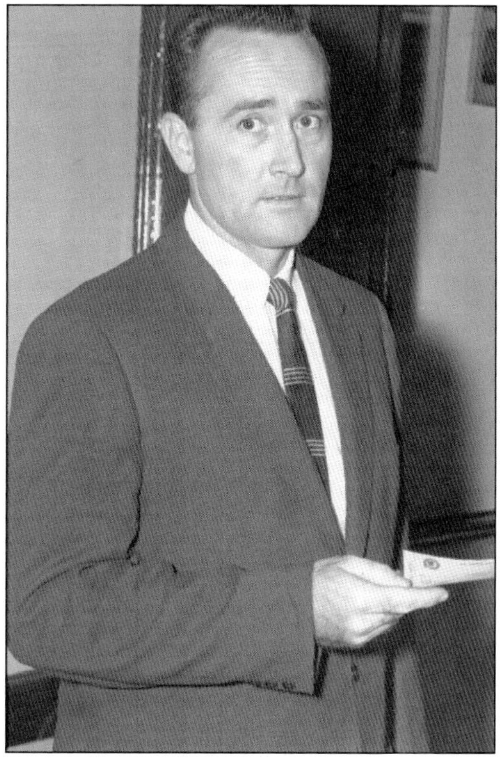

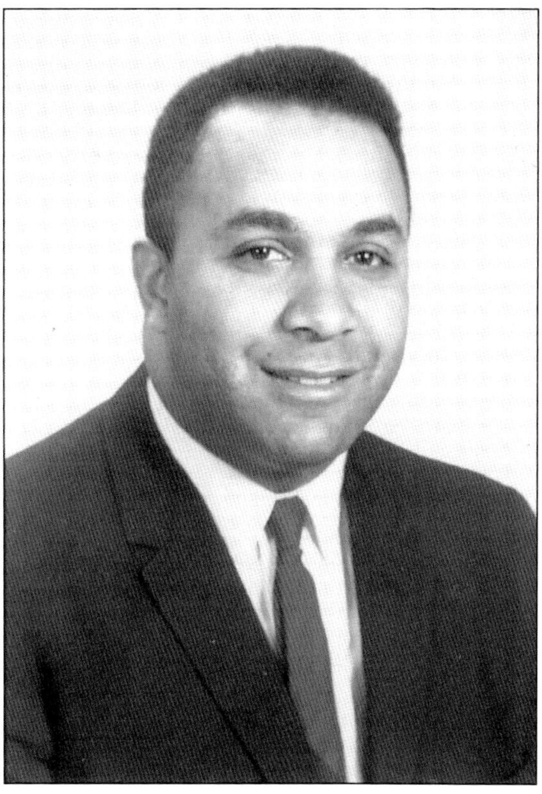

The first African-American mayor for the City of Chester was businessman Christopher King. He began serving his term in 1996 but died in office less than six months after being sworn in. This photo was taken in the 1960s.

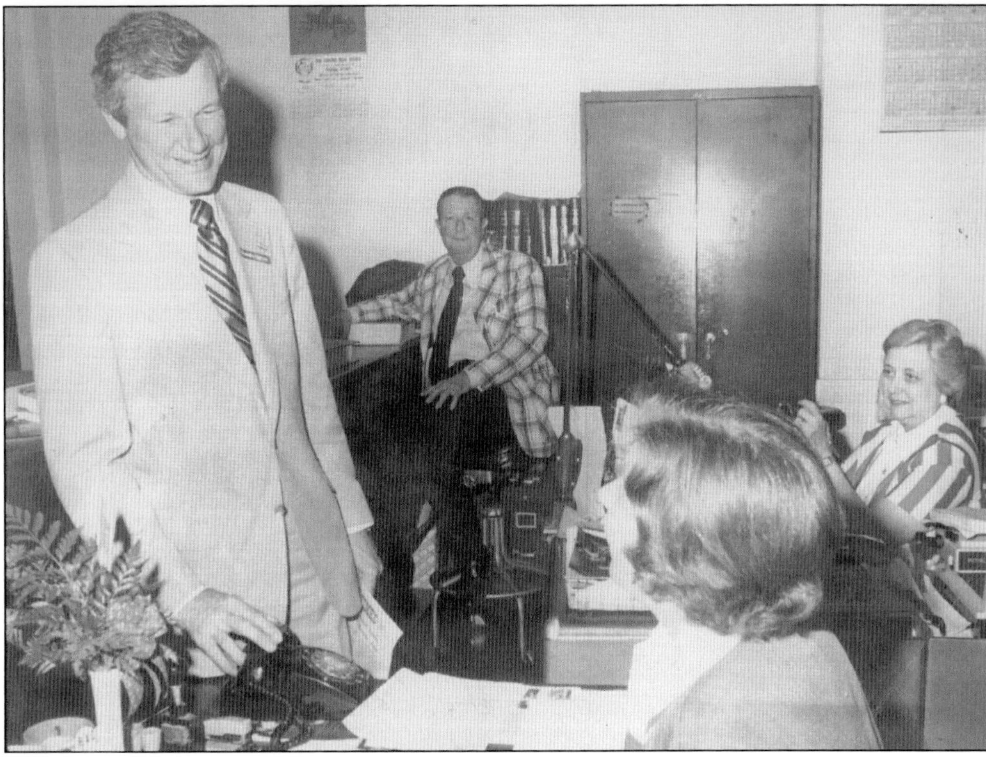

South Carolina lieutenant governor Brantley Harvey, standing left, visited the Chester County Auditor's office in May 1978 when he was running for governor. He is seen here talking to (clockwise) Chester County auditor Johnny Roberts and assistants, Ruth G. Bennett and Becky Ford.

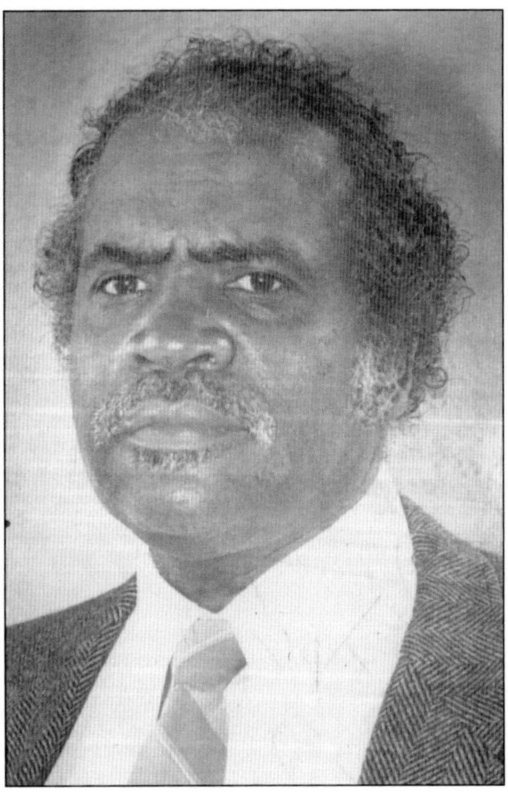

In the 1980s, George Bunny Guy was the first African American elected to the Chester County Council. Guy is still on the County Council and is one of its longest-serving members.

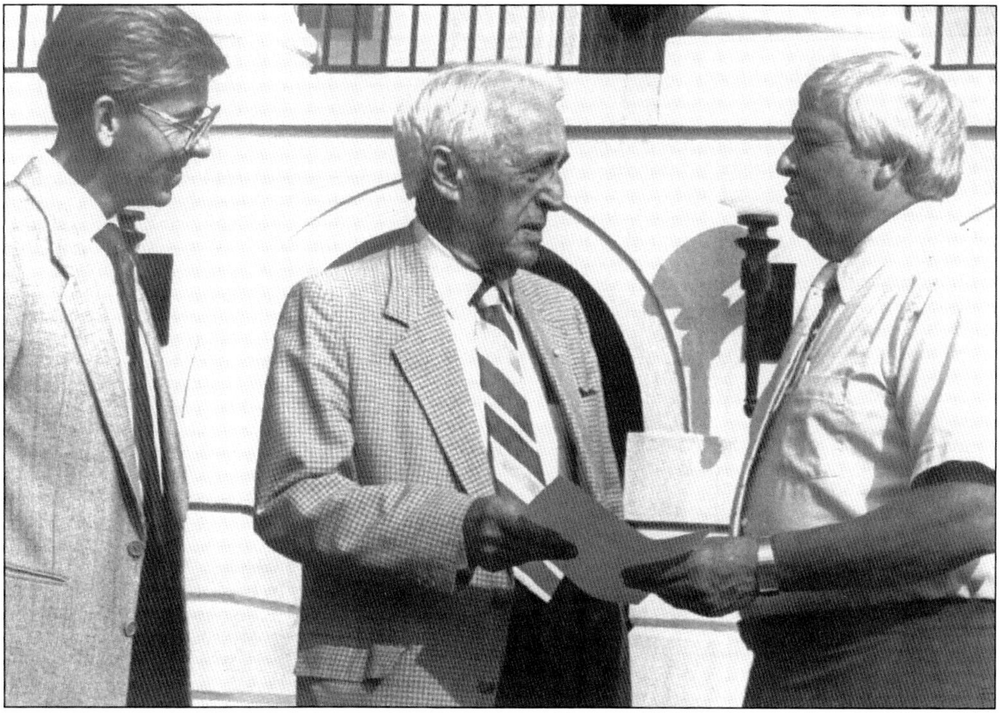

Longtime county supervisor Carlisle Roddey (1974–1998), right, presents Dr. John Newton "Newt" Gaston Jr., center, with a document proclaiming Dr. Gaston Day in 1989 while Chester County Hospital administrator, Ron Hunter, looks on. Dr. Gaston retired after 50 years of practicing medicine in Chester County.

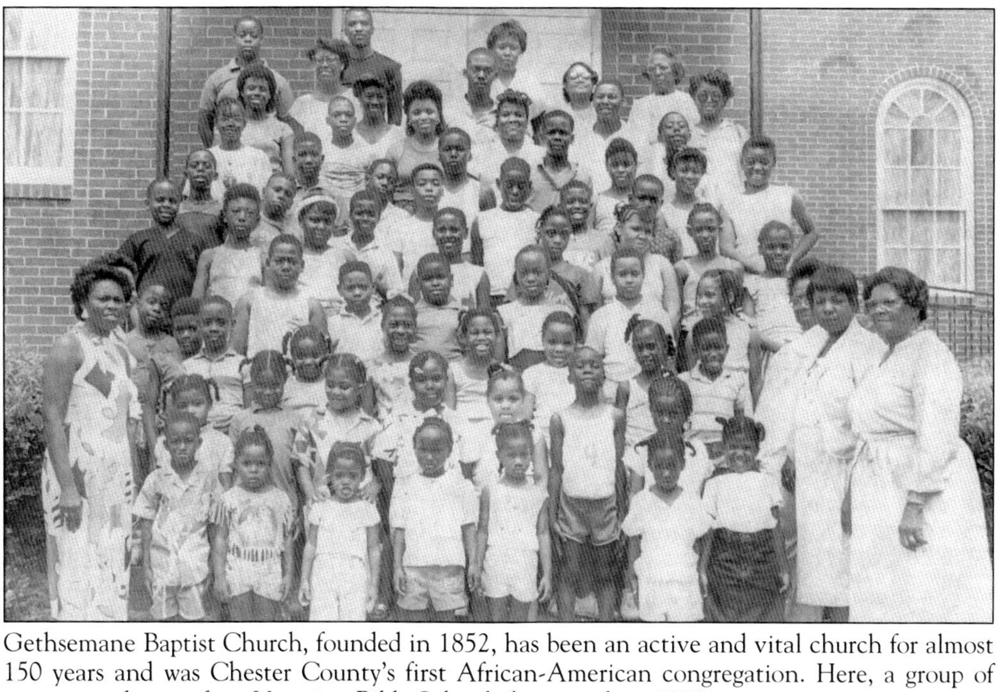

Gethsemane Baptist Church, founded in 1852, has been an active and vital church for almost 150 years and was Chester County's first African-American congregation. Here, a group of young people pose for a Vacation Bible School photograph in 1989.

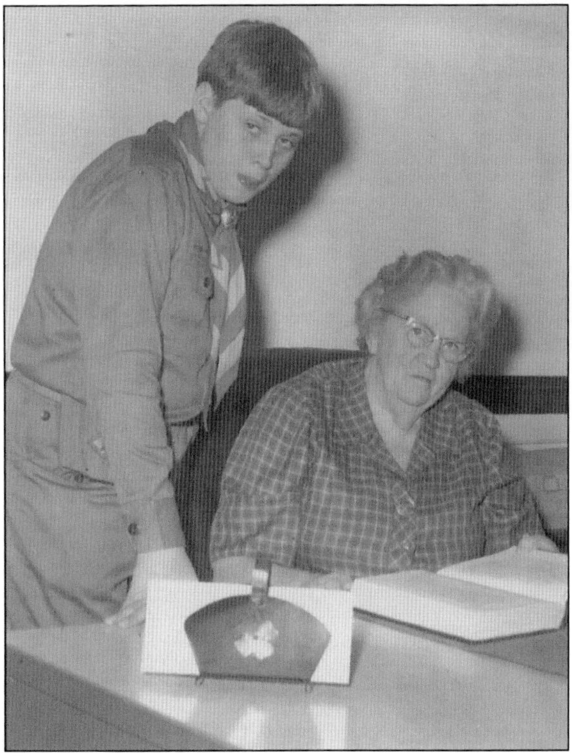

Mrs. Hattie Y. Hardin was the judge of probate for Chester County for 22 years and was the only woman in an elected position in the county at that time. Here, she poses with a boy scout who was shadowing her for a day during Government Day, observed each year by the Boy Scouts and government officials to promote a better understanding of how government works.

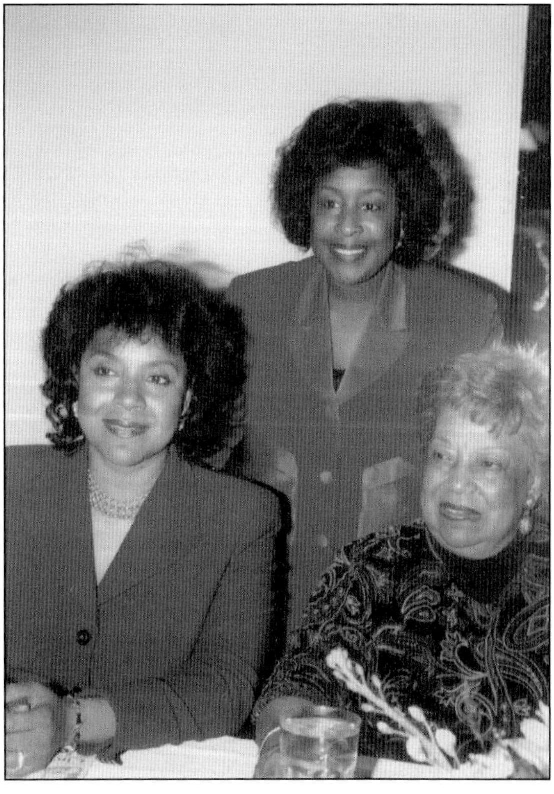

Vivian Ayers Allen, right, Chester native and 1939 graduate of Brainerd Institute, is in the process of saving all that she can of the Brainerd Campus in Chester, thanks to her famous daughter, Phylicia Rashad (left), an actress. Vivian, a Pulitzer prize winner for her poetry, and Phylicia were in Chester for a fundraiser in 2000. Standing with them is city councilwoman Annie Reid.

Five

War

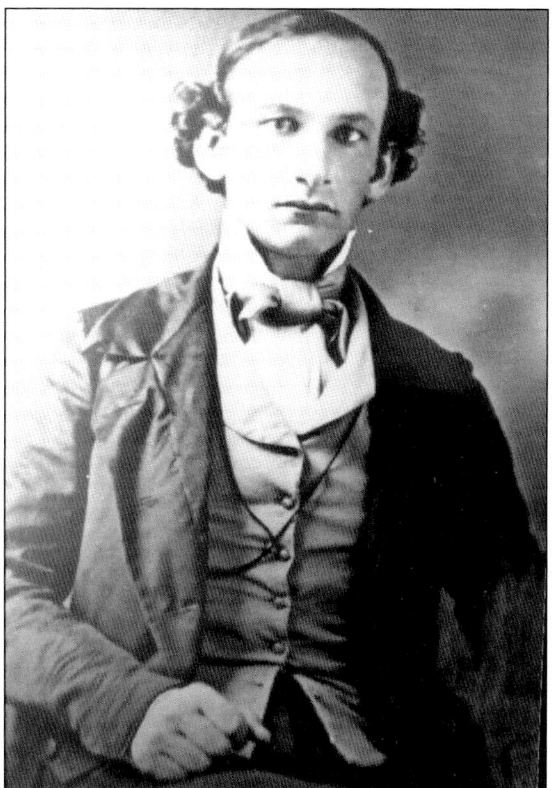

John G. Dunovant (1825–1864) was killed in action along the Vaughan Road near Petersburg, Virginia, only about a month after being appointed to the temporary rank of brigadier general in the Confederate Cavalry. He was born in Chester and also served in the Mexican War. His older brother, Alexander Quay Dunovant, was one of Chester County's signers of the Ordinance of Secession.

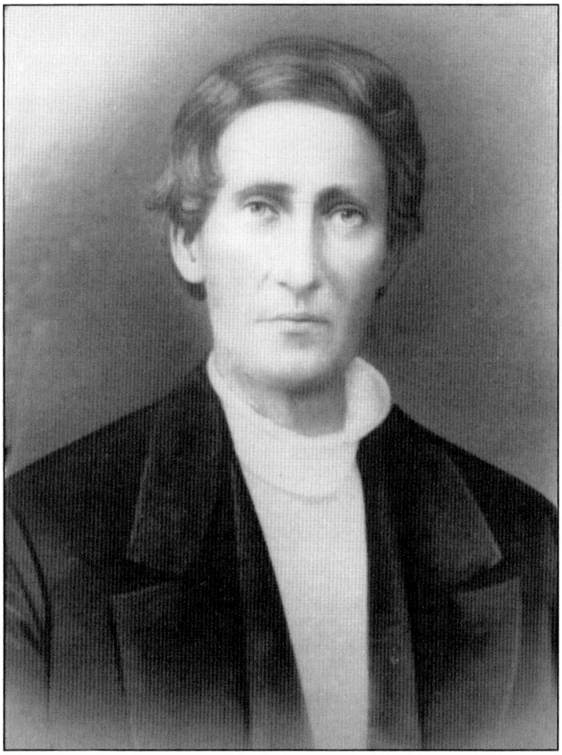

When South Carolina held the Secession Convention in 1860, John McKee of Chester was the oldest signer of the Ordinance of Secession. He was born in Ireland in 1787 and came to South Carolina in 1799 where he took up the trade of watchmaker. Clocks made by McKee are still in existence today.

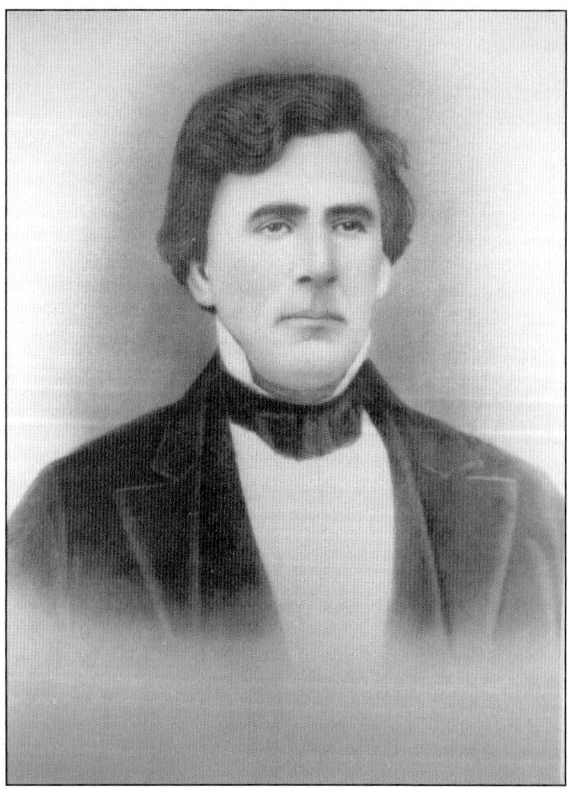

Thomas Wade Moore was also a signer of the Secession Ordinance. He was a physician, having graduated from the Medical College of South Carolina in 1829. Moore gave up the practice of medicine and became a planter. He also served several terms in the South Carolina House of Representatives.

Richard Woods was born in the western part of Chester County in 1813. The successful planter and large plantation owner was the fourth signer of the Ordinance of Secession from Chester County. He contributed to the war effort by supplying the Confederate Army.

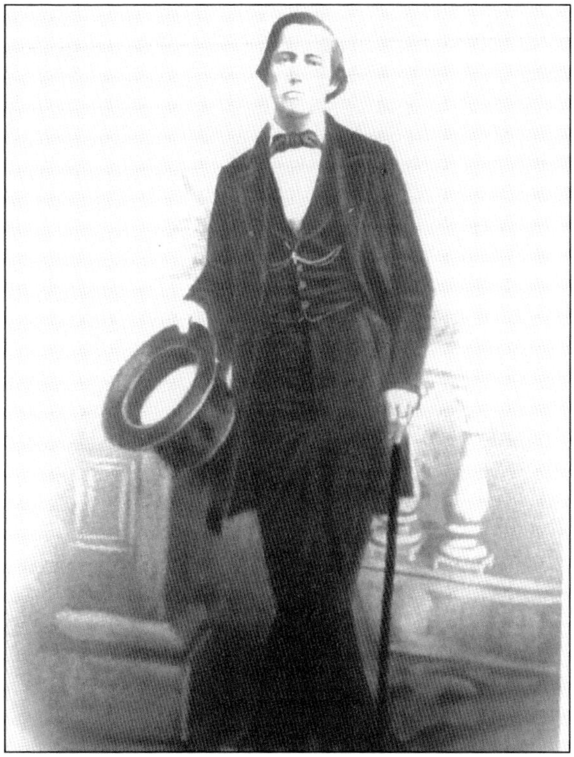

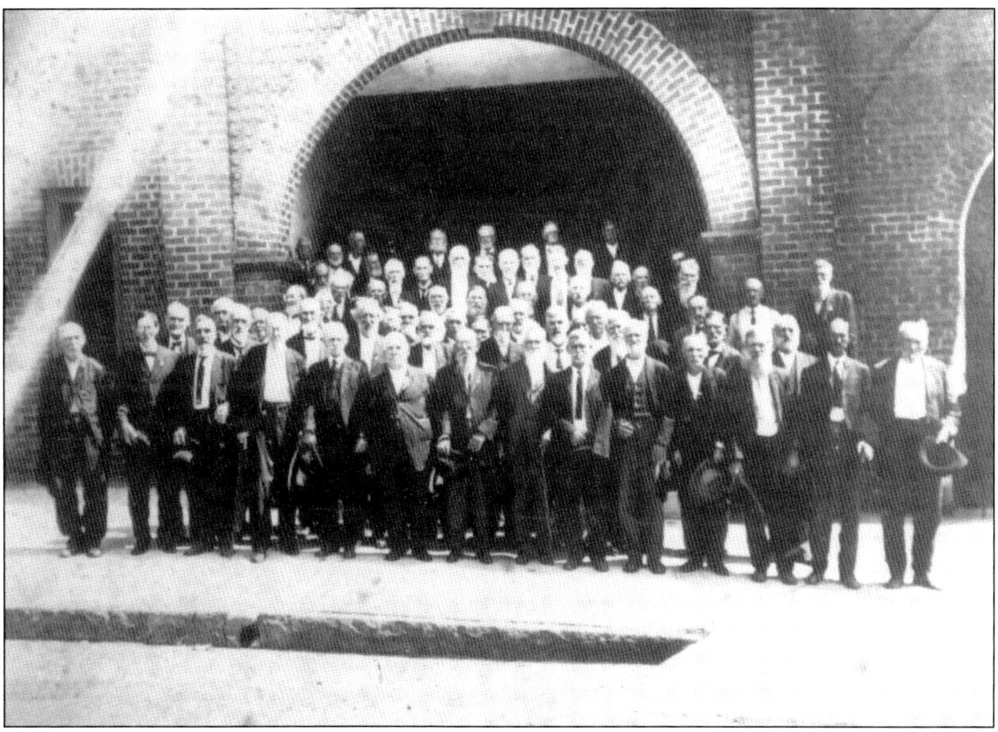

In 1909, the South Carolina Division of the United Confederate Veterans held a reunion in Chester. The group posed for this photograph in front of the Opera House, now City Hall.

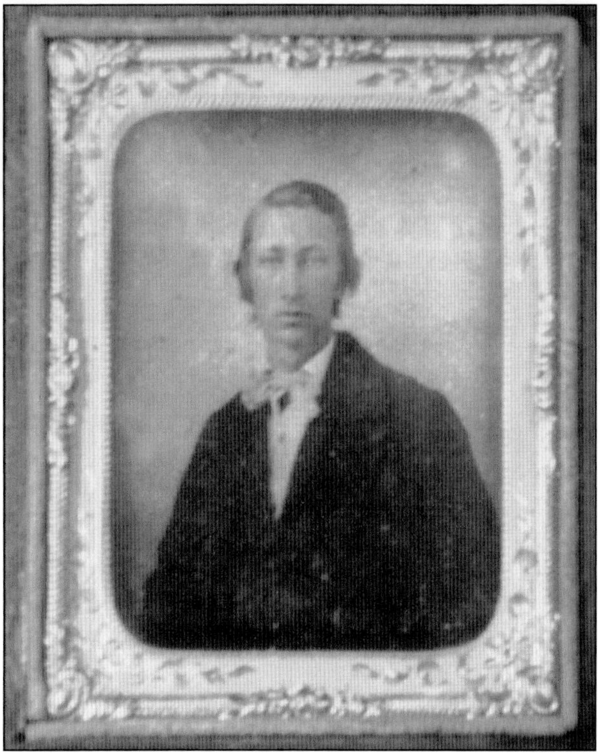

William Dunlap Knox entered the War between the States late in the conflict in 1864 when he was just 17. He was stationed at the prison in Florence. Discharged on March 5, 1865, Knox walked 123 miles back home to Chester and arrived on April 2, 1865.

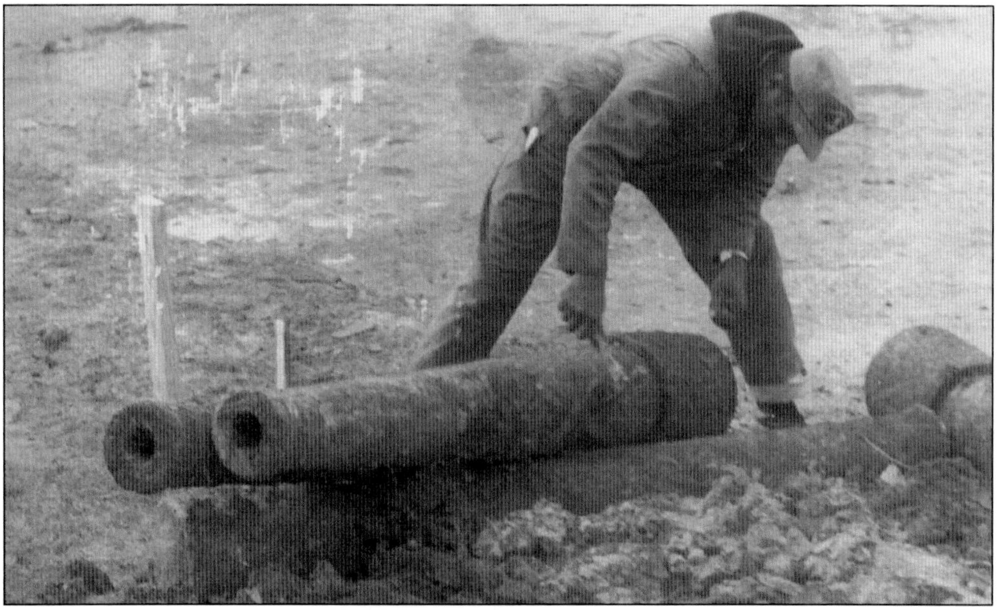

Four Confederate-manufactured cannons were unearthed in Chester in 1986. Odell Williams, contractor, pictured above, was digging a foundation for the Calvary Baptist Church Educational Building when he struck objects that he thought were sewer pipes. The cannon turned out to be spiked with shells still containing black powder. For 10 years, state archaeologists tried to disarm the guns until Dr. Jonathan Leader with the help of Scott Coleman, a local historian, discovered a way in which it could be done.

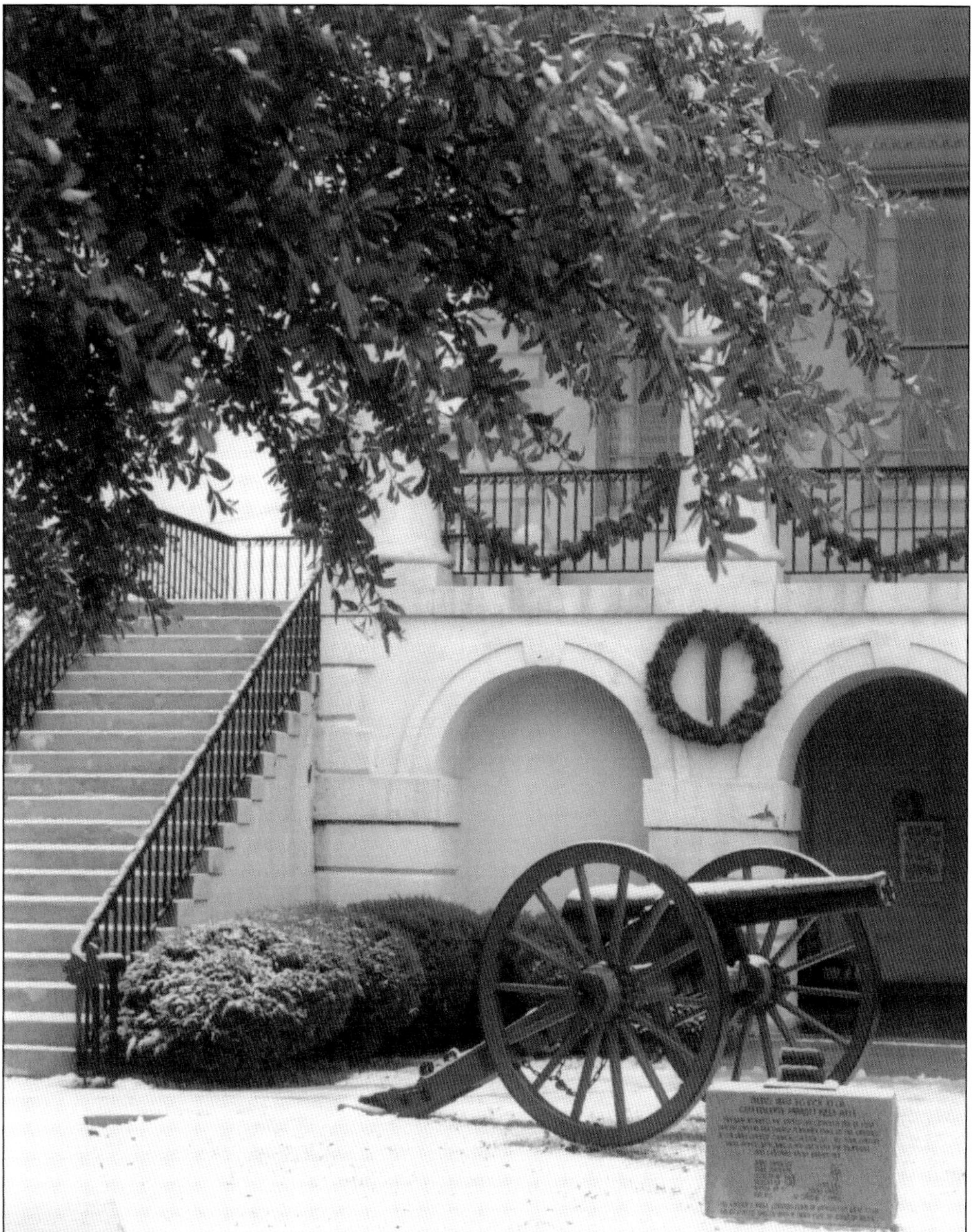

Two of the 10-pound Parrott guns, manufactured at the Tredegar Foundry in Richmond, Virginia, are on display in downtown Chester—one on the lawn of the courthouse and the other in Monument Square. A third is part of a traveling exhibit and has been sleeved, which enables it to be fired with black powder. The fourth tube is on display at the South Carolina State Museum. The cannons are rare, four of only 24 known to exist.

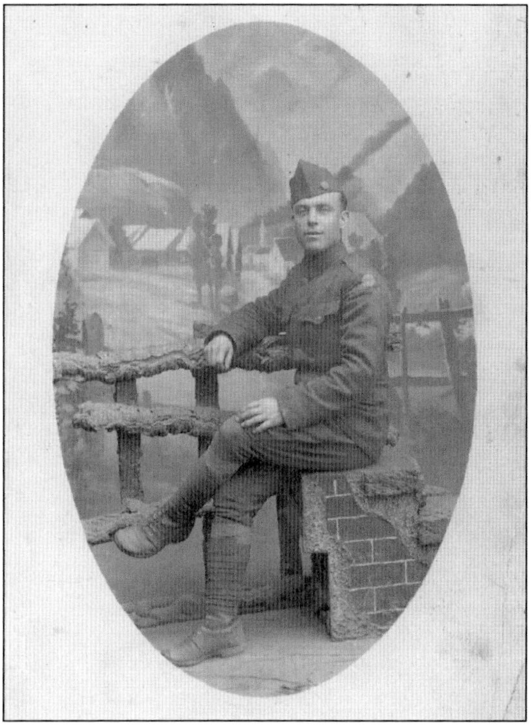

Buford Robinson, a typical looking South Carolina "Dough-Boy," served his country during the Great War. He served in France and later returned home to Chester.

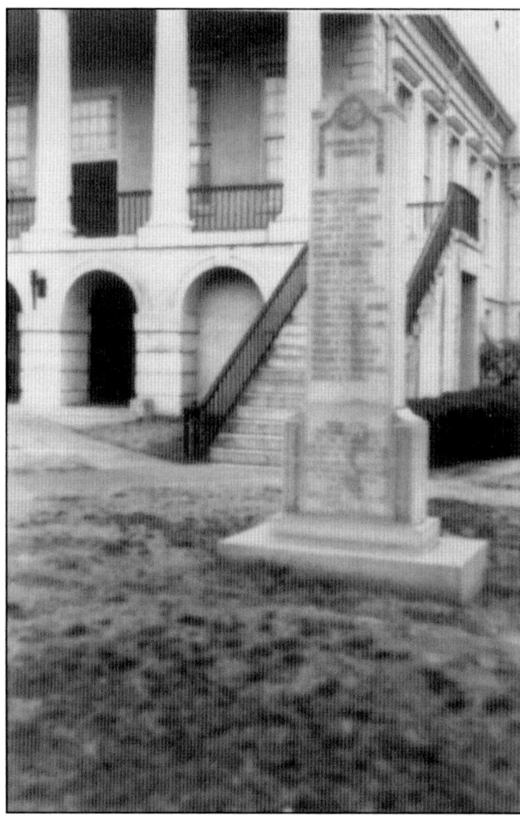

A monument to the Chester boys who made the supreme sacrifice during WW I was dedicated and placed on the courthouse lawn in the 1920s.

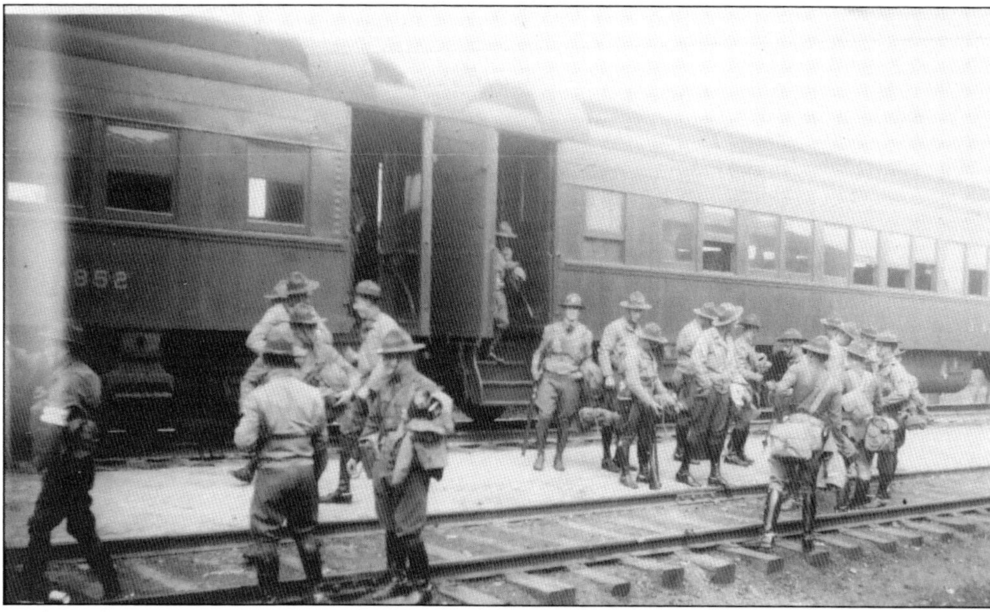

In the fall of 1941, the U.S. Army held maneuvers in Chester County. Centered primarily in the western portion of the county, the maneuvers were between the Red Army and Blue Army. Above, troops disembark from the Seaboard Coastline rail cars. Below, trucks and equipment move out to the staging area.

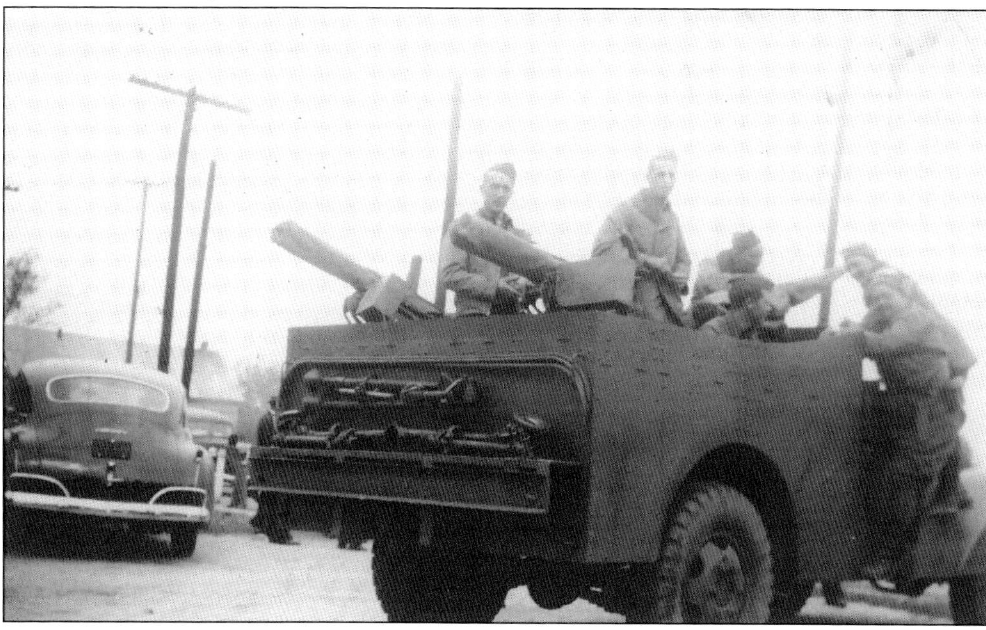

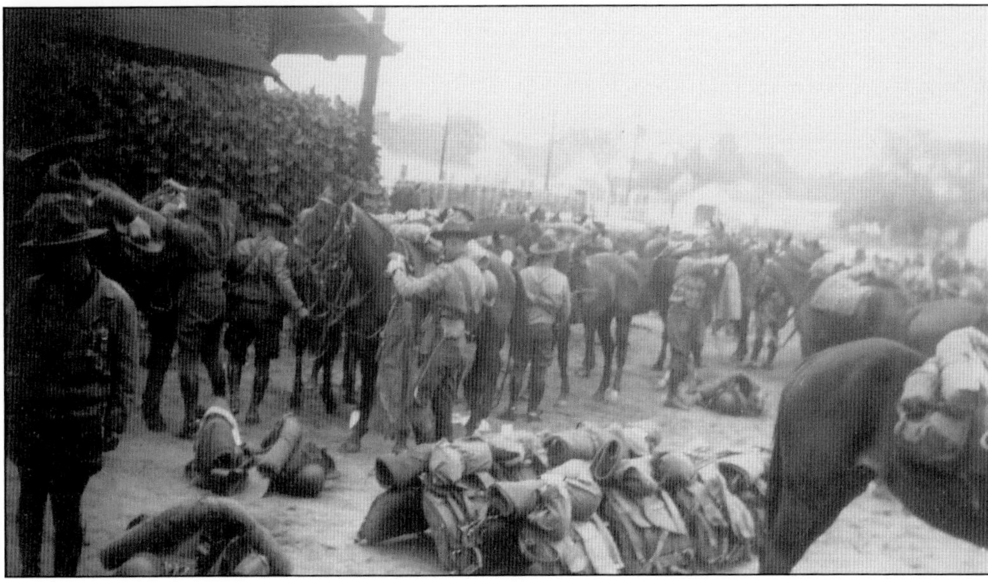

Horses and packs were unloaded from trains to participate in maneuvers in Chester County. The army soon found out that the old cavalry was not effective against the new warfare technology. Below is a sergeant astride a motorcycle, termed by some as "the new cavalry."

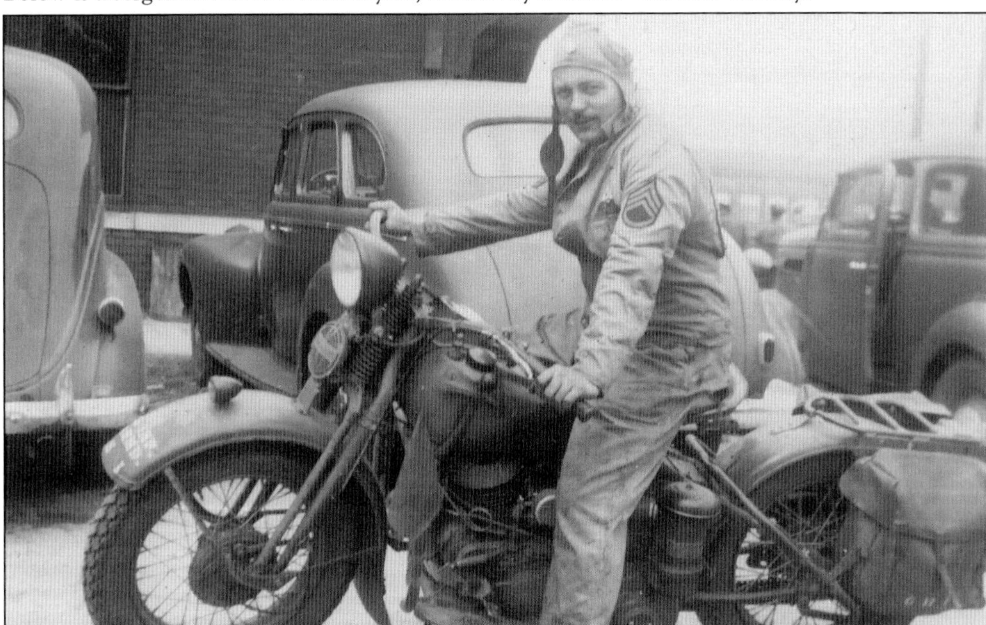

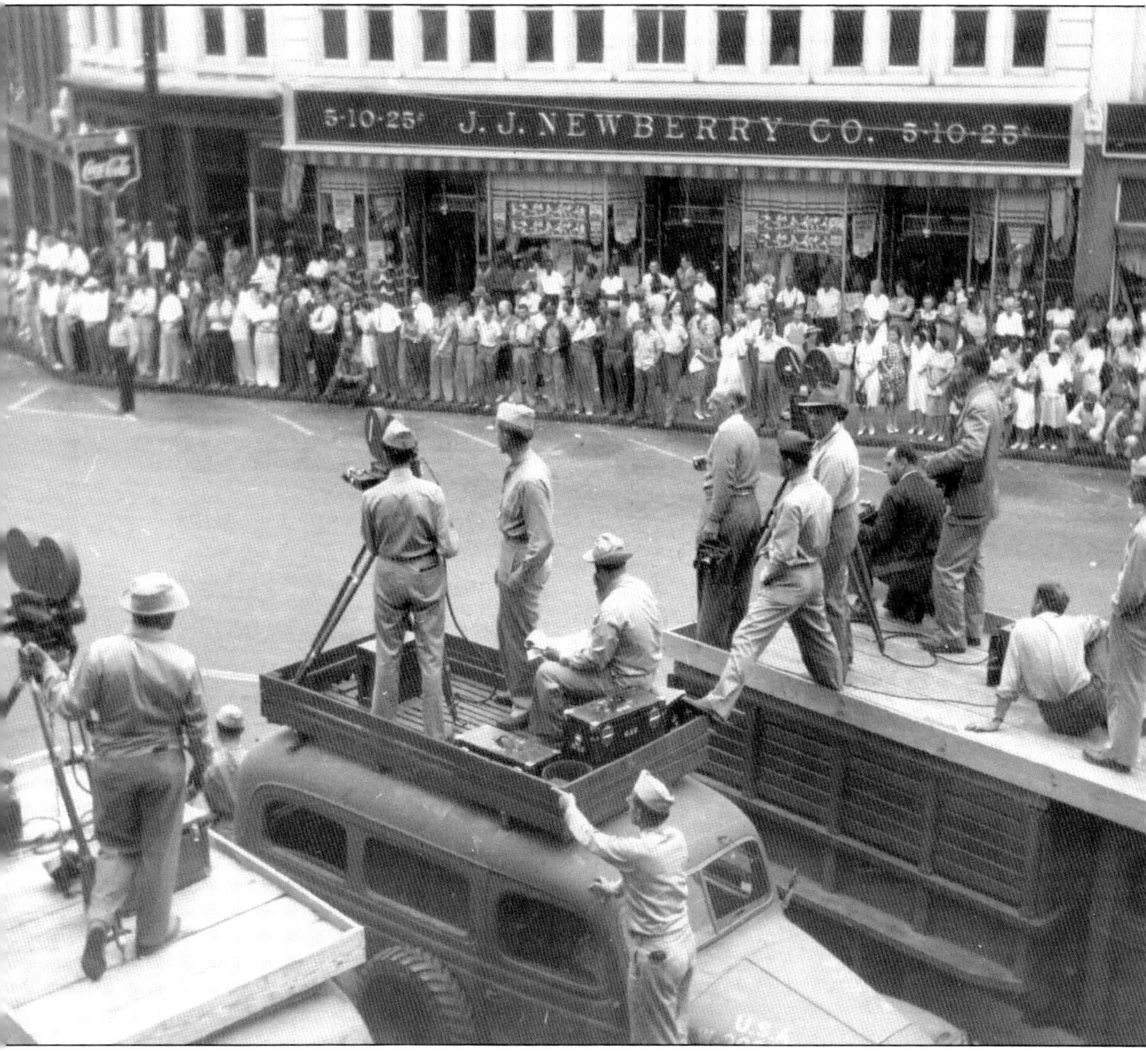

Gen. George Patton was the commander of the maneuvers in Chester County. The resolute general spoke on the stage at the Powell Theater to an assemblage of soldiers, slapping his knee-high boots with the ever-present riding crop. Army film crews took footage when Patton was paraded through downtown Chester as crowds of people looked on.

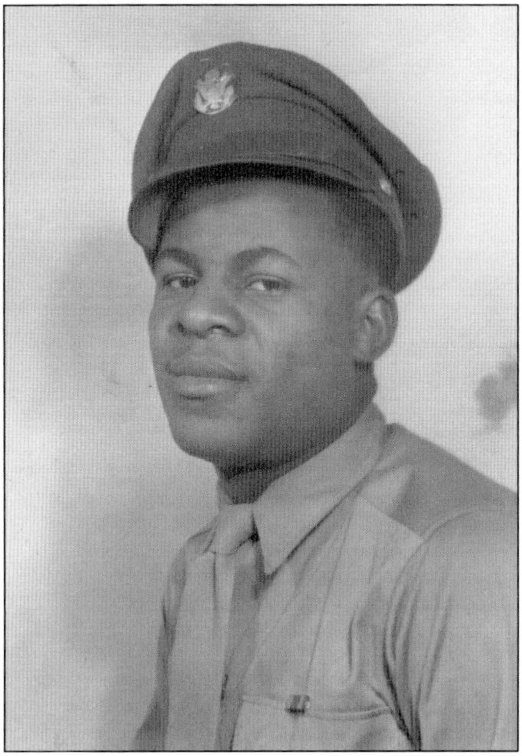

Sam Gladden was a soldier in the U.S. Army during WW II. He sent this picture home to his family and friends to see what they thought of him in a uniform.

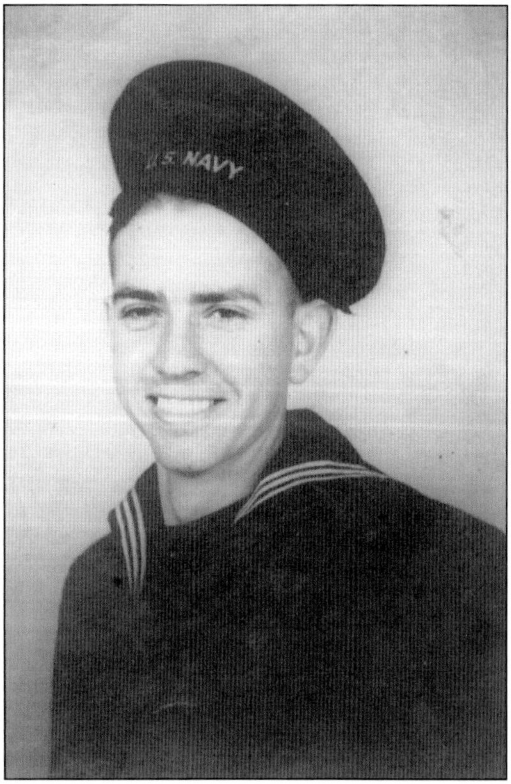

Daniel Flowers of Great Falls flashes a winning smile for the camera in 1943 in his U.S. Navy blues. Many soldiers took great pride in having their picture taken in their dress uniforms.

Lamar Kelsey served with the Army Airway Communications Systems (AACS) and was stationed in Calcutta, India during WW II. Soon after his return to Chester, he became the owner and operator of Hall Lumber Company, which is still operated by his family.

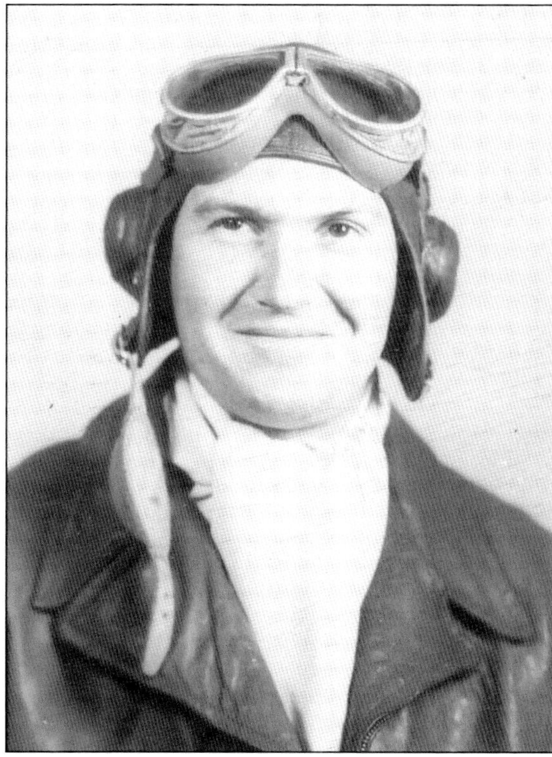

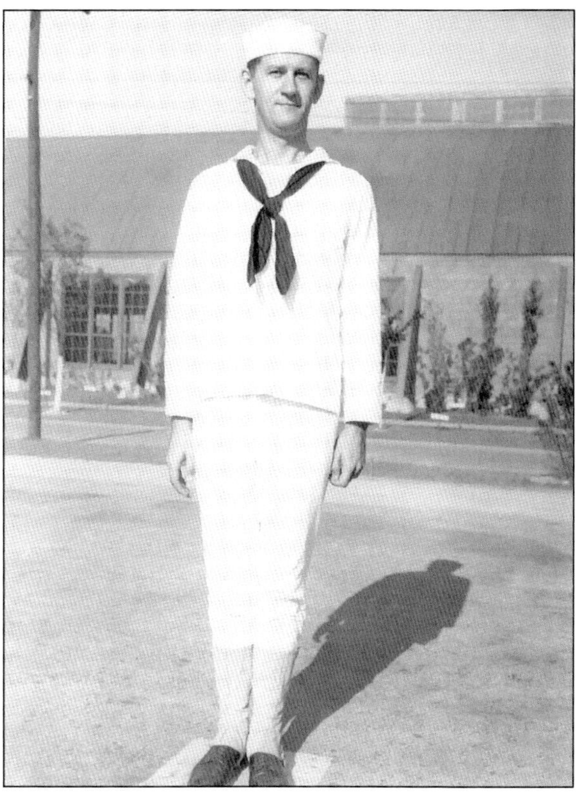

Charlton Howze stands at attention in his seaman's uniform probably at his stateside training facility before being assigned to duty.

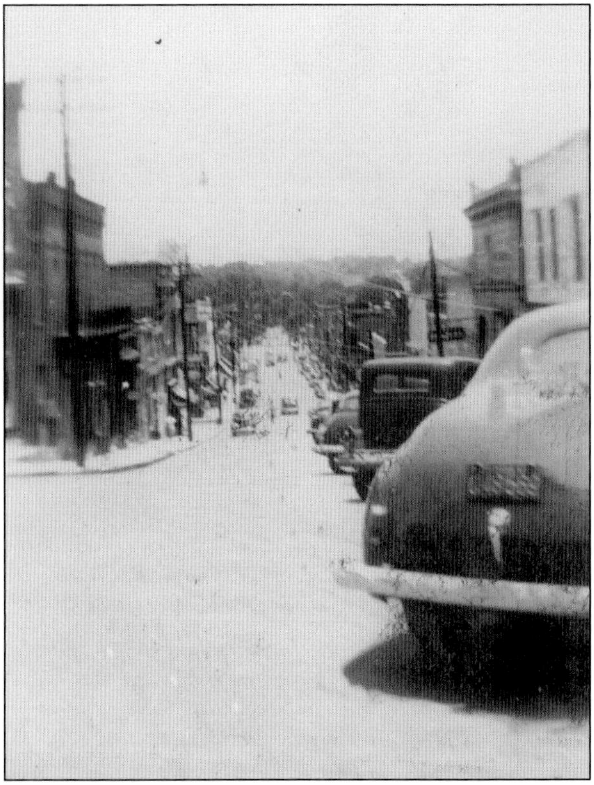

The homefront during WW II contributed a great deal to the war effort. From rationing to Victory Gardens to War Bonds, the people at home did their part. This scene in 1942 is looking down Gadsden Street toward the Valley.

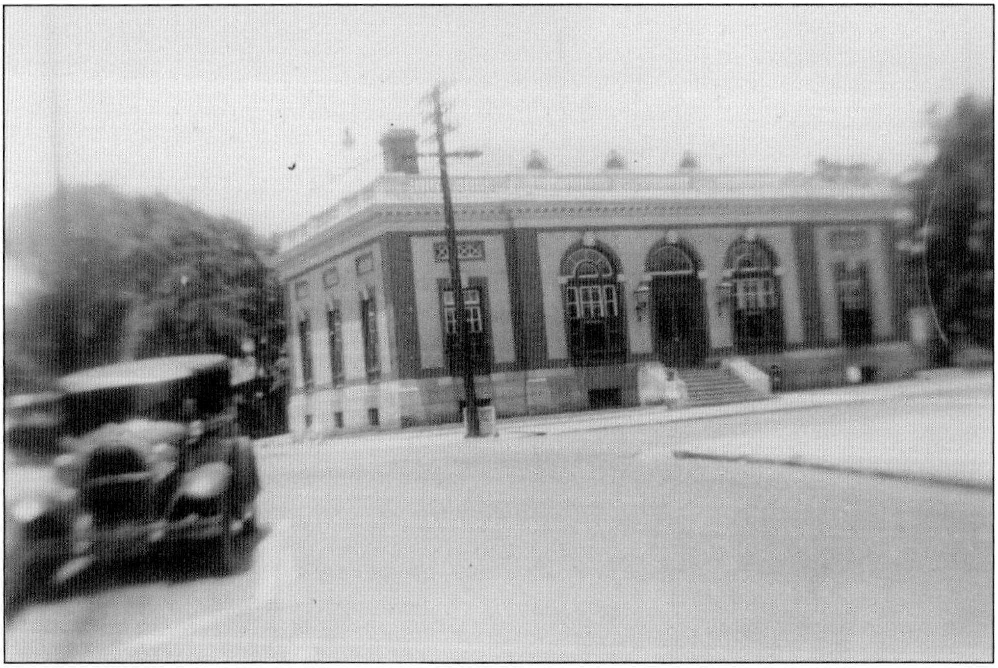

The Post Office during the war was the center of much activity. Mothers, wives, and sweethearts waited anxiously for word from their loved ones. This photograph was taken in 1942.

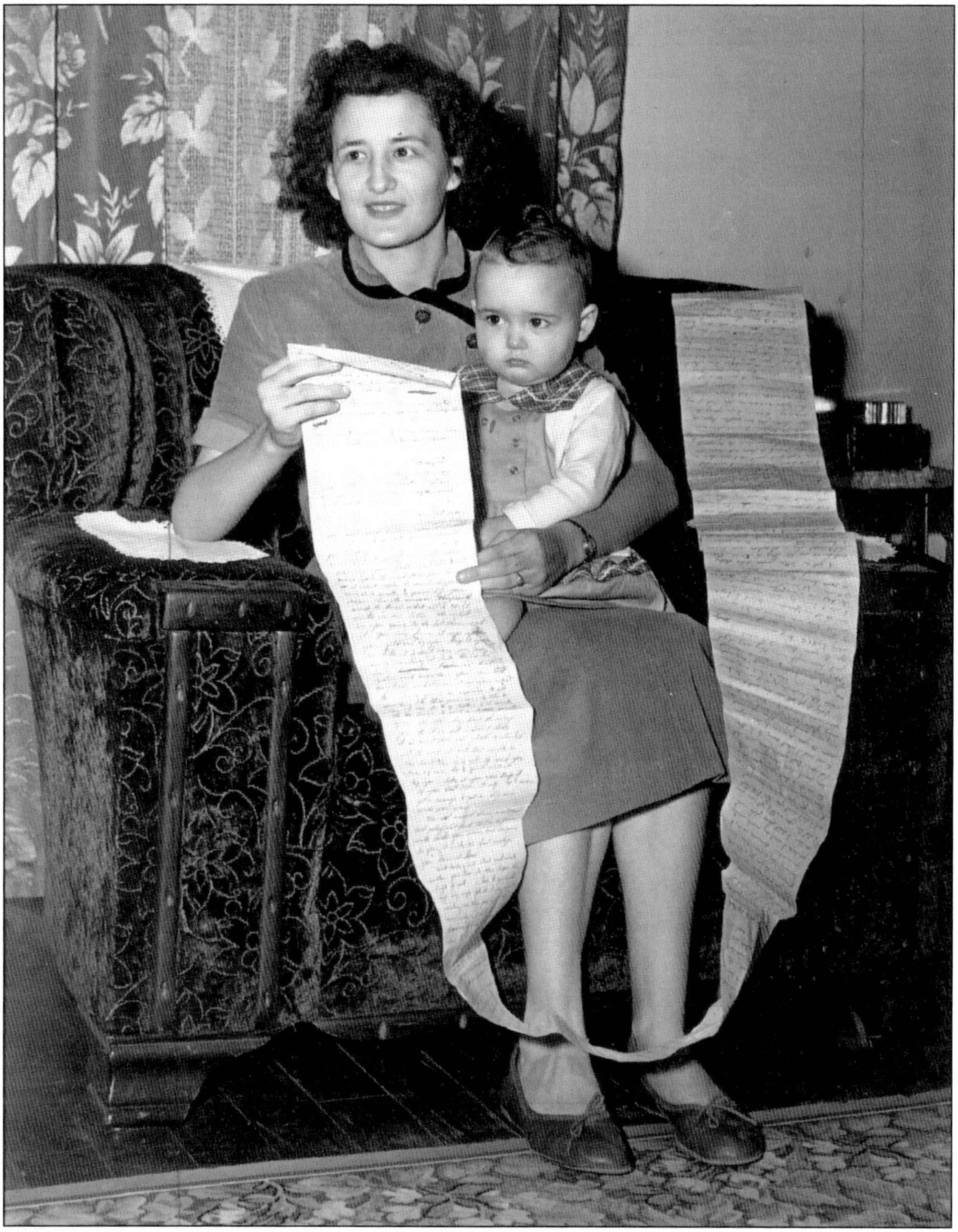

This unidentified woman and her small child pose for a photograph with an extremely long letter presumably written by her husband from overseas. He writes ". . . telling you how much I love you but that is about all I wrote. Guess you will get tired of reading it over and over, but it is still wrote down here if you don't read it." This photograph was taken by James Rape, a local photographer, for the *Chester News*.

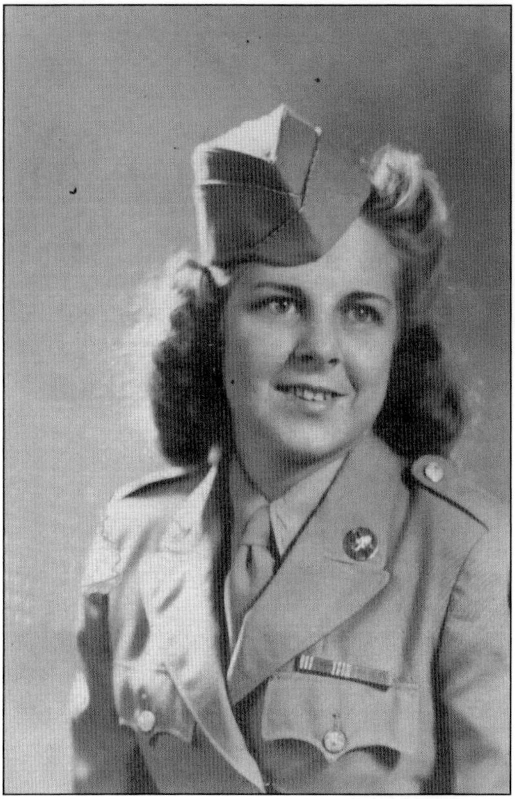

Women not only took the reins on the homefront, but they also served in the armed forces. Here Mrs. Earl Bagley, formerly Mildred Smith of Chester, poses in her Women's Auxiliary Army Corp (WAAC) uniform.

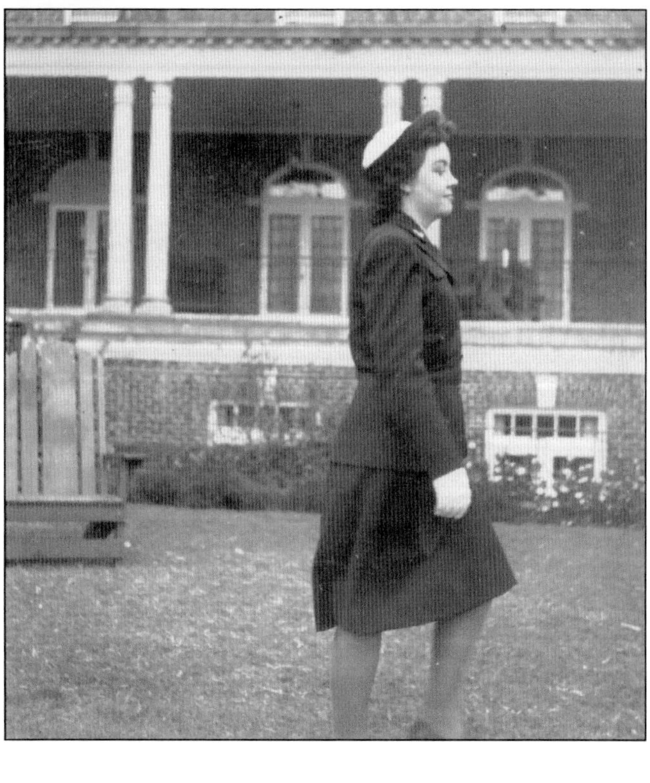

Elizabeth Anne Robinson joined the WAVES, the Navy version of the women's army corp, in 1943. She was among the first to be admitted into this group.

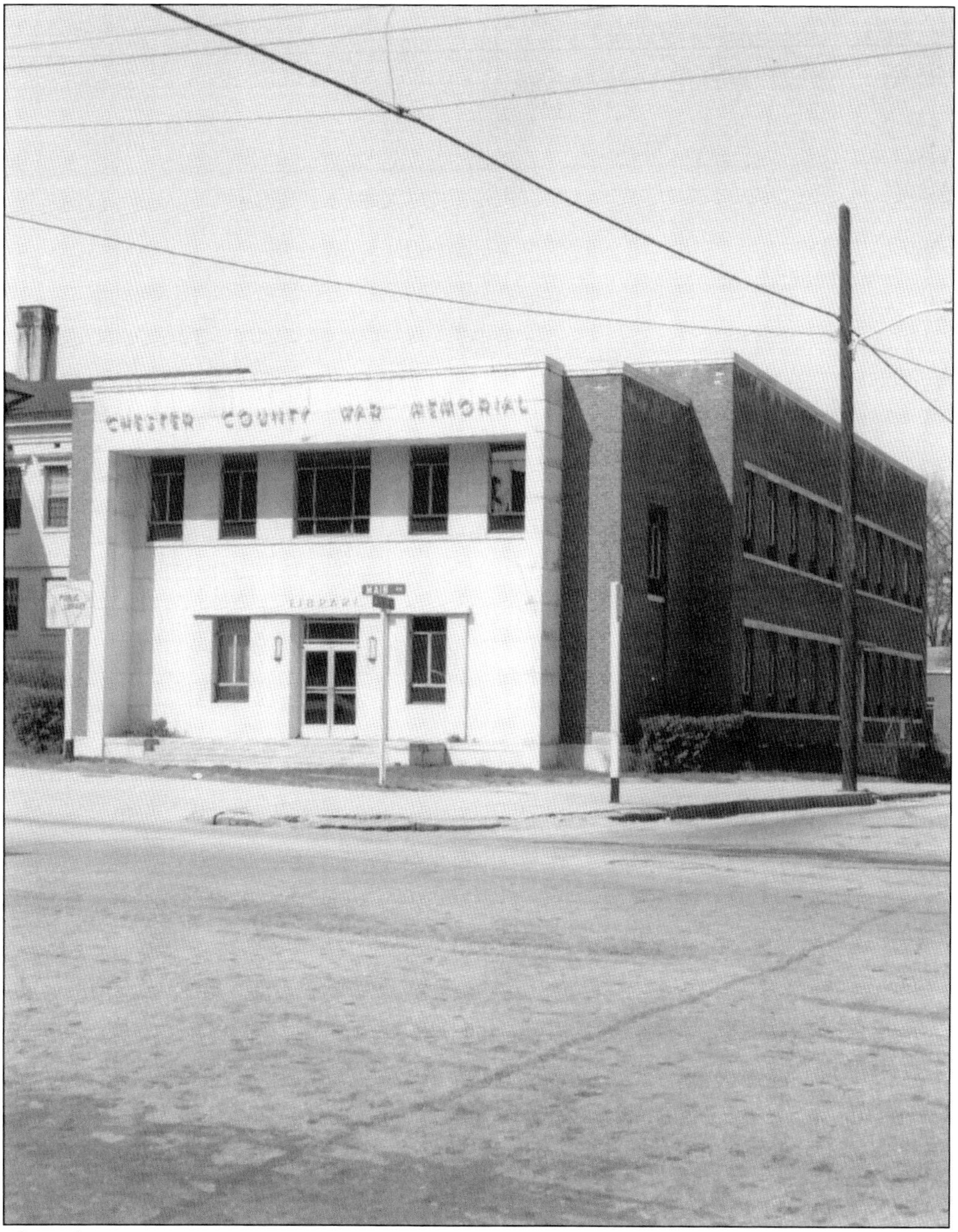

The Chester County War Memorial Building was completed in 1950 and was designed as a memorial to those Chester County men who gave their lives during WW II. Built with private donations, the building was turned over to the county and in 2000 is undergoing major renovations.

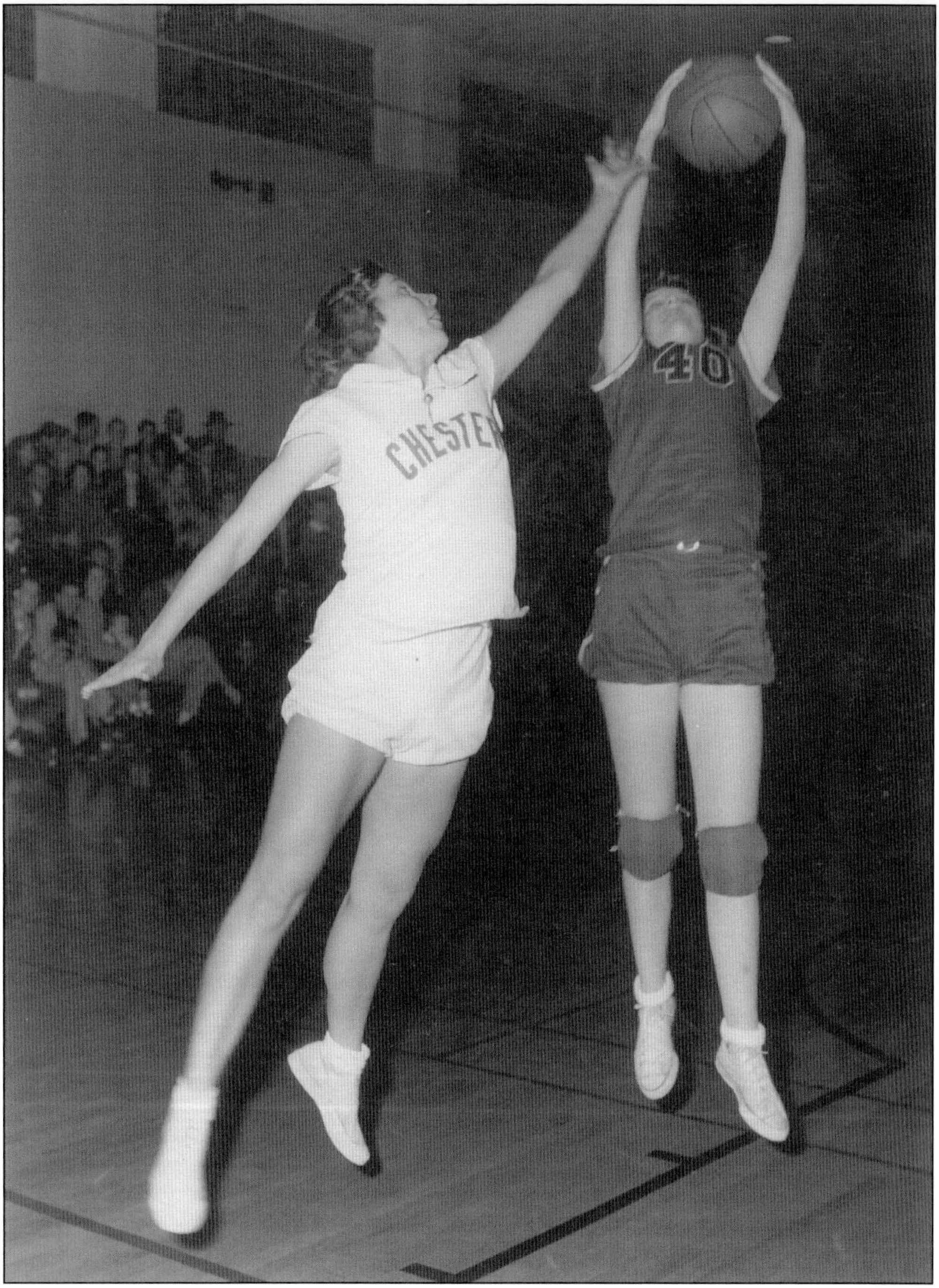

Women's Chester High School basketball has been a competitive and popular sport for decades. Pictured here is a game in the 1950s.

Six

ARTS, EDUCATION, AND ATHLETICS

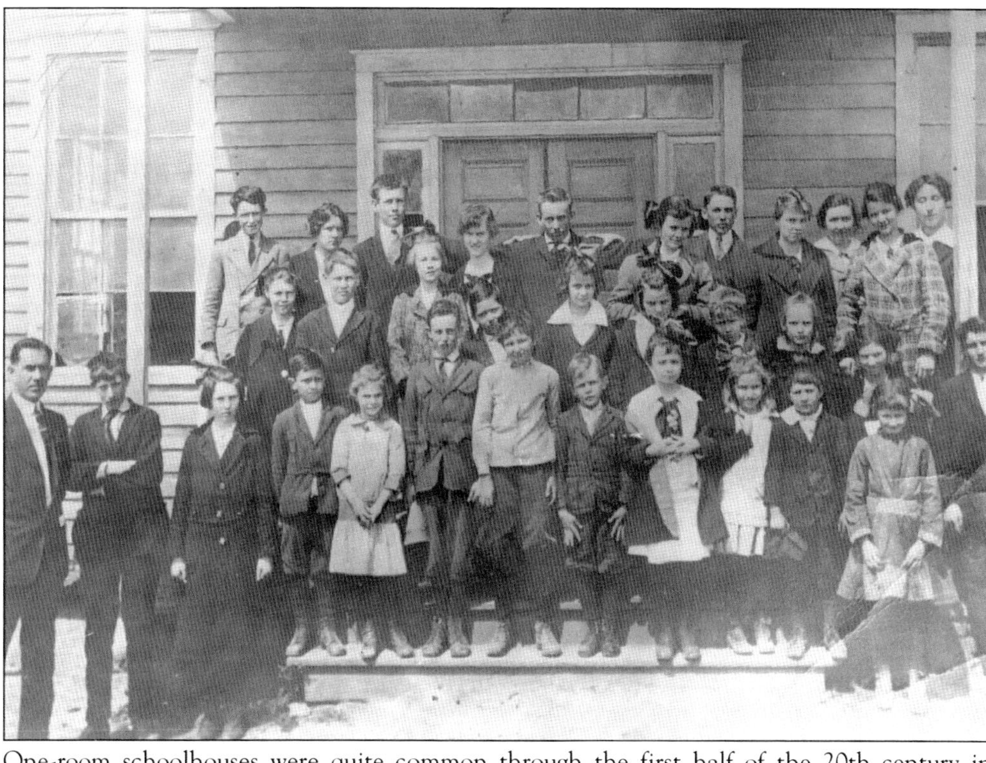

One-room schoolhouses were quite common through the first half of the 20th century in Chester County. Here, a group of students stand in front of their school in the 1910s. One teacher taught multiple grades and various subjects in a most organized manner.

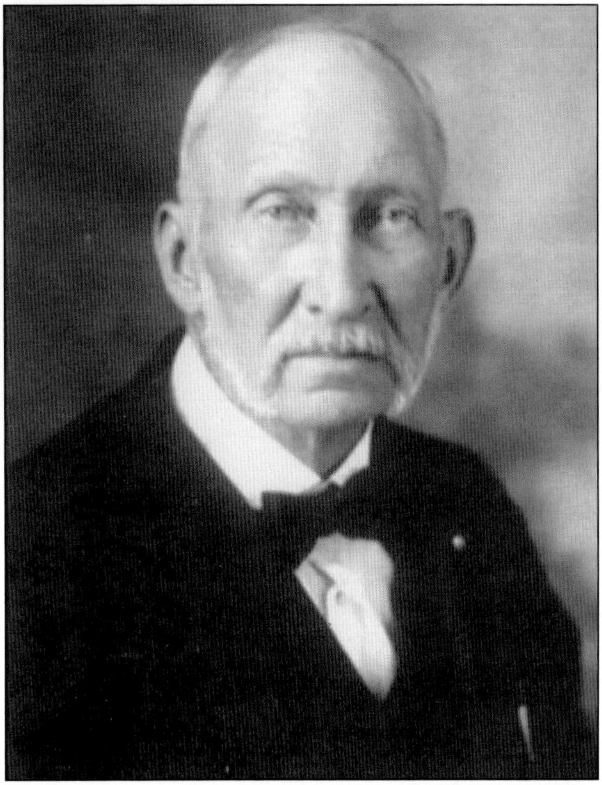

William Dunlap Knox was the first school superintendent in Chester County, serving from 1889 until his death in 1928. During his tenure he consolidated high schools, created longer terms, and began the bus system to transport students. He went from school to school in a horse and buggy and followed a strict routine. He has many descendants in the area who are still in the education field.

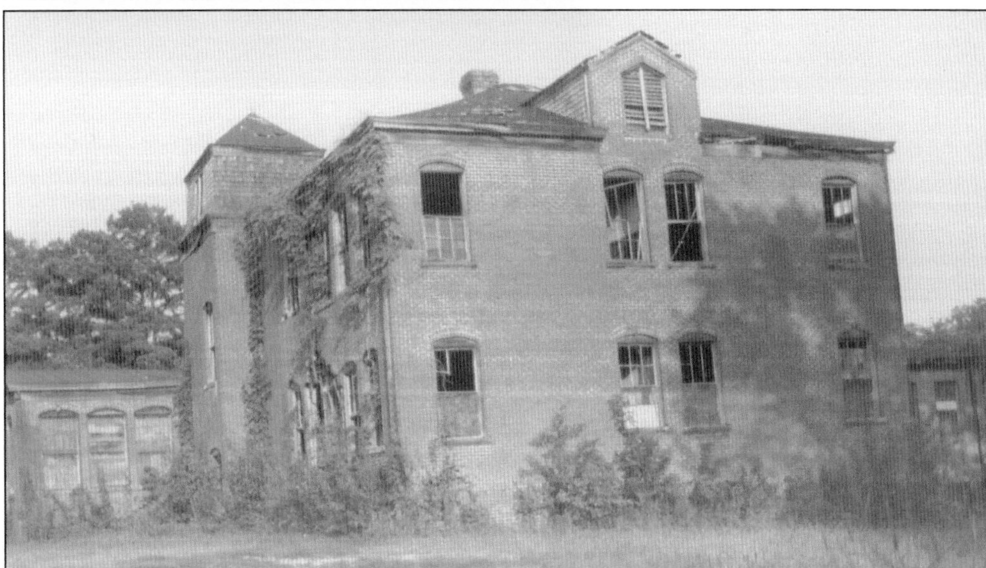

Brainerd Institute was an important element in the education of African Americans throughout the state and region. Begun in Chester County in 1866 in a log cabin, the school was operated by the Presbyterian Church to educate freed slaves. The school eventually became a graded elementary and then a high school. By the 1930s it had developed into a junior college. This classroom building is no longer standing, but Kumler Hall, the boys dormitory, is in the process of being saved.

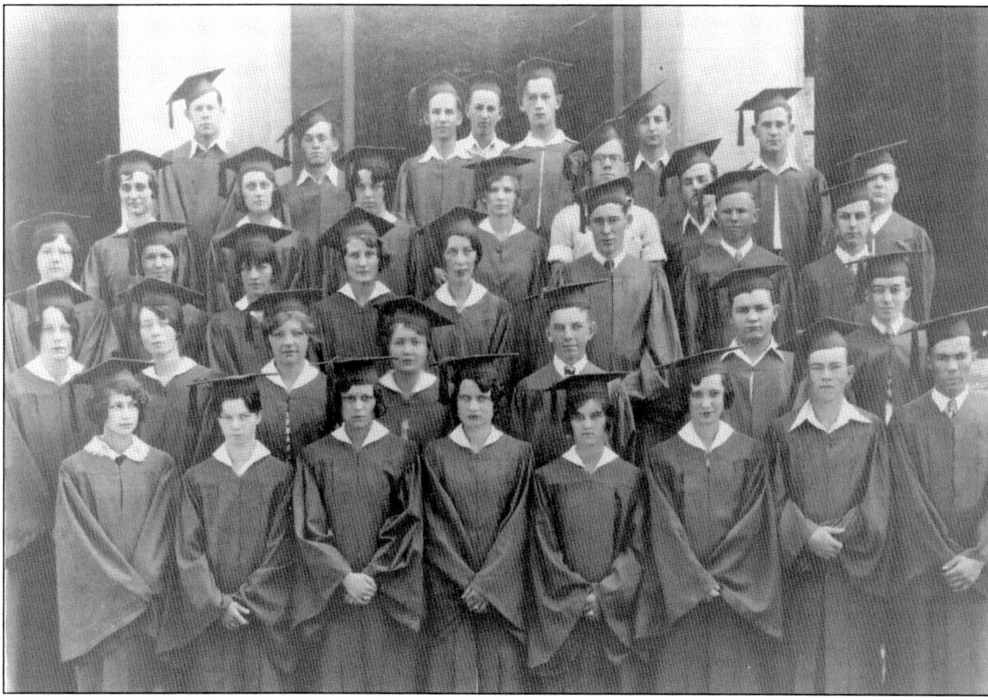

The 1930 graduates of Chester High School pose on the steps of the school on Columbia Street in their caps and gowns.

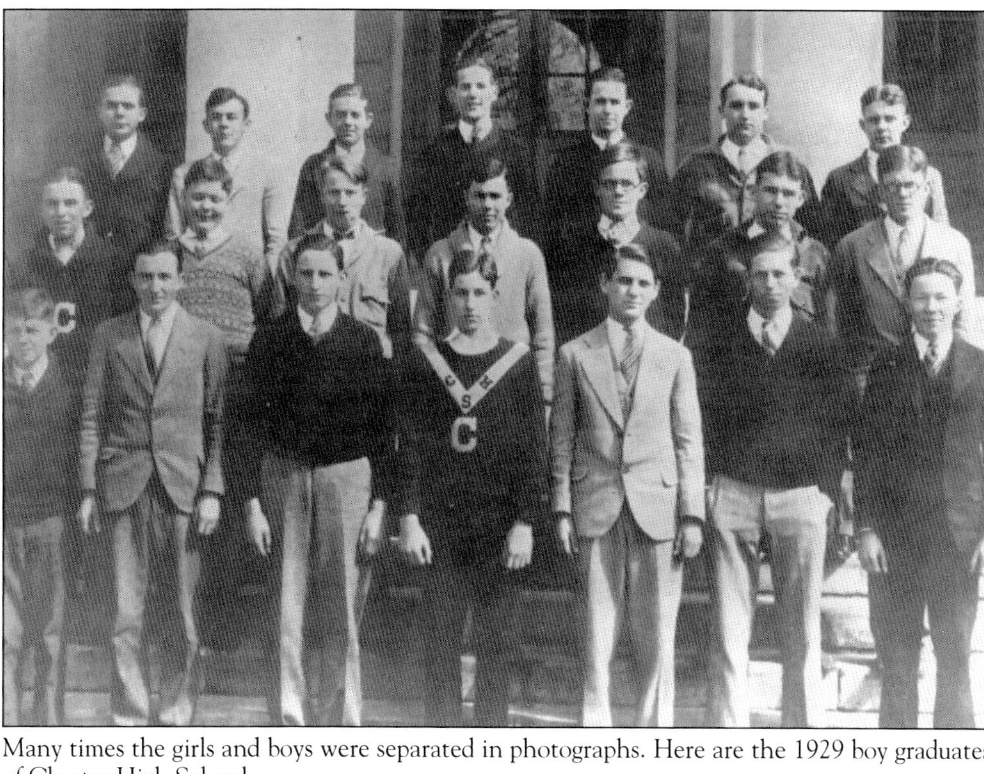

Many times the girls and boys were separated in photographs. Here are the 1929 boy graduates of Chester High School.

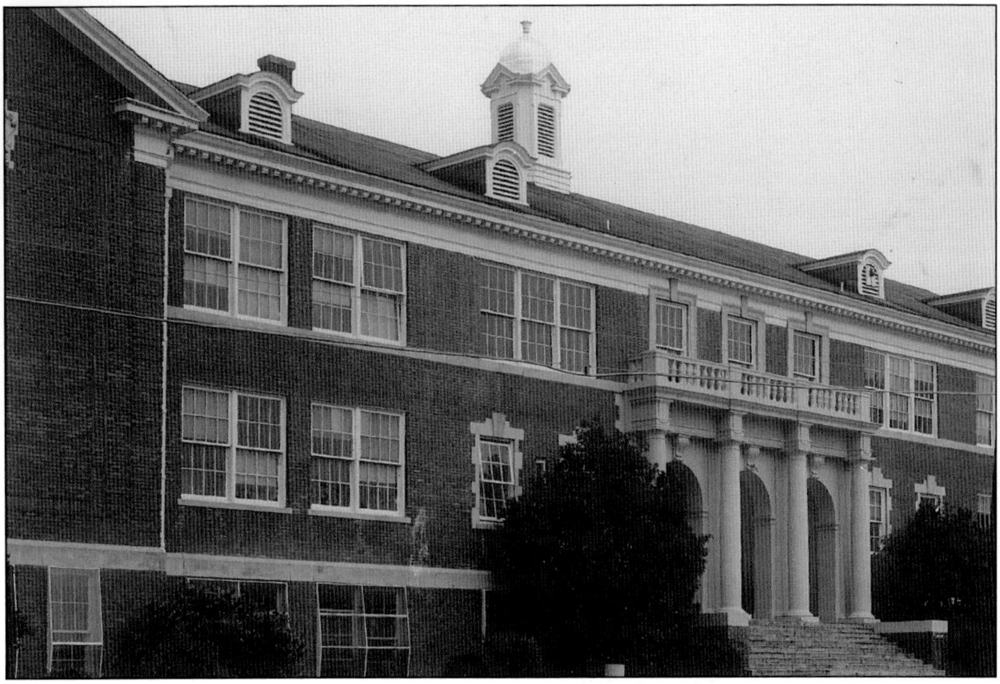

Many students attended classes within the walls of Chester High School, which was built in 1924. This building was later known as Brockman, especially when the "new" high school was built in 1954.

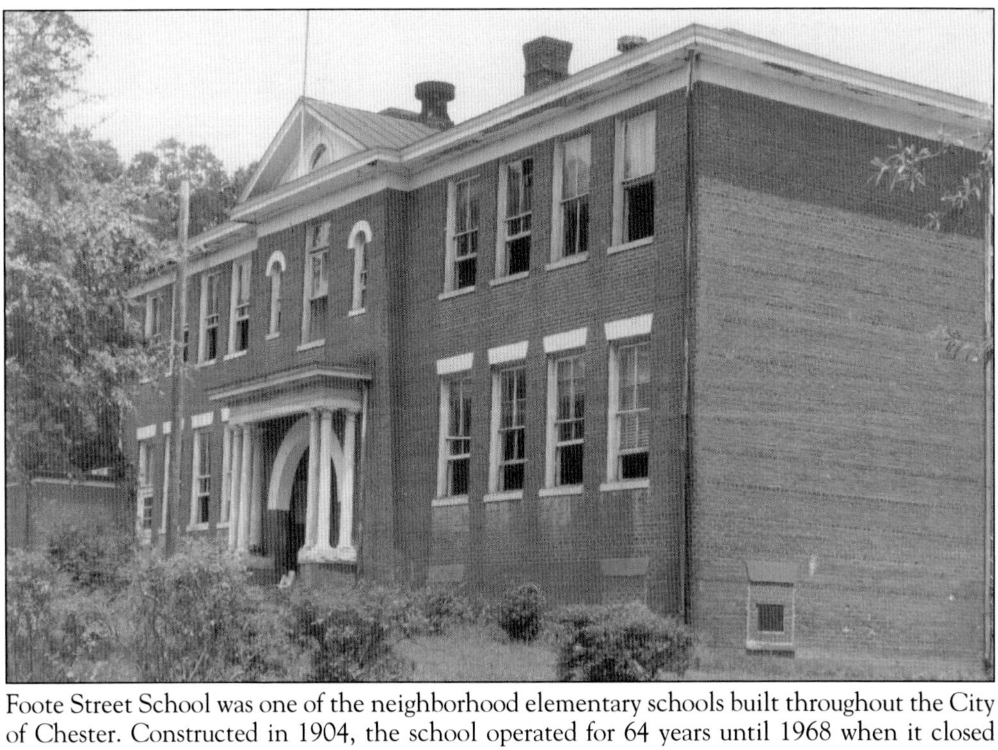

Foote Street School was one of the neighborhood elementary schools built throughout the City of Chester. Constructed in 1904, the school operated for 64 years until 1968 when it closed its doors.

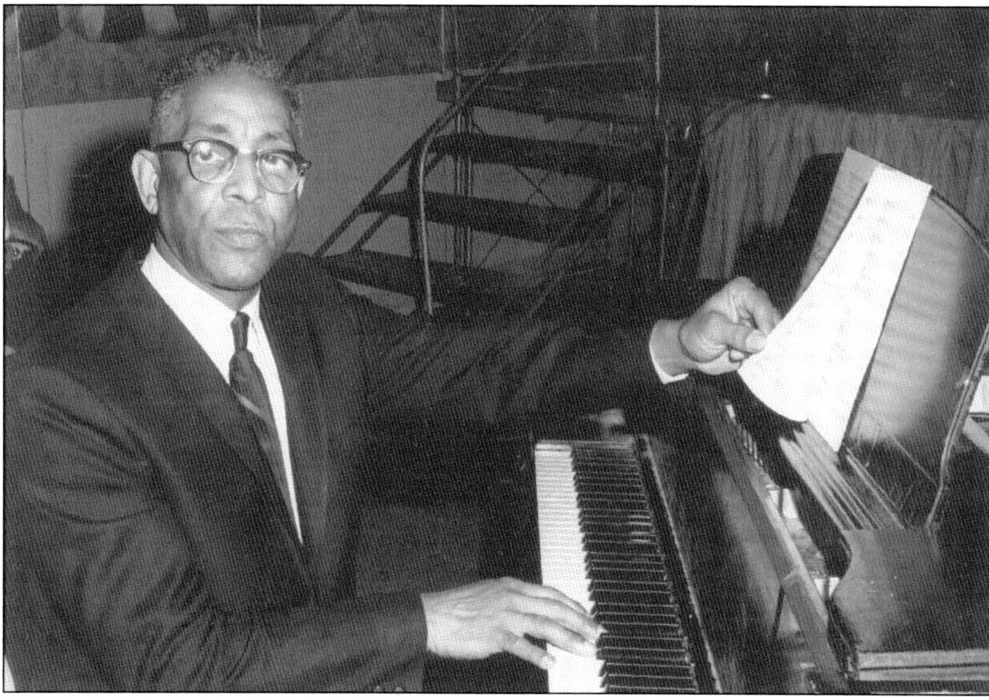

S.L. Finley was the principal of Finley High School for many years. The school was named for him in later years. He was a respected and much loved educator in Chester County.

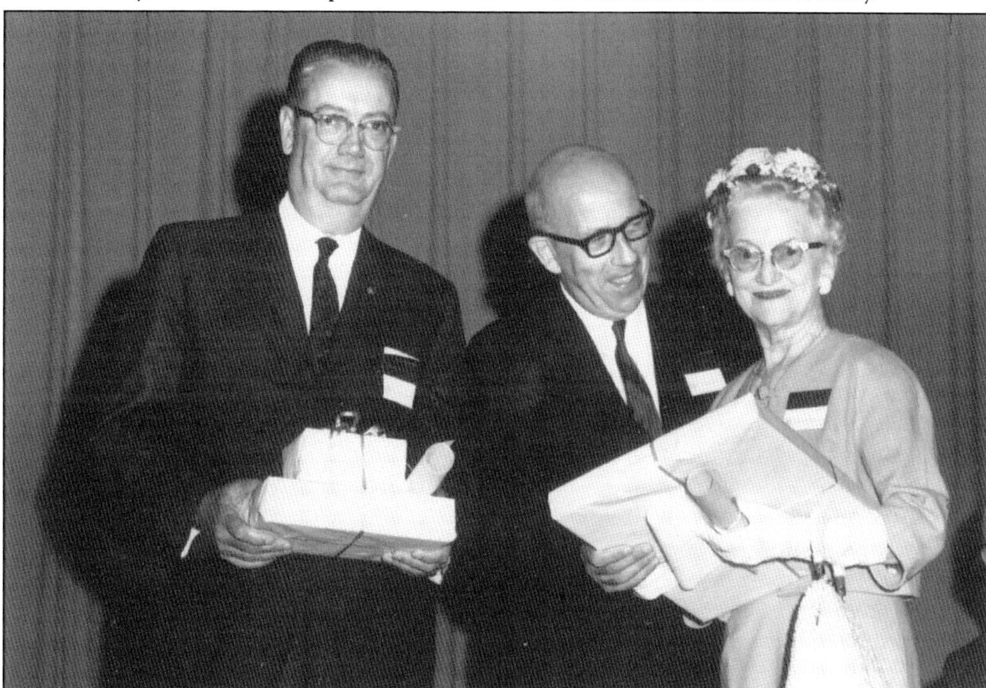

Miss Maude Bigham taught math to many-a Chester High School student over her long and distinguished career of more than 30 years. In 1957, she was the first recipient of the Bernard Baruch Teacher of the Year Award in South Carolina.

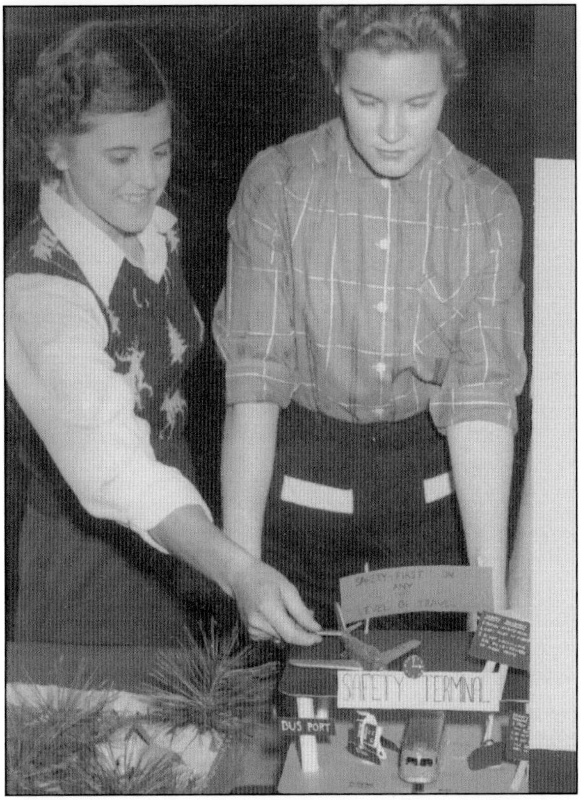

Lavinia Weir, left, of Chester looks over a safety exhibit that she and fellow classmates put together for a school display, c. 1950s.

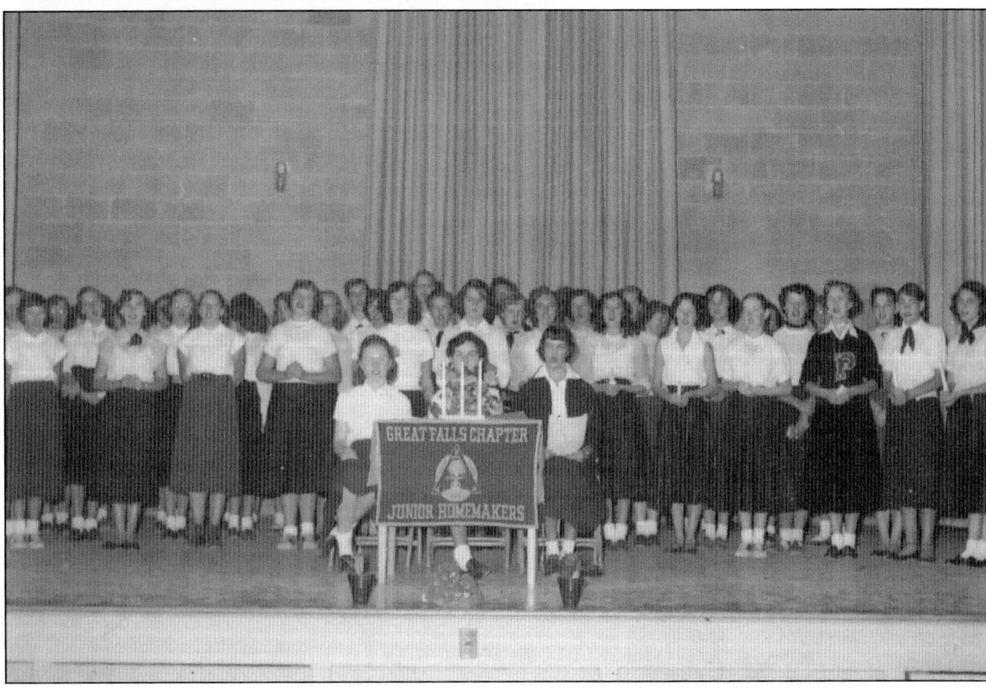

The Great Falls Chapter of the Junior Homemakers participate in an induction ceremony on the high school stage during the 1950s.

Children participate in an American Education Week program in the early 1960s.

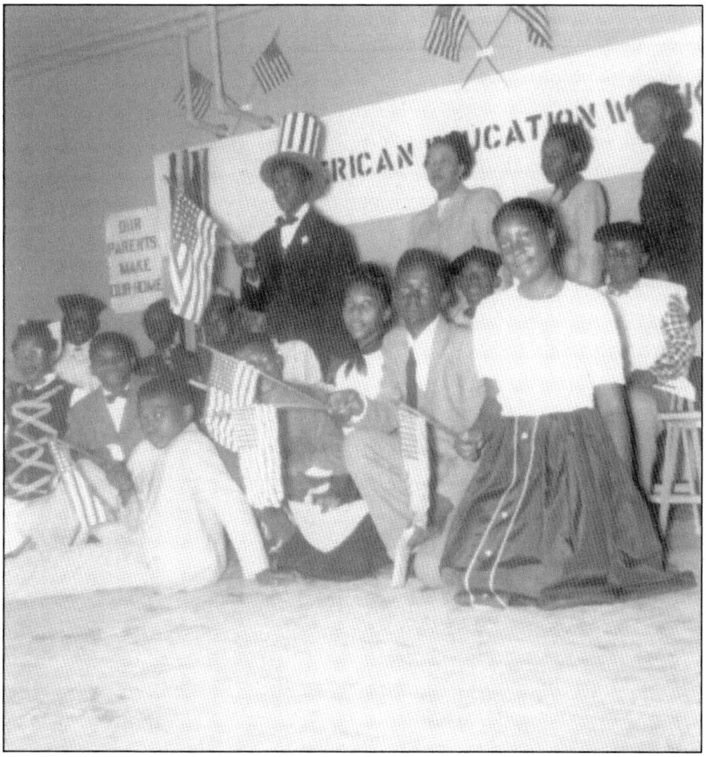

The 1957 Chester High School Marching Band poses on the steps of College Street School.

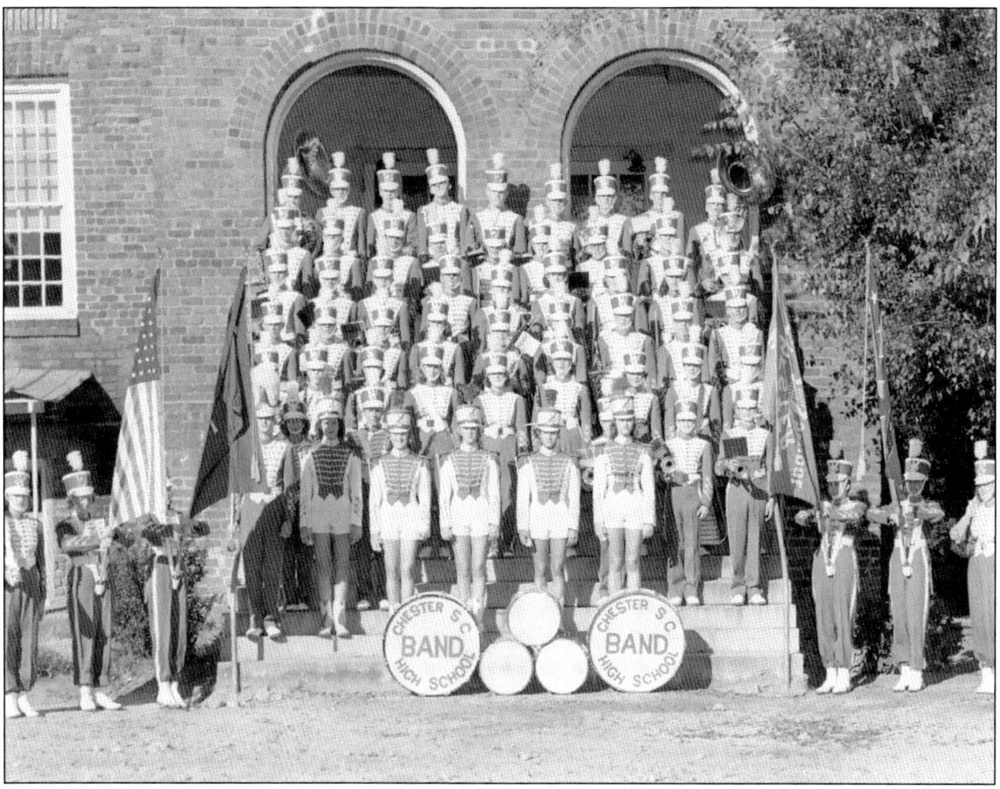

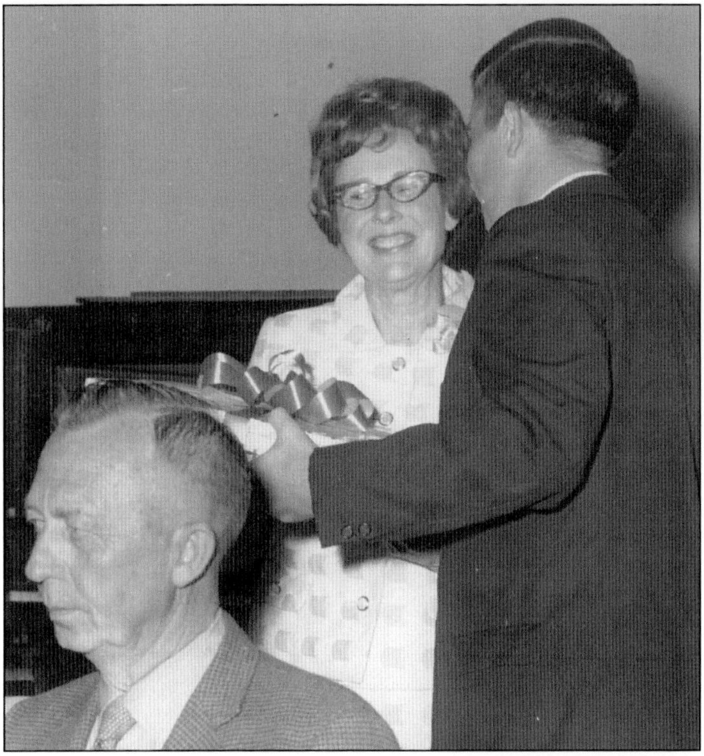

Martha Marion Stringfellow, a Chester native, was named National Teacher of the Year in 1971.

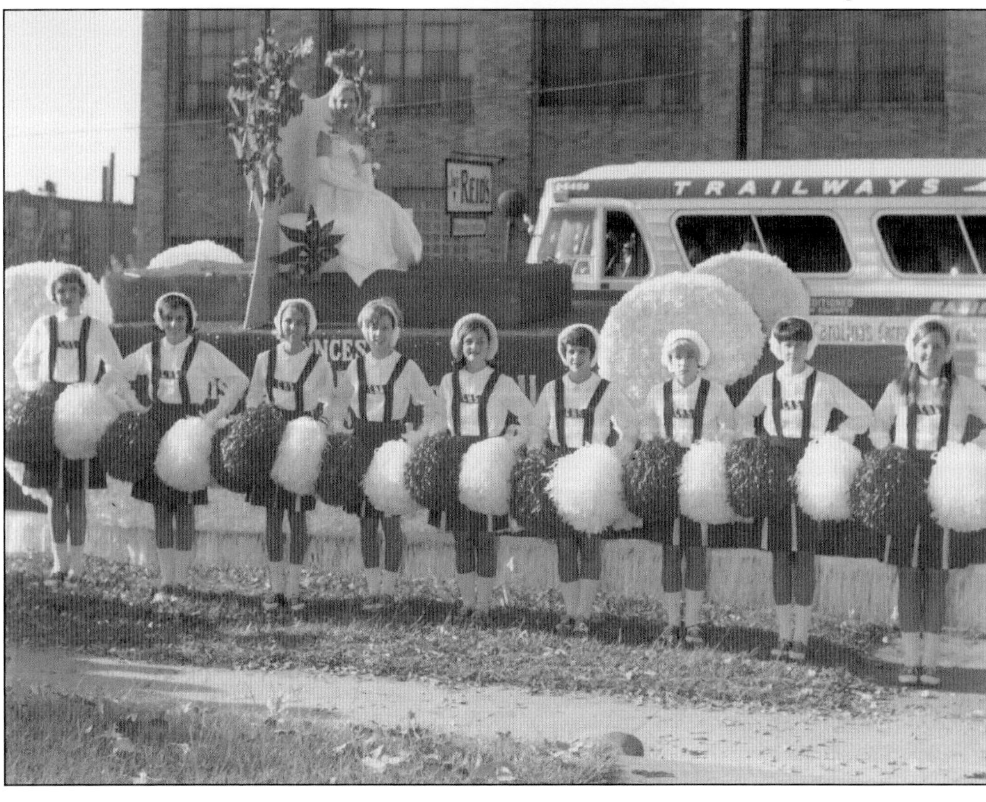

What is a football game without cheerleaders? This group of Chester High School cheerleaders, c. 1969, poses in front of a float as they prepare to participate in a Christmas parade.

Alexander Johnson was the first African American to serve on the school board in Chester County.

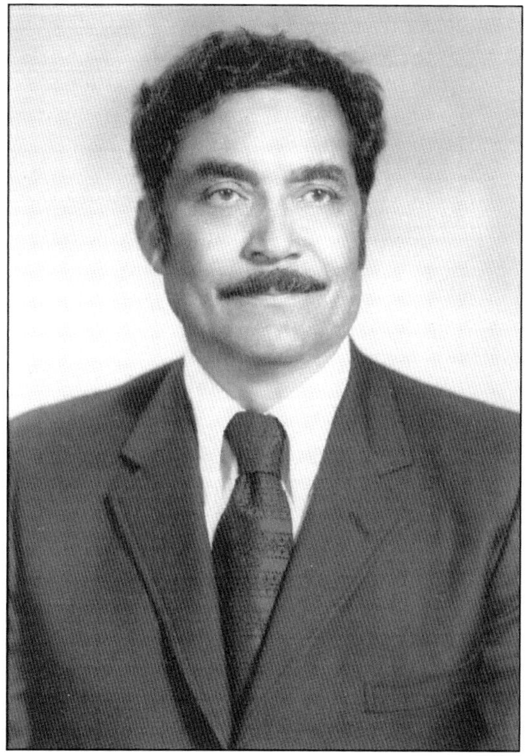

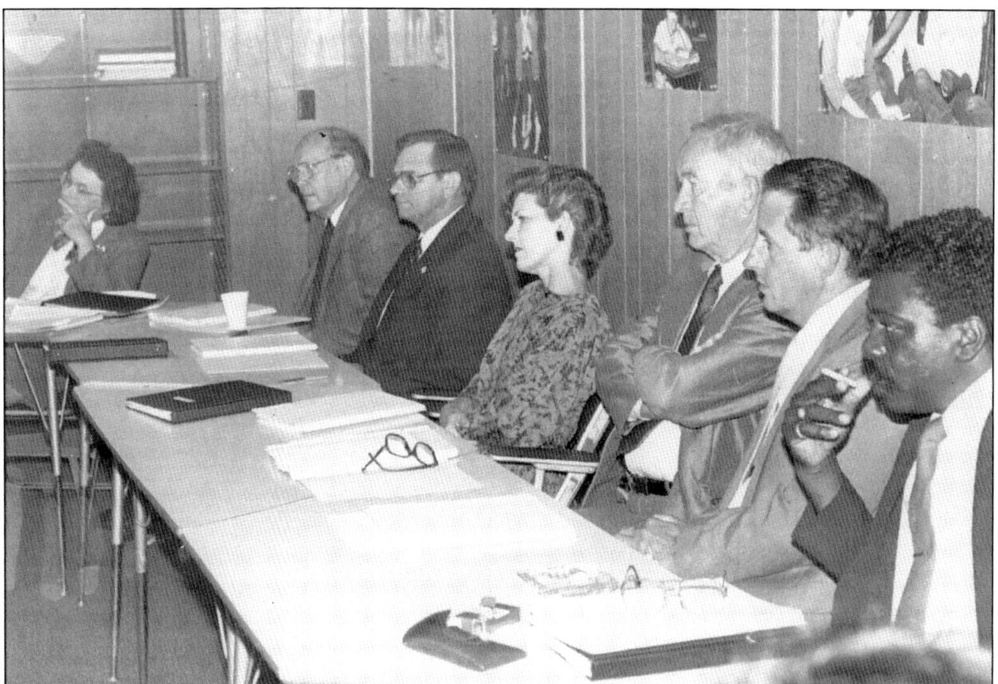

The Chester County School Board, pictured here in 1989, listens intently to a petitioner. From left to right are Brenda Fort, Willis Crain (chairman), Charles Killian, Linda Short, D.C. Reid, Hugh Berry Moore, and Rev. Bill Stringfellow.

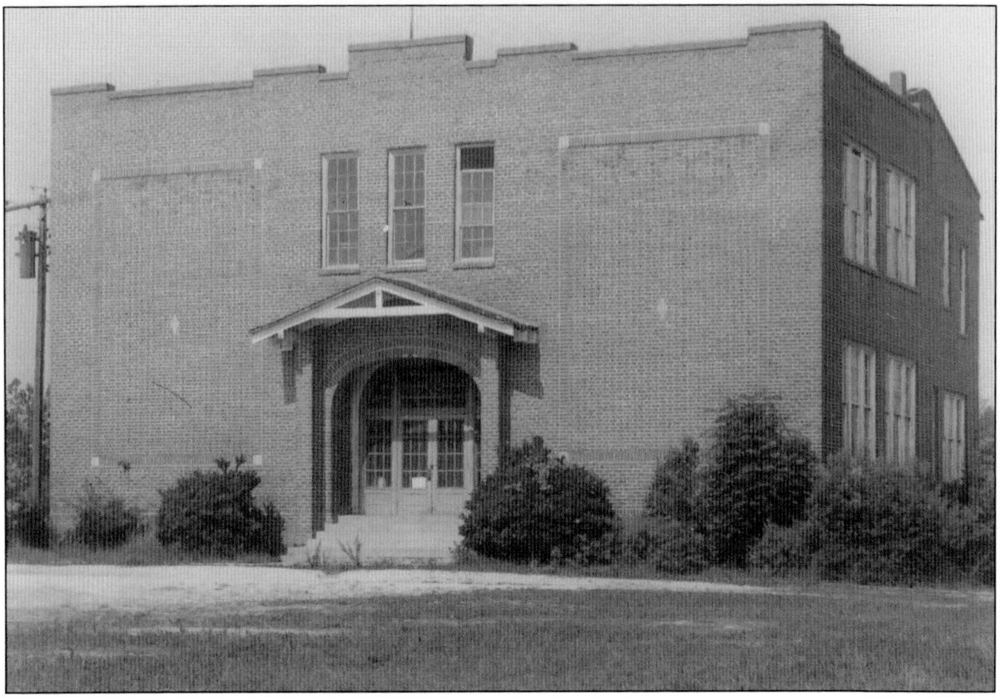

Blackstock School housed early grades through high school and educated many students in the southern part of Chester County. This is a photo of the school after it was no longer in use.

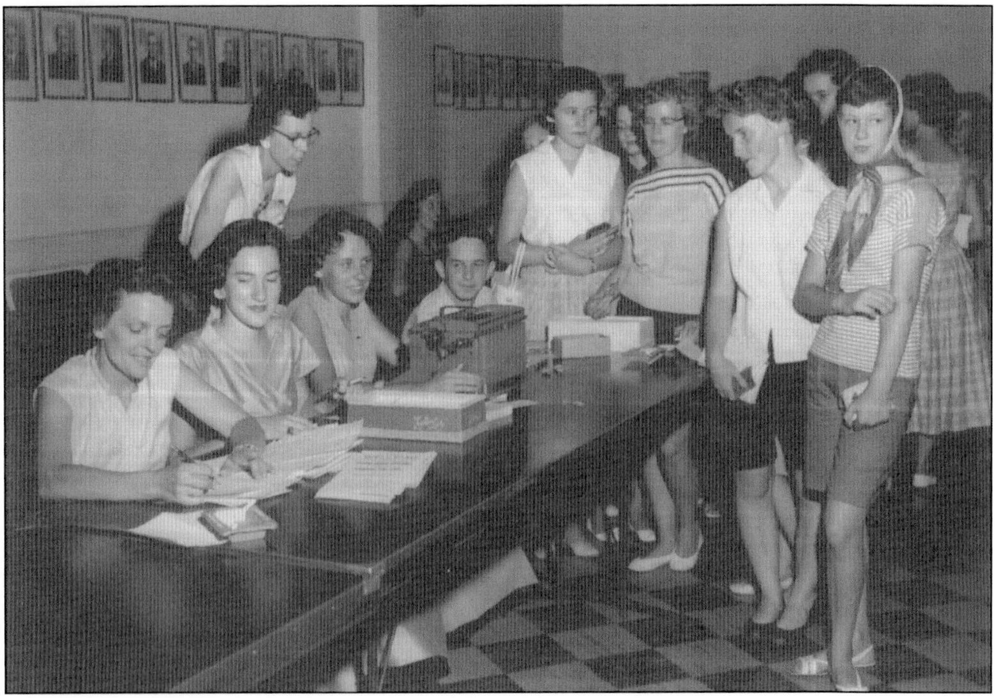

Chester Assembly No. 6 Order of Rainbow for Girls hosted the State Grand Assembly, which was basically a convention, in the late 1950s. Here, Chester Rainbow members register girls from all across the state at the Masonic Temple on top of the hill in Chester.

Members of the Gayle Mill women's basketball team pose for a picture in the late 1940s. Elizabeth Morris and Vivian Collins stand in a classic basketball pose.

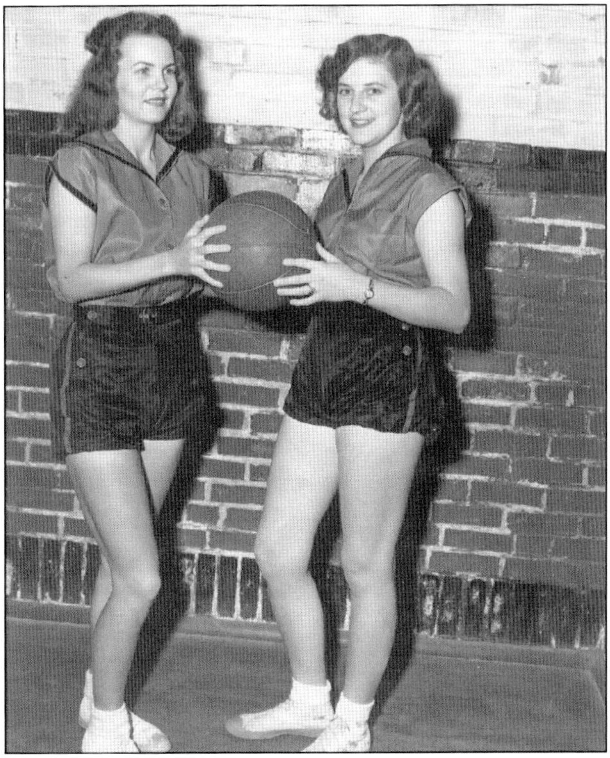

The American Legion team from 1948 posed for this picture. They are, from left to right, as follows: (front row) two unidentified men, Major Reid, and three unidentified men; (middle row) unidentified, "Red" McCollum, George Dover, Catfish Dover, Francis Atkinson, and unidentified; (back row) Barney Byars, John Cooper, unidentified, Billy Holt, John Wright, Hub Dover, and Al Shealy, the coach.

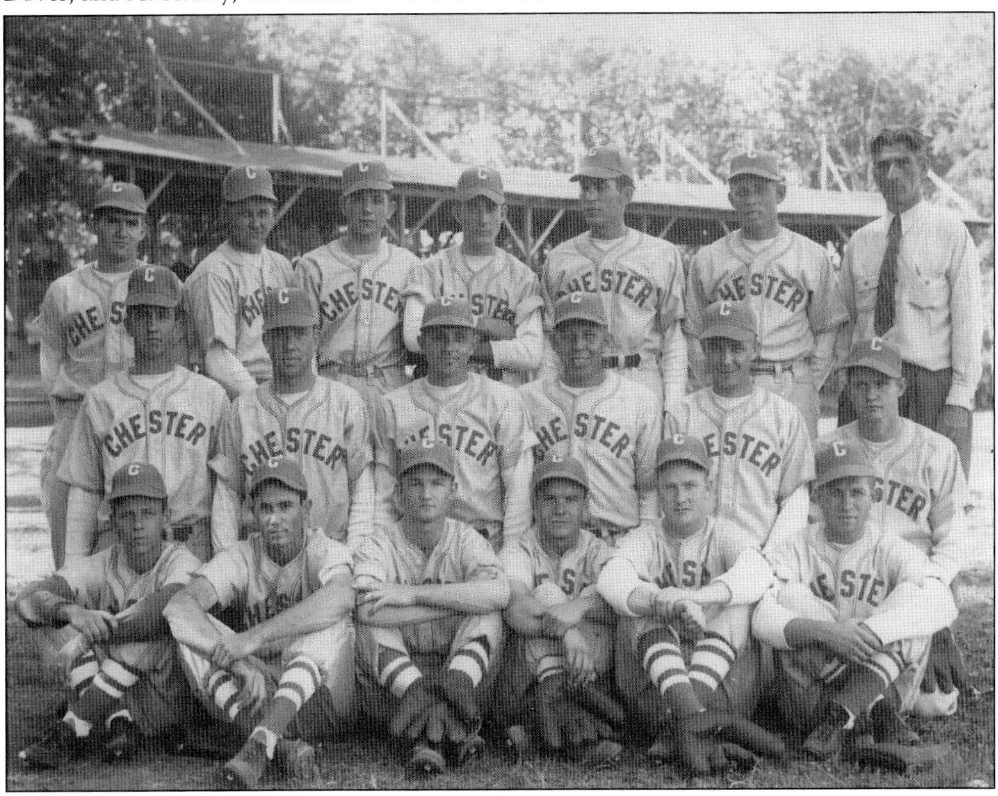

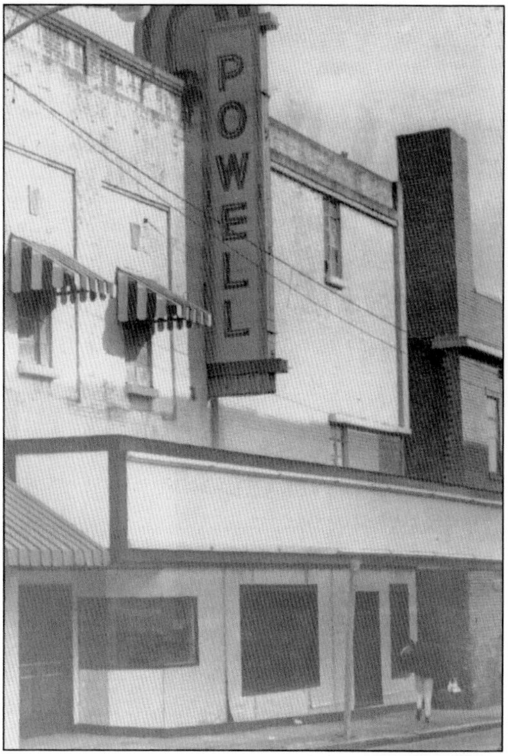

The Chester Little Theater, housed in the old Powell Theater on Wylie Street, has been presenting plays since 1972. The theater presents four plays a year including a musical, dinner theater, and a Christmas production.

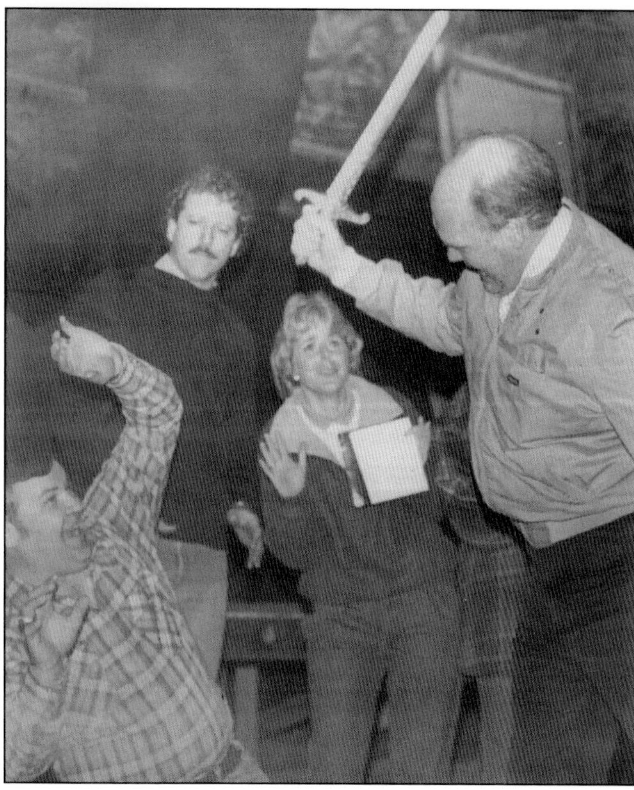

The Man of La Mancha was just one of the musicals presented at the Chester Little Theater. Portraying characters in the production are, from left to right, Jerry Kay, Butch Oneppo, Pat Wilson, and Willis Crain.